THROUGH
THE GRAPEVINE

THROUGH THE GRAPEVINE

JAY STULLER and GLEN MARTIN

WYNWOOD™ Press
New York, New York

To Our Parents

Library of Congress Cataloging-in-Publication Data

Stuller, Jay.
  Through the grapevine : the business of wine in America / Jay
Stuller and Glen Martin.
    p.   cm.
  ISBN 0-922066-11-6 : $19.95
  1. Wine industry—United States.   I. Martin, Glen, 1949– .
II. Title.
HD9375.S78   1989
338.4′76632′00973—dc19   89-5321
                                                                  CIP

CONTENTS

Section Two

A RIPENING INDUSTRY

Section Three

STRONG BACKS, ALCHEMIC MINDS AND THE PLAYERS WHO COUNT THE BEANS

CONTENTS

Section Four

THE DAVIDS,
A GOLIATH
AND A
DYNAMO NAMED BOB

Section Five

CONFLICTING
OPINIONS

Section Six

PUSHING THE PRODUCT

Section Seven

EPILOGUE: A TROUBLED HORIZON

INTRODUCTION

Why does man kill? Man kills for food. And not only for food—frequently, there must be a beverage.

—Woody Allen

Wine antedates history. Undoubtedly, Cro-Magnon and Neanderthal man made use of fermented juice—taken from the fruit of wild varieties of *Vitis vinifera*—as long as 10,000 years ago, even as the glaciers receding from the European continent signaled the end of the Pleistocene Epoch. This is because basic wine was, and is, a supremely simple beverage to make. Ripe grapes left in a stone or earthen container will ferment naturally on their own.

The pleasing taste and euphoric qualities of fruit so affected would not go unnoticed. Moreover, because of its power to stimulate conversation and lift moods, the juice may well have been vested with quasi-religious significance.

Wine also had concrete significance, for it followed man as he made the transition from a society of hunter-gatherers to a rudimentary form of civilization; indeed, wine might have encouraged such an evolution. Culled and tended vines produce more and better fruit than those growing wild and rank; once wine was discovered, early man would naturally consider it a priority. As much as the cultivation of primitive domestic grains and the husbandry of sheep and goats, the vine forced humankind to set down roots.

Grapevines also grew wild throughout the Middle East, and the Egyptians were the first true civilization to make wide use of wine. While getting more credit for building pyramids, the Egyptians initially defined the sciences of viticulture and enology. Yet their taste for wine, while long-lived, did not prove definitive, yielding ultimately to beer.

The vine continued to be cultivated along the Nile, but it wasn't until it was cultured in Europe—specifically Greece—that it achieved its first great flowering. There, wine was literally worshipped, accorded a god of its own, and the rites which accompanied homage to Bacchus were great favorites among the people. In fact, by Homer's time, specific vineyards throughout Greece were acknowledged as superior.

The Greeks made great progress in propagating grapevines, with many varieties cultivated, some extant even today. Muscat Canelli, for example, was developed during the earliest days of archaic Greece, and it is still a cultivar of great popularity in Italy and California.

With the rise of the Roman Empire, wine found boosters with enthusiasm exceeding that of the Greeks. While an adherence to the Golden Mean induced a certain moderation among the latter, such was not the case with the Romans, who were inclined to view excess as a virtue more than a vice. Indeed, drunkenness was considered a most desirable state, with citizens often accorded public esteem for their inebriate exploits.

In Rome, wine served as the lubricant that oiled that most dissolute of public functions, the Imperial Orgy. It may thus be assumed that wine played at least a passive part in the fall of that great empire.

And yet Rome, in turn, served the vine, even if wine did

not entirely serve Rome. Cuttings accompanied Roman legions as they tramped through Gaul and beyond; at the same time, various northern tribes planted cuttings on their own. And it was in central and northern Europe, in Gaul, that the vine found its most beneficent soil.

The climate and earth of central France proved better than any previous growing area for producing grapes, fruit that yielded wines of great quality. The monks who inhabited the early abbeys and monasteries in the third and fourth centuries had few peers in developing grape varieties that maximized the potential inherent in that soil and climate. Vines were also planted in Germany, Iberia and even Britain. The latter centuries of the Roman Empire were a golden age of vineyard expansion.

And yet, it was not all beer and skittles, as it were, for the empire's wine merchants. As wine historian Hugh Johnson has observed, Rome's economy was one of the first to endure a phenomenon which has plagued the industry periodically ever since: overproduction. Italian vineyards produced tremendous quantities of wine during the waning days of the empire, and this wine had to compete in the marketplace with products from the provincial fields.

Prices slumped. In response to the crisis—trouble in such a keystone commodity, as wine was to Rome, reverberates throughout the entire economy—Emperor Domitian ordered vineyards razed in some areas, particularly those that produced inferior wines. Similar injunctions, it should be noted, occurred in the Middle Ages. And while free market dynamics have replaced imperial fiat in the twentieth century, the end result is still periodically observed in today's wine industry.

By the late fourteenth century, the Dutch succeeded in controlling large parts of the European wine market, due to a formidable navy and vast system of warehouses. Bringing wine in bulk from southern producers, the Dutch blended and sold it for large profits. This, however, ran contrary to both the laws and sentiments of wine-exporting countries, which were even then assiduous in their protection of the sanctity of both vintages and individual vineyards.

This counterpoint between quality and profit is a tune

played in the wine industry even today, although improvement in wine technology and viticultural techniques have altered the rules of the game. In the Middle Ages, adulteration of product and outright fraud were common; shippers manipulated ordinary wines, and attempted to foist them off as superior vintages worthy of exorbitant prices.

Today, advances in wine science have accelerated to where fine wines are now produced in all the world's good viticultural regions. Simultaneously, the marketplace itself has become more sophisticated. Distributors, retailers and consumers alike have a better idea of what constitutes a good wine, more so than in the past, because quality has become somewhat standardized.

In the 1980s, chicanery is not a frequent problem. (The adulteration of Italian and Austrian table wines a few years ago is, however, a notable exception.) However, an oversupply of product most certainly is, for competition is no longer regional or continental, but global.

The vintages of French and Italian winemakers sit side-by-side on market shelves next to products from Germany, Spain, Portugal and Australia. Other players include South Africa, Chile, Argentina, Yugoslavia, Hungary and, of course, California, a state responsible for more than 90 percent of America's wine output. Other states, including New York, Washington, Oregon, Texas and Missouri are trying hard to become players.

The conditions that led to the wine boom of the 1970s, including the explosive growth in the number of wineries— a process that's still happening today—has set up many vintners for failure. Seduced by a wave they thought would never crest, novice and experienced winemakers throughout the world expanded vineyards. Those in California bought property at a time of inflated values and high interest rates. As wine sales leveled in the 1980s, many vintners find themselves holding costly paper with reduced means of making payments.

It could be argued that this industry has a penchant for drawing participants wholly unsuited to the hard realities of a rugged business. And make no mistake, wine is a hard business, as Roman subjects who saw their vineyards leveled by legionnaires knew well.

But winemaking in America does feature a veneer of gentility, an alluring essence that can blind one to the need for hard-nosed business acumen. In no other industry, save perhaps sports or entertainment, is the temptation for megalomania so strong. Relatively few vintners have entered the business in the past two decades for purely financial reasons, with the same drive and efficiency one would bring to managing fast-food franchises or a computer start-up company. Most figured they were buying into a lifestyle rather than a livelihood. Such dreams are inherently grand, but also brittle.

The American wine industry is a hurly-burly venue that includes cutthroat financial dealings and brutal competition for sales. Its lowliest workers, the field hands, are curiously the most appreciated, because no one else will do the labor cheap. Winery workers are fairly well paid, but the larger employers think they are paid too well, and are trying hard to change this.

This is a business which includes some wondrously rancorous family feuds and downright inept judging at wine competitions. Covered by an adoring press, which with but a few exceptions is uncritical, the industry has largely gone unexamined, particularly in terms of business competition and sordid practices. The mystique of wine, however warranted, remains intact.

The story of the American wine industry—and it's a sociology study unto itself—also involves remarkable achievements in viticulture and the craft and science of enology. There are many talented and creative winemakers producing superb beverages, wines that can stand against the best of Europe.

While the industry sports a glittering facade, an alluring romance that seduced many to join it, the economics of the grape have turned wrathful in the 1980s. Winery owners aren't necessarily destitute, but they live with constant stress and pressure, as competition forces them not only to make a good product, but to take to the hustings to sell it on almost any and every day that can be spared away from the winery.

Wine, of course, is not as fundamental a commodity as, say, petroleum. The industry's troubles do not have nearly the impact on society at large as it did in Roman times. But it is an important industry. Through property taxes on wineries and vineyards, and retail "luxury" or "sin" taxes, the manufacture and sale of wine is a significant revenue producer for governments. In fact, the way in which cash flows through the American wine industry is as absorbing as the sensory qualities of the wine itself. And money, like wine, is one of civilization's immutable fixtures.

Section One

BLISSFUL BEVERAGE— ONE TOUGH SALE

1

WHAT MAKES AND BREAKS A WINERY

Proclaimed a genius sometime around 1973, Francis Mahoney figured he had the wine business whipped. Just a couple of years after the native San Franciscan purchased ten acres in the Sonoma area, planted a vineyard and began making limited quantities of exceptional Chardonnay and Pinot Noir, he found himself on expense-paid flights to New York. Put up in elegant suites, Mahoney had only to talk to wine merchants and wine lovers about his stunning new Carneros Creek vintages, and bask in the praise.

Before the age of thirty, this former wine importer and retail salesman was a star. While a level-headed man who took this "genius" business with equanimity, he nonetheless sold every drop of wine he could produce. For nearly a decade, Francis Mahoney and Carneros Creek made all the right moves.

He then made one grievous mistake in judgment that nearly destroyed his winery. Business school grad students are rarely warned about such miscalculation. At its fundamental heart, it wasn't even financially oriented, although the fallout cost him plenty. But Mahoney's singular bad move is instructive, serving as a wine industry metaphor.

Until Carneros Creek ran aground, Mahoney rode a rather heady business wave. From his work at Connoisseur Wine Imports, he'd come to understand wine. He could also see that as the baby boom generation came of age and affluence, it would develop a taste for finer wine, leaving behind the Pink Ripple and soda-like Spanada that appealed to collegiate palates and budgets. A seemingly endless stream of young Americans had traveled through Europe in the late 1960s and early 1970s, seeking good times and finding a surfeit of cheap but high quality wines. Back in the United States, they found the wine market dominated by undistinguished jugs of Paul Masson, Gallo and Italian Swiss Colony.

There were a few producers of decent wines, among them Louis Martini, Charles Krug, Freemark Abbey and Robert Mondavi. But for every half-decent vintner, there were counters such as the flagging Beringer operation, a business on the ropes, selling what Mahoney felt was "an outrageously bad product." And yet, Mahoney also noted the emergence of some superb but very small California wineries, including Ridge and Mayacamas.

He and his partner, Balfour Gibson, knew that a small operation, making wines that truly reflected the attributes of a given grape, could appeal to a thirsty market. The big operations either didn't have the grapes of requisite quality, ignored this potential market segment, or didn't have the slightest idea it even existed.

Mahoney didn't have to worry about large-scale economies. Unlike many others who built wineries at the time and shortly thereafter—the dabbling doctors, lawyers and others seeking the romance of tax shelters and vineyards—

he didn't have $500,000 or $1 million to plow into a start-up. He didn't buy elaborate pumps, crushers and a super-speed bottling system. He didn't produce large volumes of red wines that must sit in expensive oak barrels for several years before they can be sold. Such nonproductive inventory overloaded a number of other novice vintners with less foresight, who didn't understand the capital-intensive nature of the wine business. And yet, Mahoney had a good product, and just as important, a guaranteed place in which to sell it: at Connoisseur Imports.

Starting out in 1972 and 1973 by producing only 2,000 cases of wine, Mahoney didn't bother with wholesalers. Every bottle moved through Connoisseur, direct mail and a few other specialty wine shops. Wholesalers were, however, coming out of the woodwork and looking for a piece of the action like underemployed lawyers converging on the scene of an accident. But Carneros Creek didn't make enough wine to warrant farming out for sales help. It increased production by only 1,000 or so cases each year. With the help of his wife, Kathy, Mahoney filled out bills of lading, kept the books and played the role of general contractor.

Demand for premium California wines soared, along with the prices retailers were willing to pay. In 1972, many Bordeaux wines were selling for around $3 a bottle. But Ridge began asking $5 for its Zinfandels. Beaulieu Vineyards started getting $6.50 for Cabernets and wholesalers offered $4 to $6 a bottle to an increasing number of producers, Carneros Creek included. With negligible or no marketing expenses to contend with, Mahoney watched good returns come in.

Still, the cash was never squandered at Carneros Creek. Mahoney carefully added new tanks. When he put a new chair in his office, it was a splurge. To both Francis and Kathy, these little additions were special. Within a decade Carneros Creek's business alone was worth $2.5 to $3 million, not including assets. It held very little debt. By 1983, Carneros Creek produced 13,000 cases of wine annually and had been profitable in each year of business; earnings climbed from $45,000 to $50,000 and then $80,000.

Sporting a sunburn from hours in his vineyards, this strong, compact man with a receding hairline and gap-toothed grin has the look of a farmer. Although city-born, Mahoney is clearly comfortable on the land, in jeans and work-boots, accustomed to hard, physical labor. But the articulate and university-educated farmer can also slide into a well-tailored tuxedo and blend with the movers and shakers of any business, at any elegant function. Because of his retail shop experience, Mahoney is also able to speak with and handle the most pretentious of wine snobs, responding to an obscure analogy used to describe a certain wine with an equally ambiguous, but technically correct, riposte.

However, what Mahoney most enjoyed after he began winning winemaking recognition was the security he felt that allowed him to lunch with the Napa Valley Vintners, the "in people" of his life; patrician winemakers like Joe Heitz and Louis Martini, who had endured hard times Mahoney could not even imagine. He would sit there and listen intently to the men talk about how Cabernets fetched $1 a bottle—in a good year. Mostly, the men were taking a break from hard work, making small and shop talk, discussing weather, the merits of certain bird repellants, filters and forklifts. Mahoney enjoyed the senior statesmen, but felt a bit troubled by a new breed that joined the gatherings; high-powered, almost venture capitalist types from Los Angeles and other foreign lands.

These winemakers, many of whom first visited the Napa Valley as tourists, were now the ones who most loudly and strongly fretted about "the tourist problem," and the opening of still more wineries that catered to the burgeoning crush of visitors. Other things were beginning to change, rapidly change.

The cost of land in the valley climbed rapidly as a result of the pressure of new winemakers entering the business. Nationwide, inflation and interest rates rose during the late 1970s, pressures that began squeezing the more highly leveraged wineries. Carneros Creek had gotten in on the ground floor; because of its low debt, interest and inflation weren't significant factors. Moreover, Mahoney could sell $10,000 to $15,000 worth of wine on weekends at Carneros Creek, loading cases into cars and taking the checks, as direct as sales could be. In 1979, he sold out his stock in six to nine months.

Until then, Mahoney's business—if not that for most of the premium segment of the wine industry—had been completely product-driven. That is, the wine literally sold itself. The producers made no special effort to get the product on the street, into different types of outlets and markets. But in 1980, Mahoney could see a developing need for marketing and strategic selling through a network of dependable wholesalers in other states. Competition was beginning to cut into his market. And now he'd have to cut wholesalers in on the profit, meaning he'd earn less per bottle than in California.

Winemaking has long been called the Gentleman's Game. When one asks vintners about competitors, they are quick to disclaim that they are striving against another winery. No, while Chrysler executives may get thrills taking customers from Ford or Toyota, winemakers behave—at least in public—as if their vintages all serendipitously appeal to totally different groups of customers. But wineries are locked in fiscally mortal competition for a limited pool of customers.

It is waged when product leaves the winery, outside of what Mahoney has called "the cocoon and camaraderie of the Valley." It's a battle for the ear, heart and mind of the wholesaler, who must have incentives to move one particular label among many, and who must in turn motivate retailers to continue the effort. It is also waged in the wine media, by winning attention from writers and critics.

Mahoney found himself on the road more than four months a year. Working with about fifteen wholesalers, he began to realize that this was a network in constant danger of unraveling. The wholesalers weren't trying to be difficult, but to them Mahoney was just another supplier who offered limited quantities of an excellent product. But there were lots of other wine suppliers, some of whom could offer big discounts on hundreds of cases. Mahoney discovered that people weren't as interested as before.

He had still made all the right moves, right up to 1983. By any measure, Carneros Creek was a success, on solid financial ground, with a hot reputation and poised for growth. An increasingly crowded marketplace didn't prevent Mahoney from selling all his wine. It was another thing altogether that led Carneros Creek to near ruin.

Most folks in the wine industry think that Mahoney's mistake was signing a distribution agreement with Joseph E. Seagram & Sons, the giant Canadian-based distiller. This wasn't his primary error, but it led him to the error that was. And it still could have been a good deal; Carneros Creek and four other California wineries were to be a part of Seagram's American Classics Wine Division, which eventually was merged into Seagram Classics Wine Co. These vintners had only to keep making good wine, while the high-powered Seagram troops put the products into the marketplace.

However, between 1983 and 1986, Seagram allowed these wines to languish, product lines lost in a big corporate shuffle. Seagram's inattention to the Classics devastated the reputation and finances of Carneros Creek. The winery has largely recovered. The dispute is still in litigation, however, and the claims of Carneros Creek are being vigorously contested by Seagram, which strongly disputes the validity of those claims. But this is yet another story. What compelled Mahoney to sign with Seagram is more fundamental.

It wasn't greed, although he could envision more growth with a big company handling nationwide distribution. It wasn't stupidity, although he is still chagrined that he sincerely believed the promises that were made. "Maybe," says Mahoney, "I just wanted to believe them too much."

But what Francis Mahoney most wanted was to spend more time with his family.

It's true that achievers in almost any business or profession do so at the expense of a normal family life. Winemakers often project a laid-back image, embodied in the Gallo "All the Best" commercials, with gentle strains by Vangelis, who also composed the music for *Chariots of Fire,* and gauzy images of quiet vineyards and cellars. What's actually called for is fire and energy.

Mahoney has such energy. But at the time he signed with Seagram, the eldest of his three children was about to enter the eighth grade, the youngest the fourth. He made the agreement for what he thought were sound business principles, but also to free himself from spending so much time on the road. His plan, unfortunately, backfired.

Mahoney worries that he may be considered a buffoon for what happened with Seagram. Carneros Creek had been one of the hottest wineries in the nation; its products retailed for $12 to $13 a bottle. After sitting in Seagram warehouses, premium vintages were discounted out for less than $3. The wine didn't degrade in quality, but perceptions of Carneros Creek certainly did.

However, Mahoney shouldn't worry, for he is widely admired and respected within the industry for how he held the operation together and brought it back. His recovery was Iacocca-like, gritty and well earned.

The wine business can take away much of the time for family things. This may be one of the reasons many winery families involve their children in the business. And there are many more, far less noble and truly stupid ways to run a winery into the fiscal cellar.

There are, in fact, countless things that can break a winery. The vineyard owner faces plant disease, pests and the threat of uncooperative weather. Fluctuating grape prices make financial planning tough for wineries that don't control their own vineyards. After the initial capital invested to buy the land and build a winery, grapes are the biggest cost item in a bottle of wine. Although wine is relatively simple to make, mistakes in the cellar can be costly. The basic physical force of gravity is an ever-present menace to an operation that deals in valuable fluid; the smallest leak or a blown hose connection can send many thousands of dollars down the drain.

Vintages that don't come out quite as good as intended are yet another problem. California's Kistler winery, for example, earned a near instant reputation for great wines. But within a few years of initial operation, it produced a stinker, and yet put the wines on the market. Many premium vintners who find themselves in this situation sell off the wine in bulk, for blending in cheaper varieties or plonk. They live with reduced earnings or eat the loss and save the reputation. Consumers tumbled to Kistler's blunder, and it took several years for the product line to recover.

Pricing, developing a distribution system, and targeting particular markets present an entire range of opportunity and danger. So do downright bizarre state laws that make it difficult for all but the largest wineries to conduct nation-wide business efficiently.

So, what makes a winery? When Carneros Creek started out, all an American firm had to do was create a better wine and the world beat a path to the cellar door. In the market-driven 1980s, success is much more complex, and remaining successful is a tenuous trick.

The wine industry is highly segmented in terms of price and quality. A liquor store with a wide selection of wines may in one section of the shop carry a seven-year-old $75 bottle of Ridge Cabernet Sauvignon, from that vintner's fabled Montebello vineyard. In another portion of the store, well refrigerated, is a $1.40 pint of Thunderbird. Both wines are made of grapes (although "the bird's" raw material comes from California Central Valley vines), both hold appeal to quite different consumers, and each, perhaps better than most any other segment, makes money.

Prices and quality cover the range in between, all part of an industry that in the U.S. generates from $8 billion to $9 billion in revenues annually. Aside from the fortified Thunderbird, Night Train Express, MD 20/20 and Richards Wild Irish Rose—beverages that are prized less for taste than their beastly kick—jug wines comprise the lowest end of the spectrum. Then there is the premium segment, which cost from $3 to $7 a bottle. These are what Jon Fredrikson, president of Gomberg, Fredrikson & Associates, a San Francisco wine consulting firm, calls "the fighting varietals." From $7 to $12 or so is the super-premiums, and above that, in another Fredrikson coinage, the ultra-premiums. Coolers, sparkling wines and brandies are also part of the equation. All fight for market share.

What captures market share and earns profits are quality, price and, perhaps most important in the premium to ultra-premium categories, public perceptions. Successful wineries find niches for their products, such as producing the best cheap premium, or positioning the wine as the top super-premium, without going over a price threshold that would discourage too many buyers. Except when trying to impress guests, most wine buyers like to think they're getting good value for their dollar.

At the lower-price end of the business, hard-core street salesmanship is the key. E. & J. Gallo, for example, maintains an awesome field force, salesmen who make sure Gallo products are positioned in the most and best places in a store. Gallo's "All the Best" commercials have done much to promote the company's varietals, although many in the industry consider them overpriced and not even among the best in each varietal category. But it's the field force that keeps all Gallo wines, including the unadvertised Thunderbird and Night Train Express, in front of the customers.

The vast majority of winemakers, without the resources of Gallo—or which aren't backed by big corporations such as Washington State's Château Ste. Michelle (U.S. Tobacco), California's Beringer (Nestlé) and Chateau St. Jean (Suntory)—simply try to hold down costs, reduce mistakes and hold their breaths. They hope their pricing and marketing schemes work, and that their wines win the favor of prominent wine writers.

Winemakers also compete against imports, which can be hurt or favored by changing dollar values in relation to foreign currency. And the Gentleman's Game aside, America's burgeoning number of wineries most of all compete against each other for a somewhat limited base of consumers. On the streets, where the war is waged, there simply aren't many gentlemen.

There are a few vintners who still sell every case, each and every bottle, without hard marketing. But even those who once seemingly had it made find the game turning rougher each year. "We really didn't understand that it couldn't go on forever," Francis Mahoney now says. "But when you're riding on euphoria, you're not looking at the ground."

2

THE VINTNER'S CRAFT— SHAPING THE GRAPE

Within virtually every industry, two factors are crucial to product success: quality and relative cost. On the low end of the market, jug wines are competing in much the same arena as beer. The taste and quality differences between Gallo, Inglenook, Almadén and Paul Masson jug wine are not appreciable. In blind beer-tasting tests, average consumers have an almost impossible time picking their "favorite" Budweiser from a Miller, and the same is generally true of generic wines. Thus, the consumer is much more influenced by marketing-induced perceptions such as bonhomie among retired, beer-drinking athletes or a slick picnic scene—or a fifty-cent difference in price.

However, even in the upscale end of the wine market, consumers are sensitive to price. Interest in premium Chardonnays and Cabernet Sauvignons wanes markedly when the prices climb much above $12, and there are arguments that for the standard 750 milliliter bottle, the mass market drops out at about half the price. Consequently, successful wineries spend much time and effort carefully plotting pricing strategy.

Wine prices, of course, run all across the board, from a gallon jug that fetches $3.95 retail to a bottle sold for $25. Few other widely consumed liquids demonstrate such disparity. But each product does have a market niche, targeted at a segment of consumers that through past behavior has proven a willingness to pay a certain price for wine.

However, price and quality are not linked as closely as one might think. The sticker on a bottle of wine suggests a measure of quality, but it's a number that can also be influenced by demand, status, availability, trends, hype and, in some cases, outright venality.

To begin with, wine quality is not immediately self-evident, nor does the beverage have performance characteristics that lend themselves to simple descriptions, such as acceleration rates and miles-per-gallon in automobiles. Short of its alcoholic properties and effects and these tactile considerations, wine has no other great practical function to fulfill; it doesn't break, burn out or explode like some other products, nor will it run smoothly for a long period of time. Wine can only taste good—or bad. And its quality is determined strictly by sensory perception, through sight, smell, taste and the tactile weight of the liquid in the mouth.

Herein lies some problems, for the human olfactory and gustatory senses are not standardized. People smell and taste things differently. Moreover, in sensory terms, wine is much more complicated than other foods and drinks.

For example, a chocolate eclair is a relatively easy item to judge, with flavors straightforward and simple. Even the most unsophisticated palate can determine if the cream is fresh, the chocolate of the highest, richest quality, and whether the pastry is appropriately light, flaky and delicate. But the flavors in wine can often appear dissonant to the uninitiated. Indeed, some of most highly prized flavors and aromas in premium wines are plainly objectionable to tyro wine drinkers.

Good red wines, for instance, contain a sturdy backbone of tannin, which strikes many as unpleasantly bitter. Fine white wines should contain an increment of acid, which can taste unexpectedly sour. Either element can obscure other, more subtle flavors in the wine, which is why vintages of completely different varieties and styles may taste the same to the beginner.

Furthermore, a unanimity of opinion among even expert wine tasters is so rare as to be nonexistent. In tasting competitions and sessions where wineries try to rate their own vintages against competitors' products, experienced enologists frequently express profoundly different views. One enologist's first ranked wine may be ranked tenth by another. Winemakers know that no single palate is impeccable, and thus judgments on wine quality are a matter of consensus.

Sight is the first sense used to judge wine, and this element is the simplest and most basic in the art. A wine should be clear and brilliant, though it should also possess good color. It should not be cloudy, murky or gritty. Experts never disagree on the visual evaluation of a wine.

Smell and taste, however, are another matter. A single matter, by and large, for they may in some ways be considered the same sense, as anyone who has eaten a meal while suffering from a cold is aware. When we can't smell, our sense of taste is rudimentary. In fact, we can discern just four tastes without the aid of our noses: sour, salt, bitter and sweet, but only in substantial strengths and doses. Man needs his olfactory neurons to taste the infinite variety of high and low tones that make what we eat and drink one of the major pleasures of life.

Smell is more closely allied with memory than any other sense, which is why an experienced wine taster can identify a wine he or she had tasted years before. Wine releases volatile molecules, which when inhaled greatly enhance the sense of taste.

This is a complex and subtle system, greatly influenced by past experiences. Certain aromas can call forth warm and pleasant childhood memories for one individual, or quite the opposite for another. Consequently, taste and smell, sine qua non in wine quality, is a highly individualistic consideration.

Given the variety of such experiences and memories, it would seem that a consensus on wine quality—which depends much on suggestions of multiple scents and tastes—would be impossible to obtain. This, of course, is not the case, for although there are many differences in individual taste and smell, trained enologists and tasters recognize certain touchstones. Over the years, specific qualities have become generally accepted as desirable in wines, others distinctly undesirable.

Agreement on those qualities was one thing; defining and developing nomenclature presented an even greater task. How does one arrive at precise semantic devices or word choices that accurately—or even adequately—describe smells and taste, so that discussions can at least be held in the same language?

Until recently, tasters would engage in verbal jousting contests in attempts to reach common ground on a single odor or flavor. Does it smell of truffles? Or leaf mold? Gladioli? All of the tasters discerned the specific aroma, and were even sure that they smelled it similarly. But they couldn't concur on how to describe it.

Progress in codifying wine tastes and smells has come dramatically with an invention by Ann Noble, a University of California at Davis enologist. In the early 1980s, she headed a group that developed the Wine Aroma Wheel, which in the industry has been dubbed the Davis Wheel. It consists of 132 descriptive words and phrases arranged in a series of groupings. By starting with a general impression of a flavor or aroma and working toward finer, more subtle definitions, a group of tasters all armed with wheels can agree in relatively short order on appropriate verbiage for a wine, a major step toward judging quality.

The wheel is simplicity itself. Tasting a wine, the evaluators can readily conclude that a wine is dominated by a fruity element. But what kind of fruit? Referring to Noble's wheel, they find there are a number of sub-classifications under the fruity category. For instance, there's Labrusca—the foxy taste associated with wild native American grapes, and a component of many Eastern wines—dried fruit, tropical fruit, tree fruit, berries and citrus.

Say the tasters agree that the wine is rich, lush and exotic, a distinctly tropical fruit. Under this category they find, on the perimeter and final dividing segments of the wheel, the words "banana," "melon" and "pineapple." One taster may claim the taste is identical to papaya, while another says it's cantaloupe. One says honeydew melon, still another mango, and the fifth agrees with the cantaloupe claimant. By tabulating their impressions, the tasters can conclude that the taste they're experiencing is best described as melon.

Yet fruit is not the only element manifest in wine. Sometimes there are flavors that taste bad, or "off" in the enologist's jargon. While the Davis Wheel devotes twenty-one final words to the major fruit category, it has twenty-four under the heading of chemical, which are divided into five sub-groups entitled petroleum, sulfur, paper, pungent and other. In the sub-groups are some awful descriptions, ranging from diesel to skunk, fishy, sulfur dioxide and wet dog.

Wine, then, is a collection of myriad tastes and smells that suggest many other things. It may hold vegetative tastes, hinting at olives, green beans and freshly cut straw. It may have earthy and dusty qualities, or the floral bouquet of roses, jasmine and violets.

Having a language with which to work is a beneficial development for the wine industry. Quality judgments have always been done by committee, and the Davis Wheel has helped such inherently contentious gatherings come to logical points. Even then there is argument, for in judgments of American wine, opinions of what constitutes quality have been fluid, changing like clothing fashions. The styles of the most esteemed wines of the late 1980s are much different from those of even a decade ago.

In 1975, the top American wines were characterized by their power, fruit and intensity; consumers wanted "big" wines that had formidable taste, ample smell and alcoholic punch. Such wines screamed for the palate's attention. And while they packed an undeniably good taste, the wines were so rich, chewy, alcoholic, tannic and strong of fruit that one could taste little else; the vintages overwhelmed accompanying food. They were, in the words of one vintner, "all substance and no style."

Such wines also failed to age well. High in tannic content (from both the grapes, skins and pips, and the oak barrels used to age the vintages), the delicate varietal elements that come to the fore in the world's best wines were bludgeoned to death.

Grapes with high sugar content were the primary factor in the bold wines. "We used to think that we wanted grapes at around 24 percent sugar or more," says Patrick Campbell, the owner and vintner at Laurel Glen Vineyards, a Sonoma Mountain winery renowned for its distinctive Cabernet Sauvignons. "We thought that grapes that had less sugar weren't ripe. We've since changed our way of thinking."

Sugar is a function of grape's time on the vine and climate conditions. The riper the grape, the more sugar it contains, which in the wine business is measured on the Brix scale. (A graduated scale used on a hydrometer and named after A.F.W. Brix, a nineteenth-century German inventor, this system indicates the weight of sugar per volume of solution at a given temperature.) And sugar translates directly into alcohol content, since yeasts turn sucrose into carbon dioxide and alcohol. High-sugar grapes also tend to produce wines which are very intense in fruit characteristics. Such wines are also considered "soft," in that they're relatively low in acids; grape acid goes down as its sugar content goes up.

By the late 1970s, consumers in the United States were growing tired of wines with a 14 percent or 15 percent alcohol content. They tasted hot with food, making it difficult to fully enjoy a meal. Imbibers also found that intoxication occurred much too easily.

However, at the same time, American winemakers also wanted to stretch their craft. They began to recognize that certain qualities of European wines, such as elegance, balance and longevity, were worth emulating. "We liked what made California wines California wines," explains Campbell. "We wanted to preserve their liveliness and intensity, but we wanted to also make them more complex and sophisticated, with lower alcohol content. We simply wanted to make them more enjoyable and easier to drink."

In 1980, California's vintners began considering criteria other than grape sugar to determine ripeness. "We realized that grapes from one vine could be ripe one year at 23.5 degrees Brix and 22 degrees Brix the next year," says Zelma Long, Simi Winery's celebrated winemaker. "Grape ripeness has a lot more to it than sugar. We've always looked at the acid content in grapes, but now we're paying more attention to the rate of acid decline as the sugars rise, the way grapes taste and smell, how soft they are, how easily they come off the stem, and how vines look—whether they're shutting down for the fall or now. We're devising a system at Simi for determining grape ripeness that's based primarily on sensory perceptions rather than numbers. We still check sugar and acid levels, of course. But we're more concerned about how the grapes taste, smell and feel. In this regard, we've kind of come around to the French way of thinking; they've always judged their grapes the same way they judge their wine, by putting them in their mouth."

Long believes that quality American vintners are today looking for "harmony" in their wines. "We don't want any one element to dominate," she explains. "We want a variety of flavors and aromas, all of them good, all in balance with one another. We want the flavors to lead from one to the other, so that the sensation of taste is long and sustained. We also want wines that will evolve with age, and that can only happen to wines which are made with grapes that are well balanced and not excessively high in sugar." In short, vintners want wines that taste good.

And yet, different wines taste good for differing reasons. Cabernet Sauvignon is considered exceptional when it emits aroma and flavor analogous to cassis, cedar, expensive aged tobacco, briar and a certain stoniness. Pinot Noir should have hints of cherries and truffles, while Chardonnay should display some or all of a dazzling combination that includes citrus fruit, cream, pineapple, flint, pears and butter. And on top of these varietal elements, wines also gain characteristics from vinifications and aging processes.

Some white wines, for example, have a creamy richness

that comes from what's known as yeast autolysis, which is aging the wine in contact with yeast lees. Cabernet Sauvignon gains a smoothness from maceration, which means letting the wine sit in contact with grape skins for several days after fermentation is complete. This creates longer molecular chains in the wine's tannin component, which gives the vintage a softer feel on tongue and palate. Since Pinot Noir grape skins lack sufficient tannin, many vintners ferment such grapes with the stems, which are rich in the substance. A warm fermentation process helps release them into the wine.

There are hundreds of other wrinkles, variations on the winemaking theme, from time in an oak barrel—which can also give off a touch of vanilla flavor—to fermentation temperature. Only through tinkering, tweaking and making minor adjustments in experiments can a winemaker improve his product.

And yet, one thing truly differentiates great winemakers from the ordinary, the master craftsman from the producer of plonk. Because no matter what is said and done in the winery, the product is only as good as the grapes. "The industry has finally come to realize that grapes are the primary ingredient in quality," says one winery owner. "For all the talk about superstar winemakers, their barrels, their techniques and skill, it all comes down to the fruit.

"Yes, Paul Draper is a helluva winemaker and he's done wonderful things at Ridge," continues this businessman. "But without the Montebello vineyard ... The same thing goes at Buena Vista, where they own and control some tremendous vineyard acreage. For those of us who don't control vineyards, or when we can't get guaranteed contracts with premium growers, well, no matter how great a winemaker is on the staff, we can't guarantee the same kind of quality as wineries with great grapes."

The differences between a good wine and a great wine are subtle, and often attenuated and slippery. But great wines usually spring from great places, the vineyard land that gives a vintage its quality edge, or special characteristics. For example, when an expert vintner talks of "Rutherford dust," cognoscenti know it refers to an elusive flavor found only in Cabernet Sauvignons that come from a tiny, mid-Napa Valley region known as the Rutherford Bench. The taste is dusty and earthy, like the color of the red, Rutherford soil. Perhaps one has to visit the site to understand, for comparing wine to the taste of dirt does sound terribly specious. But the grapes that grow here yield wines that are distinct and very good.

Developing into Conventional Wisdom in the United States wine industry is the thought that a winemaker's skill contributes only 10 to 20 percent toward the product's ultimate quality. Europeans have long held this view, and rarely venerate winemakers. They respect the power of the grape, something Americans are just beginning to comprehend. A winemaker can, of course, totally screw up the world's greatest fruit, effectively fashioning a sow's ear out of a silk purse. On the other hand, ordinary grapes can be elevated only so far. Therefore, a wine's origin has much to do with its quality and the price it commands.

For instance, only a limited number of French wineries make true bordeaux and burgundies, since there is only one Bordeaux and one Burgundy region in the world. Indeed, in Europe, each wine's nomenclature is rigorously determined by its area of origin. The finest wines will be designated by individual vineyards or estates, such as Château Haut-Brion, while a good but less prominent wine may be identified with a small area surrounding a village, or a particular slope or river valley. Everyday wines of pedestrian quality may carry an appellation that embraces a vast winegrowing region; bottles simply marked "Vin de Bordeaux" or "Vin de Loire" are examples.

For Americans who haven't studied French wine, this causes some confusion. Consider Mouton Cadet, which has a reputation in America as an excellent wine. It carries a Bordeaux appellation, but it is not the same thing as Château Mouton Rothschild. In France, it's considered a wine of modest virtues. But the Rothschild family exports about two million cases of the stuff each year, primarily to the U.S., and makes a great deal of money from the product.

The Europeans have had centuries to both define and refine their appellation system. Over the years, those areas which were superior for the production of specific types of wine grapes have been identified through trial and error. At times, only a few feet may separate a vineyard which is accorded a top designation and one that's relegated to secondary or tertiary status. No matter; the differences have been noted over hundreds of years, and the indicated status, for the most part, reflects reality.

Things are different in the U.S.—very different. When American winemaking finally took serious root in the mid-nineteenth century, growers were serious about matching specific varietals with specific microclimates and soil types. (Microclimate is a term used to describe the consistent weather conditions varying from place to place.)

Robert Louis Stevenson vacationed in the Napa Valley in the late nineteenth century and commented at length about the experiments of local wine grape growers. Yet in spite of the assiduous efforts, progress wasn't dramatic until the early 1960s. What had been learned before Prohibition had been lost, and recouping and expanding that knowledge in the aftermath took nearly three decades.

Until then, many thousands of acres of varietal vineyards were planted in areas for which they were completely unsuited. Pinot Noir, which needs cool temperatures, was planted in the Calistoga area of the upper Napa Valley, which is more suitable for varieties that thrive in warmer weather, such as Zinfandel and Petite Sirah. Cabernet Sauvignon, which requires relatively thin soils—since it tends to put out excessive vegetative growth in better dirt—was planted on ground rich enough to generate cabbages the size of bushel baskets. As late as the 1950s and 1960s, California growers were planting grape varieties based on their readings of grape market conditions. They planted what they thought would make the most money, and not the varieties best suited to their land. Such growers probably didn't even know they were sacrificing long-term profits for short-term cash flow. The quality of the fruit and wine suffered.

That began to change in the mid-1960s. The recognition that great wines are grown as well as made came gradually; indeed, the first wineries to embrace the doctrine were the smallest. The larger vintners were still enamored by technology and a sense of alchemic manifest destiny. They were of a mind that the deficiencies in the grapes could be corrected by technical expertise in the cellars.

Most small wineries didn't have access to the sophisticated equipment that was standard at the bigger operations. Therefore such vintners traded on the French doctrine of *goût de terroir*, which literally means taste of the soil. It's an idea that vests soil and climate with a sort of mystical ascendancy. In this view, only Mother Earth can produce great wines, and in a way that usually transcends human science. Of course, these winemakers also didn't have the capital to invest in technology, which made it financially expedient for them to cultivate a vineyard supremacy philosophy. Still, it's probably fortunate they didn't have great capital resources, for their acceptance of this notion, for whatever reason, has led to some great American wines.

Joe Swan, a Sonoma winemaker who specializes in Pinot Noir, is one such vintner. Swan is a devotee of red burgundies—those velvety French wines made from the Pinot Noir grape. From the very beginning, Swan was adamant about matching microclimate, soil and the proper clonal variety. His ten-acre vineyard was planted in one of the coolest regions in Sonoma County, near Forestville; some people thought the area was more suited to artichokes than wine grapes.

Swan, however, was convinced that the finest Pinot Noir fruit came from areas so cool as to border on chilly. He demanded spare soil for his vines, at a time when vegetative vigor was vineyard fashion. Swan's vines certainly didn't look pretty. Pinot Noir is a shy vegetative producer anyway, and Swan planted his vines densely and pruned them in a manner that was a variation on the Burgundian vertical cordon style. "These aren't ornamental shrubs," he growls. "My pruning system puts sun on the fruit, and that concentrates the type of flavors I want out of Pinot Noir."

While Swan's vineyard looked rather scrubby, controlled studies have recently shown that "putting sun on the fruit" does indeed yield a different grape and wine flavor. In any event, the fruit that came off Swan's vines produced some of the best Pinot Noirs made in the late 1960s and early 1970s. In the purest sense, his wine is his fruit.

Since the early 1970s, the importance of grape origin has become increasingly recognized in the American wine industry. In 1978, a regulatory change in the Federal Alcohol Administration Act allowed vintners to file for appellation recognition. An appellation is a U.S. viticultural district, defined as a grape-growing region that ostensibly has geographic features that make it distinct from other, nearby areas. Administered by the Bureau of Alcohol, Tobacco and Firearms (BATF), which falls under the U.S. Treasury Department, appellations are generally recommended by the industry. Wineries granted such recognition were allowed to note on their labels the origin of the fruit crushed for the wine; it usually denotes a fine wine grape region.

And yet, this appellation business is something of a weird development, particularly in California. Ever since the repeal of Prohibition, the industry has attempted to attune the public to varietals. Now that a California Cabernet Sauvignon or Pinot Noir has a strong identity—as do Napa Valley or Sonoma County wines—vintners are confusing the issue by carving up territory. In trying to position themselves as being superior or separate from wineries in other nearby geographic settings, with different microclimates and soils, they may be Balkanizing a marketing asset.

"What we were really looking for was label authorization for estate-bottled wines," says Wendell Lee, the legal counsel for the Wine Institute. "But the only way the Bureau of Alcohol, Tobacco and Firearms would give it to us was through a regulation outlining requirements for entire viticultural regions. After that, the petitions started piling up."

Of course, the American appellations were themselves designed to help marketing and boost sales. For example, the Carneros Quality Alliance, a group of more than sixty winemakers and grape growers in parts of Napa and Sonoma counties, is promoting the Carneros viticultural region.

But there are some liabilities in this system. For one thing, an appellation thrives on the image of the best winemakers and growers within it. Weaker growers and vintners within the appellation territory have the right to use the designation on their label. They are, in a sense, hitching a ride; although the lesser wines can't command the same price as the best, their returns are boosted appreciably.

Consider that more than twenty Napa Valley vintners and growers petitioned BATF in 1985 for recognition as the Stag's Leap District, the third sub-appellation since the general Napa Valley viticultural area was established in 1980. The first two subs, Howell Mountain and Carneros came in 1983; Stag's Leap would be the first in the immediate valley.

Stag's Leap is a name that's magic in super and ultra-premium wine. The district is kind of a sub-valley in Napa Valley, along its eastern hills. Its soil includes rich, ancient volcanic deposits, which when combined with the micro-climate in the 2,500-acre area yields equally rich Cabernet-Sauvignons, Merlots and Zinfandels. The proposed district includes growers such as Joseph Phelps, Dick Steltzner and Warren Winiarski, and Stag's Leap Wine Cellars, Stag's Leap Winery, Clos du Val and the Robert Mondavi Winery. But others wanted in, and asked the BATF to expand the boundaries. Lawyers, geologists, historians and a load of experts clashed at federal government hearings.

The American appellations, says Wendell Lee, "essentially are a device for wineries to separate themselves from each other on the shelves. Theoretically, appellation authorization should be a good marketing tool. In practice, I don't really know if that's the case." Despite the wine knowledge that does exist in the general public, Lee believes that consumers by and large "don't know that much about grape varieties, let alone their viticultural requirements or those areas in the country where each one does best. The whole appellation question goes right over their heads—it may even confuse many of them."

What this suggests is that the winemakers are playing to a very selective audience, the true aficionado who would consider such information appropriate, even essential. To be sure, this is the audience that provides vintners with the most feedback, the critiques and psychic stroking. But wine snobs, it's been said, rarely buy wine; they just go to tastings. Creating appellations may be akin to a government bureaucracy or a session of Congress that responds to a vocal special interest which commands attention through stridency but represents relatively few citizens. The interests of the general public and the government are then not well served.

However, appellations in the U.S. wine industry are here to stay, in California and, increasingly, in other states that develop their wine industry and identify differences between regions and try to capitalize upon them. The public could learn; thirty years ago, the Napa Valley had no great significance as a viticultural area, but now even a casual wine imbiber recognizes that it stands for quality. Value, however, is another matter.

3

YOU GET WHAT YOU PAY FOR, OR SO YOU THINK: PRICING AND THE PERILOUS ECONOMICS OF WINERIES

As he sat through the wine business seminar nearly ten years ago, Dennis Marion lamented that he'd paid Marvin Shanken $500 to hear what was proving to be mostly common drivel. Shanken is the editor and publisher of *The Wine Spectator*, and his New York–based communications company also publishes a number of respected industry trade magazines and directories. With a circulation of about 70,000, the *Spectator* does a superb, honest and lively job of reporting on the industry. It's even honest enough to occasionally make growers, vintners and wine merchants kick in protest. But Shanken's seminar wasn't telling Dennis Marion much of anything he didn't know.

However, he heard one line that almost made the $500 worth it. It was said that 98 percent of the people in the U.S. who buy wine look for bottles that retail for $6 or less. Marion's prices were about a buck higher. "Six dollars was the magic number," he now says. "Knowing that, I based my entire company on the premise. I wouldn't want to give him all that much credit, but it is the only thing Marvin Shanken has ever done for me."

Marion already had a sound idea of what he wanted to do with the blending and bottling business he started in 1978, which has since made him one of the more successful American négociants. Négociants, who have operated in France for centuries, buy surplus wines that are average quality or below, and blend or "elevate" them into good but reasonably priced wines. Négociants may also buy grapes and make their own wine. Once looked down upon in the States, American négociants didn't come into their own until the early 1980s.

Considering his background, one would figure Marion might go in a different direction. After graduating from San Francisco State University with a bachelor's degree in Art, Television and Film, he went to work at a Sausalito retail wine shop. Self-taught in wine arcana, he was hired by Mountain View's Gemello Winery to buy and import European wine for its retail outlet. Marion handled clarets that were bottled before phylloxera hit the Continent's vineyards more than a century before, burgundies from the 1940s, wines worth hundreds of dollars and more. He continued to move top-end wine through his pair of Pacific Coast Wine Company retail shops, in Palo Alto and Los Altos, a business he founded in 1973. Needless to say, the Silicon Valley–Stanford corridor on the San Francisco Peninsula contains a well-heeled pool of wine consumers.

Marion enjoyed bidding on rare wines at Christie's in London, but he was shrewd enough to recognize that an American négociant could develop a high-volume business, getting good values on surplus wines and aiming at the lower portion of the fighting varietal segment. Under his M. Marion label, he began selling small quantities of different varietals. Marion's wholesale prices translated into wine that retailed in the $7 range. After Shanken's seminar, he dropped his prices by a dollar or two, adjusted his profit expectations and attempted to blend the best wine that could move for less than $6.

The figure is just as significant today as a decade ago; 98 percent of the wine sold in the U.S. still goes for $6 or less. Marion's prices are still primarily based on this one marketing consideration, and an abiding faith in consumers' common sense. Marion is a businessman not burdened by a winemaker's ego, although his Domaine M. Marion winery is now producing his own vintages as well as *négociant* blends. Every winemaker in every segment claims their products are of high quality, but Marion is forthright enough to add that he's providing value for the dollar, with no high-minded claims. Ego, he explains, is one of the industry's biggest problems.

"The doctor or lawyer turned winemaker who is out to make the greatest late harvest Chenin Blanc in the world figures that it must be the consumer who's off-base if the product doesn't sell," says Marion. "But if the wine doesn't sell, it's not a successful product. People have to realize that the consumer is God; they drive the industry."

There are some vintners who ask consumers to pay ungodly prices for their wines. A few surely deserve the premium, for creating rare and wondrous wine that meets the caviar wishes, champagne dreams and hefty pocketbooks of a very small segment of the public. An allocated supply and high demand for a great wine allows it to command high prices, as is true with any product. But other vintners get $14 for a wine that's not appreciably different from an $8 or $10 bottle. Certainly they won't sell as much, but the bottles will sell unless the wine is eviscerated by reviews, because there are probably enough consumers who think that if the price says $14, it must be worth $14. As Marion explains, one should never underestimate the impact of perceived quality.

No one, of course, perceives great quality differences

between generic wines selling for between $3 and $4 a jug. Sales in the low cost segment are very market driven and price sensitive. The province of very few corporations—including E. & J. Gallo and a handful of imported brands, each of which controls about a quarter of the market, and to a lesser degree companies such as Seagram & Sons, Canandaigua Wine, National Distillers and Brown-Foreman—it's a segment of significance to grape growers, distributors and retailers. In terms of pricing and quality debates, it's simply not as interesting as the action surrounding premium table wines.

Certain pricing strategies, some observers feel, are harming the industry as a whole. "The biggest problem with pricing," says James Laube, a senior editor and columnist at *The Wine Spectator*, "is that it's way too high, for just about everything." Laube, who fears that many winemakers are making the beverage downright unaffordable for even weekly consumption, says: "It's becoming a luxury product."

Laube tastes dozens of wines each week and understands the sensory differences between a $6 and $20 wine. A more expensive wine usually gets more "handmade" treatment and, by most measures, is a better product. "But a $20 Cabernet Sauvignon," he explains, "is simply not two or three times better than a $10 Cab." There are differences between a $6 and $10 bottle, although the quality level, if even greatly discernible, may not mean that much to a consumer looking for something pleasant with which to wash down a good plate of spaghetti. "But the lower you get in price," adds Laube, "the closer you get to the reality of economics."

Winery economics, as much as market considerations, are often the major factor in the price of a given wine. The quality of the raw materials and enological skill that go into a wine are critical if it is to successfully remain in a price segment. But where it's placed in a segment can often depend on when a winery was built, and how it's financed, equipped and operated.

Since the mid-1970s, the capital costs of starting an estate operation—which includes vineyards and a winery—have grown astronomically. Wine is one of the most capital intensive of all industries, demanding a considerably higher investment-to-sales ratio than either automobiles or steel. For example, for every dollar it generates in sales, USX has a buck invested in property, mills and other hardware. Micro-electronics companies often invest about $2 in capital for every dollar in sales. But this is about the minimum for a small winery, and a three- or four-to-one ratio has become common.

Prime vineyard land is the foundation of a whopper investment. In the Napa Valley, this can amount to $40,000, $50,000 and more per acre. Of course, land isn't so costly in many other parts of the nation; in Washington's Columbia Valley, which has helped make this state the second-leading wine producer in the nation, good vineyard ground can still be had for $3,000 to $5,000 an acre.

In addition, the U.S. Department of Agriculture estimates that it costs $3,000 to plant an acre of wine grapes, plus $1,000 for annual maintenance. Industry consultants quote much higher costs, up to $10,000 per acre. Consider that the vines don't start producing fruit for several years, and that a winery's other expenditures are loaded up front, with cash flow several years down the road, and profits even further.

Take the case of Dennis Groth, who had been the chief financial officer at Atari while it was crushing tons of money out of the video game industry. In 1986, Groth went public with his winery's costs and revenue projections. Five years before, this former CPA acquired 121 acres near Oakville, in the Napa Valley, and added forty-three acres the following year. Even then it cost him more than $20,000 per acre. Building the 30,000-case-per-year winery Groth envisions will take some $2 million—although he had the sense to delay this expenditure—and still more for cooperage, stainless steel fermenting tanks, fork lifts, trucks, a bottling line and other equipment. Groth figures that by the time he reaches 30,000 cases in production and sales, he will have invested nearly $8 million to generate $2 million in annual sales.

When that times arrives, his projected expenses don't leave much for him to take to the bank. Indeed, on a $13 bottle of wine, he figures that retailer markup would consume $4.33; the distributor markup $2.17; selling and business costs $1.74; grape production $1.43; wine production costs $1.19; interest on loans $1.46; and federal and state taxes 34 cents. What remains is a net profit of 34 cents per bottle, or not much more than $122,000 per year. There are certainly easier and more prosperous ways to invest $8 million.

Of course, there are also different ways to establish a wine business. One path is to construct a showpiece winery, another is to begin with a modest prefab building, generate sales and then expand. It's amazing how frugal a vintner can be.

University of California Berkeley economist Kirby Moulton conducted a survey of small wineries in the early 1980s. He compared their construction costs—including the value of buildings, cooperage and equipment—to their output on a dollars-per-gallon basis. The range was tremendous, with construction costs of less than $4 per gallon for the smaller, flexible operations where the owner substituted his labor for capital equipment, to nearly $22 for the bigger enterprises. Other surveys in the early 1980s suggested construction costs of more than $30 per gallon, and costs are higher today.

Napa Valley vintner Mike Robbins went the full nine yards with his Spring Mountain winery, which includes terraced vineyards and the restored 1880s mansion in which Angela Channing of television's *Falcon Crest* ostensibly lives. Although Robbins started in a small cellar under the old house, he expanded by constructing Victorian-style buildings on sites carved out of the side of a mountain. He went for premium equipment and, as he admits, turned a large fortune he'd earned in real estate into a much smaller one. In business for nearly two decades, he earned operating profits during only one or two years. "It's been a nonprofit corporation," he has said, "that wasn't designed to be that way." Like many vintners, Robbins will have to sell his winery to gain any of its financial fruits.

Daryl Sattui, on the other hand, started his operation on the cheap. Sattui had a plain 4,000-square-foot building and only forty-five wine barrels. He tried to rent out the extra space not just for the money, but to make his place look more like a winery. In turn, he rented most of the equipment he used for winemaking, including a little basket press for $10 a day. Only after his business was well established did he buy his own equipment and upgrade the facilities.

Production costs also vary, depending on what the vintner spends for filters, bottles, corks, capsules to cover the top, labels, shipping cartons and for labor. Other things eat into a winery's budget, including marketing and advertising. Even tastings—for consumers who visit the winery, distributors and retailers—can drain a surprisingly large volume of wine.

"Tastings will kill you," says one winery owner. "Every time one of our salespeople makes a call on a distributor, or a major client like a supermarket chain, the boys and girls there want to taste the wine. Come back just a month later and they want to taste again. Wine writers are always asking for bottles, charity groups want wine for tastings, dinners and auctions. I don't begrudge a reasonable amount of this, but it can get to where you bleed."

Tastings are important because they allow the consumer to taste wine without spending ten bucks. And yet, on crawls through winery-intense regions, some folks do nothing but taste, and are called roadies or tipplers.

To stanch some of the bleeding, a growing number of wineries in the Napa Valley are charging from $1 to $5 for tastings. They'll usually toss in a small glass sporting the winery's logo. But since roadies don't like to pay for anything, a fee, however small, is a magnificent deterrent.

Within a year of opening its tasting room in 1985, "the party animals were finding us," says Stag's Leap Wine Cellars tasting room manager Steve Hare. The winery felt compelled to offer samples, he says, because "if we didn't have tastings they [consumers] felt either we were cheap or we didn't have good wine." But when Stag's Leap Wine Cellars realized that a big percentage of roadies didn't even know which winery they were in, or care, the freebies stopped.

When the winery started charging $2 for a small glass in

which to taste, traffic at Stag's Leap dropped off by a third. And yet, tasting room sales went up by a corresponding amount. Apparently, with the obnoxious crowd out of the way, the serious could linger, ponder and then buy.

There are plenty of little things that wound a winemaker's budget, from spills to unexpected refrigeration unit repair bills. But grapes by far represent the largest single production cost. For some super-premium vintages, grapes account for 60 percent of the winery's operating costs, and average about 40 percent for most small wineries. In recent years, Napa Valley Chardonnay grapes have been going for $1,000 to $1,300 a ton, and more from the most favored vineyards. Cabernet Sauvignon prices have crept upwards from an average of about $800 a ton in 1981 to nearly $1,000 in recent years. (Colombard and Thompson seedless grapes, from which generic jug wines are made, come in, as might be expected, at about $100 to $130 a ton.)

In an interview with *The Wine Spectator*, the venerable Louis Martini said he prices his wine "pretty much based on our costs of production." As a rule of thumb, he added, "I've always figured that you're not going to lose any money if you charge what it costs you to buy grapes divided by 100. In other words, if the grapes cost you $600 a ton, you should be able to put out a $6 bottle of wine with all the full markups."

By and large, wine pricing is an ephemeral thing, although Dennis Marion's approach is about as concrete as one can get; he targets a market segment and works back from there. But other winemakers go the opposite direction, tacking a profit on top of production costs that can be desperately high. It doesn't matter that those costs are outrageous because the winemaker paid too much for vineyards, a showpiece building, took out loans at astonishing interest rates, bought the very best fork lift money can buy, vacations in Europe each year, and simply mismanages the business.

This is not to say mismanagement is behind every super-premium wine, for there are plenty of honest vintners whose sweat is their equity. At Congress Springs Vineyards in Saratoga, California, it took Dan Gehrs a decade before he made a modest profit from wines that range from $5.50 a bottle to $15 for his best Chardonnay. He makes the most of crushing equipment that would embarrass a Bulgarian peasant. And he turns out vintages with sensory qualities equal to their price.

Some vintners count on perceptions of their lifestyle to carry over into their wine's perceived quality. It has worked for Robert Mondavi, who built an aura around his wines by sponsoring cultural events at his winery and spending a ton on promotion. He still trades off a high-toned mystique, and the prices match the illusion. Gehrs holds festivals at his winery in the Santa Cruz mountains and trades off the image of the small, hard-working winemaker.

Premium wine buyers are always on the make for something new and different, to generate the fresh talk that enlivens wine consumption. A vintner can fool the public some of the time, or until the fools in the public move on to the next brand that seems to promise super quality at a startlingly steep price.

Still other vintners use comparative tastings to position their wines against the competition. That is, they'll buy the wines of several competitors in a certain range of prices, taste them, and try to figure out where they should be among that group. Most think their wine is better, and thus tack on a dollar or two. Smart newcomers, on the other hand, bury their egos and price their wines cheaper, just to win a following.

Since there often isn't a noticeable difference between an $8 wine and a $10 wine, and a $10 wine and a $12 wine, a syllogism would suggest that $8 and $12 wine are pretty much the same stuff. There can and should be quality differences between the two, if wine pricing were totally logical. But it's a fact that liquor and grocery stores sell wine with $12 worth of quality for $8, and bottles with eight bucks of quality for twelve. And some consumers not only get what they pay for, but what they deserve.

One area where consumers aren't getting their money's worth is in restaurants. As New York food and wine critic Robert Finigan complains, house wines are frequently marked up by ten times the wholesale cost. "A 1.5 liter bottle of standard California wine will seldom cost a restaurant more than $4," he writes. "At approximately fifty-two ounces to the container, the restaurant can pour thirteen four-ounce servings. If the price per glass is $3, then the establishment has grossed $39 on a $4 investment." An increasing number of restaurants serve name varietals by the glass, a trend hastened by the spread of nitrogen dispensing machines that preserve opened bottles of wine for as long as the liquid holds out. But unless a diner wants only one glass of wine, and wants to spend only $3, the ordinary house wines aren't the greatest deal. Premium wines, too, are often marked up to unconscionable levels.

So, how do consumers know whether they're getting a good or bad deal on a particular wine? The appeal of a given wine is extremely subjective; what's wonderful to one person may seem off or foul to another, the same as with food. Consumers turn to advisors like Robert Parker and *The Wine Spectator* simply because they either lack the confidence to make such judgments, or fear wasting money on trial and error. Still, trying different brands is half the fun of drinking wine. When an individual finds a brand that he or she likes, and which fits the budget, then that person finally has one answer to the price-worth question.

Consumers can face some daunting choices not only in price, but also in an absolutely stunning range of brands and varietals. In a grocery or liquor store that emphasizes wine, one side of an entire aisle can be stocked with bottles, a wall without one duplicate label breaking the variety. For one thing, established wineries keep diversifying their lines—adding popular, hot-selling products such as White Zinfandel and other blush wines—and expanding with second labels. A big wine outlet may feature a couple of hundred different Chardonnays or Cabernets. Moreover, despite the high capital costs, there has been an explosive growth in new wineries in recent years.

The number of bonded California wineries has nearly doubled since the early 1970s, from not many more than 300 to nearly 700 today. According to the Bureau of Alcohol, Tobacco and Firearms, the number of American wineries has grown from less than 650 in 1976 to nearly 1,500.

Wineries don't all compete against each other in every

state. In fact, about the only significant nationwide players are wines from California, imports, a couple of brands from Washington State and the high-alcohol wino varieties out of the East; and much of the juice for these still comes from the Golden State. Wines made in other states largely stay home; the volumes are not great, and if a vintner isn't economically compelled, the trade barriers and hassles of interstate wine commerce aren't worth the trouble.

The increased competition is making life tougher for vintners, along with a reduction in the number of distributors. Indeed, as an increasing number of midsize and even large distributors go out of business, or are bought out by larger entities, power is being concentrated in fewer hands. In one way this is an efficiency, in that a big distributor can more easily handle the nuances of myriad state liquor regulations. In another, wineries cannot command as much loyalty or attention from a business that's handling perhaps dozens of other vintners. To get any kind of edge in the clutter, wineries are forced to offer greater discounts to grab distribution and sales attention, further cutting already thin profit margins.

Explains George Schofield, the former chief financial officer at Robert Mondavi Winery and now a financial consultant to roughly fifty small- to medium-sized wineries: "These wineries simply make far less money than people think. And the owners that have trouble probably underestimated their capital needs. They simply ran out of money. Most of these folks are very intelligent people, and some have marketing abilities. Some don't. Most all of them have the ability to move a limited amount of cases. Anybody can make and sell 5,000 cases of wine, but where they get in trouble is when they try to go from 10,000 to 30,000 cases." Schofield feels that wineries are at best "a 7 percent business," although such a return on total assets is wishful thinking for an awful lot of vintners. It's said that as many as half of all premium California wineries are earning a very minimal financial return. And Schofield feels for those who are, as he says, "just working for the banks."

He does point out that the businessmen who hold on, even if they're just scraping by with a marginal return, "have that underlying appreciation of winery and vineyard land." This is true, and as one vintner ruefully concedes: "Yeah, I'll finally get to sit back and enjoy being a wine-maker after I've sold my winery." Others, however, don't even get to enjoy it, after being forced to sell out to avoid bankruptcy. And there are usually good buyers for a good winery that's failing in marketing and finance.

Corporate-owned wineries, such as Washington's Château Ste. Michelle and Beringer, have purchased other labels to expand their business. These are premium to super-premium wineries, and Ste. Michelle President Allen Shoup believes that beyond a half-million cases of production, even the best big premium winery risks a drop in quality. "Therefore, we think it's better to expand by building or buying other wineries and allowing them to operate the winemaking separately," he explains.

Banks don't like to run wineries, although the Bank of America found itself temporarily sharing the Ste. Genevieve Vineyards with University of Texas, after the owners of the business defaulted on a loan. Located in West Texas, Ste. Genevieve is that state's largest, with 1,000 acres of grapes leased from the university and a $15 million winery. Although *The Wine Spectator* reports that sales of Texas wines are on the increase, the state's battered oil patch businesses—which have defaulted on loans like crazy since the early 1980s—have left Texas banks in shambles. In turn, these institutions don't have the capital to fund winemaking enterprises.

California bankers follow their wine loans closely. It's what they call proactive management. Nervous management is an equally apt description. As Janet Basu noted in *San Francisco Focus*, even when business loan interest rates dropped to about 9 percent in 1986, banks were still asking vintners for 13 percent. "Lenders continued to lump wineries in with the rest of agriculture as high-risk businesses," she wrote. But bankers say there are changes in the wind. "The kinds of clients we're getting today are different from those of four to five years ago," says Bank of America vice president Dave Meddaugh, of its Napa Valley St. Helena office. "Instead of doctors and lawyers out to make a mark in wine, we're hearing from more foreign interests, customers who have done intense financial research, who know the industry and have substantial resources."

Just a bit ominously, the current financial climate in parts of the premium wine business is driving vineyard owners to once again plant grapes that they think will be part of the hottest-selling niche four years hence, disregarding what is best suited for the land. While such decisions on grapes could create liabilities down the road, the reactions are understandable, given the squeeze in which many vintners find themselves.

At a time when competition demands price cuts, bank debts force wineries to seek higher prices; one estimate suggests that a $2 million bank loan adds a good $10 to a winery's case price. But that's only if the business can get it, for some wines aren't sold until long after their most profitable time.

The extra warehouse aging is unintentional. Although certain varietals such as Cabernet Sauvignon and Merlot develop complexity and quality in the process, they can't be held forever. Storage costs eat up whatever value they retain long before they spoil. So, such wine must eventually be dumped at bargain basement prices, $8 wine that can be had for $4.50 or less.

They're fairly easy to spot. The clue on the shelf is when the wine's vintage year is about two or three years older than comparable brands. That is, if it's a 1982 or 1983 Cabernet and the vast majority of other Cabs are 1985 releases, then it's a wine that's just escaped from the Twilight Zone. Reserve wines are often a little older than the majority of releases in a varietal category, but they'll be higher priced than the Zoners.

These warehouse refugees once again present the consumer with a price-quality dilemma: Is the wine cheap because poor quality made it a market failure when first released? Or was it originally just a marketing and pricing failure, a pretty good wine that's now a steal? A low price can make it look suspect; and yet, the consumer may be getting an extra measure of pleasure off another's misfortune.

For example, in the late 1970s and early 1980s, Stephen Zellerbach's Cabernets and Merlots captured their share of gold medals in contests. But his business constantly struggled, pinched by rising costs and high interest rates on the winery he started building in 1981. (Prior to that, with grapes from his own vineyard, Zellerbach had another winery make wines under his label.) But no matter what he did, no matter how much time he devoted to marketing, Zellerbach could not sell much more than half the volume he expected to move. Today, in some California grocery stores, one can find seven- and eight-year-old Zellerbach wine for less than $4.

When a winery deploys all its investment capital, cash flow stops during the year's slow period, and it must borrow to cover day-to-day operating costs, it's the start of a death spiral. Some do pull the operation back up, but others, like Zellerbach, eject before the crash, selling the business and its assets. Winemakers under such stress also just plain wear down, another reason they punch out instead of hanging on.

However, some of California's premium wineries are making a killing. Many of these operations were founded prior to the soaring land price increases of the 1970s, the rampant inflation during that decade and construction costs that get worse every year. And their best vintages illustrate that while some older wines go down in price, others climb at a wondrous rate.

Indeed, certain wines from the most esteemed vineyards and wineries—including Jordan, Sterling, Mondavi, Caymus, Heitz and Ridge—appreciate in price by 20 percent or more each year. George Schofield has predicted that the price of a Jordan 1982 Cabernet Sauvignon will fetch more than $73 a decade later, appreciating by more than $56.

However, some other wineries that are doing extremely well have wines that are among the easiest to acquire—the cheapest fighting varietals such as those from Glen Ellen, Fetzer and Sutter Home, which virtually flood stores with bottles that may sell for as little as $3.49 a pop. These new, high-volume players drain business from others in the premium segment, and it puts additional pressure on wineries in the $5 to $8 category to lower prices. The squeeze gets even tighter.

While the low-priced dry table wines are considerably better than jugs of generics, any wine drinker with even a moderately refined palate can tell the difference between an ordinary Sutter Home or Glen Ellen and a legitimate super premium. But for just three and a half bucks, the consumer can be fairly assured that the quality, as Dennis Marion says, provides value for the price. Such wines almost scream to be taken home and consumed with regular, just-the-family meals on Tuesday and Wednesday nights.

And this is something that the American wine industry, after all, has been wanting to happen for, well, just about a hundred years.

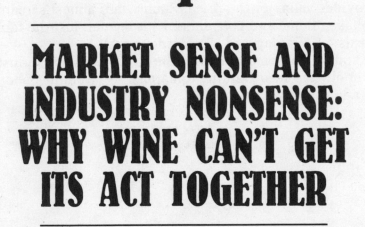

4

MARKET SENSE AND INDUSTRY NONSENSE: WHY WINE CAN'T GET ITS ACT TOGETHER

Don Payne tried to put it another way, with an analogy that everyone at this glittering and gala assembly could understand. Tall, lanky, and sporting a white beard and one of his dapper, trademark bow ties, Payne is an affable Ph.D. psychologist, and an executive vice president of Oxtoby Smith, a New York–based consumer research and consulting firm. In 1985, his company conducted a $275,000 market survey for the California wine industry; a few people in the business found the study useful, although many considered it a waste of cash. Still, Payne was invited to sit on a discussion panel before the most important gathering of the industry's eagles in a century.

It was a stifling hot afternoon in late August 1987, at the Buena Vista winery near Sonoma. The excuse for the affair was the winery's one hundred thirtieth anniversary. Founded by Agoston Haraszthy, a legendary name in the business, Buena Vista is now owned by A. Racke International of West Germany, and is operated by Marcus Moller-Racke and his wife, Anne. Buena Vista has called the soiree "Vintage 2000—A Challenge to the Future."

Nearly every big name in the business of growing grapes, making and selling wine, consulting in the business and writing about it was there. The guest list read like a directory to America's greatest wineries, and even included old Ernest Gallo, who looked surprised at himself for being there, if not a little lost. On the panel with Payne were several winery executives, including Robert Mondavi, a wine-prescribing physician and Kaiser Permanente hospital director named David Whitten, and U.S. Congressman Robert Matsui. Their discussion was moderated by Gourmet magazine wine editor Gerald Asher, a diffident, plump British fellow who is known as a perspicacious wine importer as well as an elegant prose stylist.

Don Payne was trying to explain why more Americans don't drink wine. "You are trying to reach a reluctant audience, which is very difficult to do," he said. "Wine is kind of like Guatemala." Wine has been compared to a countless number of things, although likely never a Central American nation. But Payne pressed on.

"You see, we were recently approached by the Ambassador of Guatemala about a survey. He was concerned about a lack of tourism and asked, 'Why do Americans hate Guatemala?' Well, it's pretty obvious that Americans don't hate Guatemala. It just never occurred to them to go there for a vacation." American awareness of the nation is so low, explained Payne, "It doesn't exist on the list of alternatives. And so wine is like Guatemala."

Sitting several seats down the panel from Payne, Robert Mondavi's eyes were heavy. He hadn't said a word in ten minutes and in the heat looked nearly asleep. But suddenly, as if goosed, he bolted upright and began railing, convinced that his words carried truth. "Why can't we get a single, simple program?" he fairly shouted. "An on-going program. When it's so simple to get to all the people, and we just do restaurants. I just don't see that! I'm amazed."

Mondavi was referring—in a short-hand kind of manner, of course—to the lack of a big campaign, a nationwide push to put wine in front of the American consumer. But what he meant was understood. And ignored.

The discussion moved on and the panel got into a rancorous and drawn-out debate on ingredient labeling on wine bottles. At the moment, labeling is a problem for the industry, not a minor one, but certainly not disastrous. The panel never returned to Guatemala, or why Americans don't drink more wine.

Vintage 2000 was a good idea, but the mass had not gone critical, and a rare opportunity slipped away. Expecting more was perhaps a chimerical notion. Individuals in the wine business often know where they, individually, are headed. But as an industry they go in hundreds of different directions, and collectively, to be blunt, they show about as much vision as Ray Charles.

However, the past decade has been good, very good to the wine industry. According to figures released by the Wine Institute, the American wine market increased by 210 million gallons in that time, from 376.4 million gallons sold in 1976 to 586.6 million gallons in 1986. While dessert and appetizer wines slipped from 21.9 percent of the market to 9.5 percent in 1986, the low-alcohol segment—which consists of table wine, champagne, wine coolers and natural wines—grew remarkably, from 294.2 million gallons to 531.1. The growth rate of wine sales in this period exceeded that of most other beverage groups, both alcoholic and non-alcoholic.

Moreover, boosted by a sharp drop in the dollar's value against foreign currencies, American wine exports increased 64 percent in 1987 over the previous year, to nearly twelve million gallons, about 95 percent of which came from

California. The value of these exports amounted to $60.8 million, as opposed to $34.8 million in 1986. Canadians purchased the greatest volume, some 3.3 million gallons worth almost $11 million. But the Japanese, who tended to buy more expensive wines, bought 2.25 million gallons worth $14 million, almost double what they had spent a year before. Even the United Kingdom nearly doubled its American purchases, from 962,000 gallons in 1986 to 1.9 million in 1987.

In addition, a number of California wineries were riding a boom right through the first nine months of 1987. Indeed, Sutter Home had registered a 63 percent sales increase, or 1.6 million more gallons, over the same period in 1986. According to a Jon Fredrikson survey, other moderately priced varietal producers also had big sales jumps: Geyser Peak had a 36 percent increase, Fetzer 34 percent, Wine World (which includes the Beringer and Los Hermanos brands) 23 percent, and Glen Ellen with a stunning 83 percent jump.

As Fredrikson told *Wines & Vines* magazine, "Many smaller wineries marketing super-premium and ultra-premium varietals also posted volume gains in the 10 percent to 15 percent range. Pine Ridge was up 85 percent in the first nine months, William Hill 81 percent, Dry Creek 42 percent, Kendall-Jackson 59 percent, Cuvaison 94 percent, Buena Vista 25 percent and La Crema 151 percent."

The export increases and figures from individual wineries, however, mask some fundamental problems. The U.S. wine market has, since 1986, slumped to about 575 million gallons annually, and most industry analysts figure the growth curve has flattened to a plateau. Wine coolers, which had a 36.8 percent sales increase jump from 1985 to 1986, now seem to be cooling off. Sales of generic jug wines, which represent about 80 percent of the wine market, have been dropping 2 percent to 3 percent a year throughout the 1980s. (Imports peaked at nearly 142.4 million gallons in 1984, capturing more than 25 percent of the U.S. market. The percentage fell to 18.5 percent two years later, but imports will likely always take at least this much of the U.S.

market, through low-end Italian wines and French and German premiums that do well along the Eastern Seaboard.) And despite its decade of growth, wine remains one of the least popular beverages in America, ahead of only spirits.

Even more alarming, there was a precipitous 1988 decline in wine consumption in that bellwether state, California. For the first time in thirty years, wine consumption dropped—a hefty 3.8 percent, to 4.5 gallons per person. Most of it occurred in bulk wines, continuing the national trend. Nevertheless, this figure carries ominous implications for the premium end of the industry as well. It indicates that those Americans who are most inclined to drink wine already are; few new wine drinkers are coming into the marketplace. And by and large, as California goes, so goes the national industry.

According to *Beverage World* magazine's 1987 Beverage Market Index, Americans are guzzling more refreshment fluids than ever, some 22.54 billion gallons' worth in 1986. By far the most favored fluid was soft drinks, accounting for about 48 percent of the total. Beer finished second with almost 26 percent, with fruit juices, drink mixes and bottled water all coming ahead of wine, which had a 2.6 percent share. Their figures didn't even mention milk.

Furthermore, roughly half the wine sold in the U.S. is consumed by the residents of just nine states; California quaffs 20 percent of it, while the others include Illinois, New York, Massachusetts, New Jersey, Texas, Florida, Ohio and Pennsylvania. Thanks to its burgeoning in-state industry, Washington is climbing, but on the whole, this concentration suggests weak nationwide marketing.

But even the industry's gains, while certainly significant, fail to impress one Louis Roos Gomberg, a man whose opinions are worth hearing out. In the wine business, he is a singular kind. "If you look at this from a couple of other perspectives," he explains, sitting in his comfortably cluttered office on the seventh floor of a building on San Francisco's Market Street, "you'll see that the United States is only a speck or a dot in the world of wine. From the standpoint of per capita consumption, we're something like thirtieth out of the thirty-five leading industrial nations.

Some of the big wine-consuming nations have recently had consumption declines, such as France, Italy and Spain, and they're still averaging around twenty gallons.

"Chile, Switzerland and Austria average ten to twelve gallons," Gomberg continues, "while the U.S. finally reaches 2.4 gallons after a twenty-five-year climb from four-tenths of a gallon. But if you don't include Thunderbird, Wild Irish Rose, Muscatel and Vermouth, just eliminate the junk and consider dry table wine, then it's only about 1.6 gallons per capita. So is that such tremendous growth? When you reach my age, it gives you a different perspective."

Gomberg's age is eighty-one, and he's been an active player in the American wine industry since 1935. At the time, the Wine Institute was just getting started, and it was looking for an administrative assistant who would essentially be a director of research. The person, Gomberg was told, needed five qualifications. First was a grounding in economics; Gomberg said that was his college major. Second, a background in statistics; "My minor," he replied. The person had to be a writer; Gomberg had just spent nine years as a newspaper and Associated Press reporter. Legally trained? He had picked up a law degree along the way. Well, how about experience with trade associations? "Well, the AP is kind of a trade association," he offered.

Gomberg actually took the job—perhaps just to spite the damn prerequisites—and when he didn't receive a paycheck at the end of his first month, and was told, only then, that he was on "a three-month trial," he still stuck around. Gomberg plunged into his work and got his hands on a copy of a book called *Supply and Price Trends in the California Wine Grape Industry, 1869–1918*, what he now calls "my original bible." He still has it, along with his first statistical report on the number of bonded premium wineries in the state and 1934 export and import figures.

Since then, Gomberg has fiddled with virtually every statistic coming out of the business and law that has affected it. After leaving the Institute he invested in a winery that lost its entire inventory in a 1953 mudslide that crushed its cellar. He founded Gomberg, Fredrikson & Associates, which provides consulting services to wine producers, marketers, advertising agencies and investment firms. He's got perspective at his age, all his faculties and when one gets him rolling—and it isn't the least bit difficult—the man is a certified rare vintage.

He's often in his Gomberg, Fredrikson office on weekends, when not off at meetings on international law, United Nations policies or international understanding seminars with the likes of Ted Turner. Balding and with a full, snowy beard and black-rimmed glasses set on a wondrously prominent, drooping beak, Gomberg is sitting there wearing a yellow, red and blue madras shirt, a pair of red slacks, and he's not on his way to a golf match. No matter, it's a casual kind of day, and he speaks in a gentle, pleasant and charming voice that rises in pitch when he grows enthused, which is often.

According to Gomberg, the wine industry is a long way from deliverance. Two major things adversely affect it, aside from the Guatemala thing, although both problems have an impact on the public's lack of what might be called "wine awareness." One is the trade barriers between the states. The laws prevent wineries from shipping directly to customers across most state lines, though they make life cushy and comfortably monopolistic for relatively few distributors, which along with the state liquor control boards have no incentive to see the system changed. The other problem is an absolutely abysmal lack of an industry-sponsored, well-funded and big-time American wine promotion.

In his heyday at the Wine Institute, Gomberg had twenty-seven assistants working to compile statistics and summaries on state laws and regulations. "There is no group of products in this country," he says, "that is more highly regulated and subject to more diverse laws and regulations than alcohol. And wine regulations are just as complex as those covering spirits and beer. It's a very complex set-up and no two states are alike. Some states have taxes and fees that are three to four times higher than others. And now that so many states have their own wine industries, they seem to be developing preferential treatment for local wines, with higher taxes and more regulations for those made out of state." An Oklahoma winemaker, for example, pays a $75 annual license fee; an out-of-stater who wants to sell there, $625.

The United States Department of Treasury's Bureau of Alcohol, Tobacco and Firearms administers most of the federal regulations covering the wine industry, while the Food and Drug Administration, of course, is the guardian of health concerns. But state regulations are the most encompassing and difficult to deal with. As economist Kirby Moulton noted in a chapter on wine industry economics, written with Gino Zepponi and published in a 1987 Academic Press book called *Economics of Food Processing in the United States*: "The philosophy and character of many regulations stem directly from America's Prohibition period. When Prohibition was repealed, individual states were granted rights to regulate the production, marketing, and consumption of alcoholic beverages. Such beverages were effectively removed from the protection provided to other goods under interstate commerce laws."

There are myriad regulations on what kind of establishments can sell wine, in what form, on what days of the week and at what times. New York and Pennsylvania do not allow wine to be sold in grocery stores; if they did so, goes the industry consensus, U.S. wine consumption might double. Blue laws still exist in a number of regions, and some states provide a local option for a county or town to remain dry. Prohibition still wiggles, squirms and is alive.

About two years ago, an Eastern sales manager of a California winery attended a large tasting affair being held at a New Jersey casino. The law in that state maintains that such tastings must have an educational or cultural raison d'être. Moreover, all the wine used must be bought from a licensed distributor or wholesaler. It can be served only by licensed bartenders or cocktail waitresses, who, thanks to the licensing process, know they can only dole the fluid out one ounce at a time, while keeping a pot of fresh, hot coffee on hand, lest they face The Consequences. So, when the sales manager learned that the casino didn't have his wine that was supposed to be tasted, he went to his car to get a case. Busted by a Division of Gaming Enforcement agent, his wine was taken away, he was threatened with a $5,000 fine if he did it again, and then let go. Say all the nice things you will about New Jersey—and the state has its charms—but this is rather ludicrous considering the cash it extracts from drunk gamblers, and quite hypocritical.

Fees, which are essentially taxes, are yet another burden. In its state budget passed in June of 1987, Ohio set up a new fee structure that requires a $600-per-year fee for each out-of-state supplier of beer, mixed beverages and wine. The structure also includes a $35 registration fee, and $30 to cover a lab analysis of each label. For small, out-of-state wineries, this can be quite a financial burden.

As Ohio wine distributor George Hammer told the Cleveland *Plain Dealer*, a small vintner who might allocate ten cases to the state is, with just the $600 fee, looking at a $5 per bottle boost in price. Wine that would otherwise make its way to the finer restaurants in Cincinnati—and for folks on the Coasts, these do exist—won't even get into the state. The fees, groused a Cleveland retailer, will preclude the consumption of fine wine in Ohio.

States that maintain controlled liquor stores have a semi-monopoly on the wine trade. State operations can wrangle good bargains from producers and concentrate on selling a high volume of relatively few wines. Since they're not market-driven, these stores are not compelled to carry a large number of choices for consumers, nor discount prices. Their interests are protected; if you're caught bringing wine across Pennsylvania state lines, the minimum penalty is a $25 per bottle fine.

In fact, only those few states that have signed bilateral and reciprocal trade agreements allow direct wine shipments to consumers across state lines. Although selling wine by mail order is an increasingly important marketing tactic within California, sending it to many other states would be a crime. Appearing before a California state Senate select sub-committee on the wine industry in November 1987, vintner Sandy Obester explained that visitors to her winery near

Half Moon Bay on the San Francisco peninsula almost daily ask that wine be shipped out of state. She frequently must decline.

"If I were producing drugs," she told the committee, "I could drop them into the mail box, but the law forbids me to send wine that simply." In fact, Obester asserted that the United Parcel Service, spooked by even the slightest possibility that underage kids would get their hands on mail-order wine, refuses to accept shipments to states where such trade is legal. The liability fears are understandable, but truly dubious products—from breast enlargers to "guaranteed" hair-growth potions—zip through parcel channels.

Most of these states that prohibit out-of-state mail order wine require that vintners send their products through licensed brokers or distributors. If the states allow grocery stores to sell wine, and the chain is big enough to support a high volume, it, too, may be able to acquire a distributor license. "The idea of having distributors control the wine coming into a state is that it's a central source from which to collect taxes, which makes the job easier for the state," explains one California winegrower. "Nothing gets past them that way. And it's a darn good symbiotic deal for those distributors when they don't have to compete against direct shipments. They don't even compete much against each other where states set minimum wholesale prices. The territory is carved up and maintained with minimum effort. So both the liquor control boards and distributors like to keep things just the way they are." And there are others who don't particularly mind.

For a small winery, dealing with the downright Byzantine state regulations is a monumental hassle. If a winery in New York, Washington, Texas or California wants to sell its wine in Ohio, it must make sure that its bathrooms are up to Midwestern ideals of codified cleanliness. Under the imprimatur of Governor Richard Celeste, and Rule 4301:1–103, Article V, Section 1: wineries must operate in a building "(e) In which all toilet facilities shall be partitioned off from any part of the manufacturing department or bottling department," and "(f) Which is provided with handwashing facilities consisting of a lavatory, soap, and individual towels." Ohio law also specifies how often the floor of the winery must be scrubbed, and then reiterates that the toilet and lavatory "shall be maintained in a state of complete efficiency, and shall be cleaned at all times."

This doesn't mean Ohio regulators are obsessive; to be fair, these are reasonable health standards. But there's also a portion of the Ohio regulations that states that "No person suffering from a contagious or infectious disease shall work . . . in the manufacturing or bottling of wine." The state requires that winery workers have physicals from a licensed physician, and certificates showing them as free of such ailments; Ohio inspectors can demand to be shown such certificates at any time.

This brings up some interesting questions. AIDS, technically speaking, is infectious, although it would be absolutely impossible for it to be transmitted through wine. Given the epidemiology of the disease, it's almost certain that there are winery workers with AIDS at facilities making wine that's sold in Ohio. Should Ohio get itself into an AIDS panic, mount a hunt and try to push this one, denying a permit to a winery with an AIDS-afflicted employee, it could face an awfully nasty civil rights and restraint of trade lawsuit.

The real upshot of these regulations, of states that control distribution and sales of wine, and of every little tax and trouble levied against the product, is restraint of trade. Winegrowers have a tough time generating sales when they don't get cooperation from, say, a state store. Moreover, state liquor stores actually establish physical and psychological barriers to the purchase of wine.

Savvy grocery store managers know that wine is an impulse buy and thus try to make it as convenient as possible for a customer to grab a bottle. At a Lucky grocery market in Hayward, California, bottles of Chardonnay are in hanging racks near the fish section, Cabernets are poking out everywhere in the cheese case, while bottles are lined in a row beneath the meat counter, are piled in bins near the crackers, sit in racks virtually everywhere, and also take up most of the liquor aisle itself. "Hey, it's one of the more expensive items in the store," says an assistant manager. "We get a 25 percent markup on it and this stuff just flies out the door. We make it real easy for people to toss a bottle in the cart and take it home for dinner."

But if a consumer in New York wants a bottle, says Gerald Asher, "He or she has to make a conscious decision to walk into that store and ask for it. It's not only an inconvenience, but the message is that this is not a part of everyday living . . . and it's slightly tainted." It's a wicked purchase, not relaxed and casual. About half of Pennsylvania's liquor stores still have counters that separate consumers from the wine.

Some of this is changing. From 1969 through 1985, restrictions were eased in Washington, Maine, Idaho, Alabama, New Hampshire, California, Montana, West Virginia and Iowa. The year after it deregulated its state store system, the volume of wine going into Iowa increased by nearly 60 percent. Every state that has eased restrictions has seen an immediate consumption increase.

Despite lobbying efforts by California's Wine Institute— one of its major charges is to fight the trade barriers between states and those that exist in foreign nations—all too many states make it costly and tough to market and sell wine. If tax revenues are indeed what the states are mainly after from wine, this may be a product where supply-side economics truly works; by lowering taxes and making it easier for folks to purchase wine, the increased volume will boost revenues.

Though the industry has found it difficult to fight the statehouses, it does have a few allies. There's a group, for example, called Pennsylvanians for a Responsible End to the State Store System, which in 1986 had 2,500 members. But as its chairman told The Wine Spectator's Neal Ewing, "Many people who support us philosophically won't get involved politically." In other words, the industry's trade barrier problems and how it hinders winery marketing simply doesn't jingle the public's hormones.

Guatemala doesn't jingle American hormones, either. But the blame for this doesn't rest with the American public. This is a public that gobbles Twinkies and fast-food burgers whole, buys expensive BMWs, cheap Hyundais, VCRs, and watches MTV and PBS. The American public buys good books, *People* magazine and the appeals of slick television preachers. The American public spends billions and billions of dollars on the dumbest, most useless items imaginable. They're so open with minds and pocketbooks that they'll go for just about anything if it's pitched right.

That the wine industry can't sell them on wine to a greater degree is almost unfathomable. Even trade barriers aren't to blame, because if the public really wanted the wine, a lot of barriers would fall. No, the fault rests with an industry that's never gotten its collective act in gear. It's a subject, though, that puts Lou Gomberg into overdrive.

"There was an industry program for twenty years, from 1938 to 1958, to get more people to drink wine, and it was a very modest program, designed to offend no one," says Gomberg, moving to the edge of his chair. "And its message was, essentially, 'Mrs. Gotrocks serves wine, so why don't you?' And the only people encouraged to try wine was the elitist and semi-elitist trade."

Consumer attitudes toward wine were made fairly clear in a 1955 industry-commissioned study done by Elmo Roper. It was in many ways highly flawed, says Gomberg. The Roper staff was given little training in the complexities of wine, which obviously hindered their interrogative and analytical abilities during interviews. "The three most popular wines among regular home wine users were port, kosher Concords and sherry," Gomberg laughs, "so you know there had to be something questionable about the data-gathering and analysis. But the Roper staff also interviewed 5,000 Americans, and asked each about 400 questions. And it turned out that the word 'wine' had some very interesting connotations for Americans."

Asked if they thought wine was a drink for Americans, about 90 percent responded with a flat no. "Then, they were asked if it wasn't a drink for Americans, who do they think it's for," Gomberg continues. "Well, the first answer was that wine is for rich people, not Americans. Number two, it's for foreigners, not Americans. And three, it's for drunken bums, not Americans."

That one can't be rich or a drunken bum and still be American is a notion that may have reflected some perversely strong middle-class values of the 1950s. But while American bums patriotically pickled themselves on domestic Thunderbird, the elitist trade ensured that the growth rate of imported wines was substantially higher than the growth rate for U.S. brands. Meanwhile, until 1955, Gomberg explains, the California wine industry had a policy of not recognizing distinctions between premium and cheaper wines. And the Europeans loved this, for it made it incredibly easy to snootily dismiss all California wines as being alike. The worst dragged down the best.

That year, about thirty-five California wineries started the Special Public Relations Program for California Premium Wines, and the industry went along. It worked, to the degree most of those wineries shipped much larger volumes, at a growth 50 percent higher than the imports. But grand, industrywide efforts to push wine languished.

In 1937, California vintners had established a Wine Advisory Board, a marketing order established to fund research and promotion activities, most of which were carried out by the Wine Institute under contract. It lasted until 1975, when changes in how the state administered the program made it unworkable. It never worked all that great anyway, or wine would be more popular. At various times, growers in California and New York tried to get commissions and marketing orders under way, only to have them torpedoed by wineries. As Moulton and Zepponi note, "Fears arose that growers would organize into price bargaining groups after a marketing order was initiated."

Grape growers and vintners got it together in 1984 for a new marketing order. With a broad base of about 6,600 members, it was set up so that it couldn't influence grape price bargaining between growers and wineries. And by raising something like $8 million, it had some cash to invest in wine promotion and marketing.

It hired Julia Child, of all people, to hawk California wine on television. While a wonderful lady, Child is often reticent to endorse much of anything. She didn't even really want to do this, but as Jim Laube noted in one of his *Wine Spectator* columns, took the California Winegrowers $100,000 and delivered a "soft sell and a watered-down message about California wine that few people paid attention to." They also funded Don Payne's Oxtoby-Smith study.

For $275,000 the industry received the results of a survey of 1,176 adults who drink wine at least once a month, boiled into a seventy-one-page document, with big type, and between 30 and 150 words per page, numbers included. It revealed that wine is a woman's drink, or that 56 percent of the wine drinkers are women. It revealed that 72 percent of the subjects don't often read or study newspaper or magazine articles about wine, and don't really care. It revealed that there are six different kinds of wine drinkers: "simplifiers," who go for the cheap, mostly California jug wines; "self-assured, modern drinkers," who think wine is special and who are predominantly female; "sophisticated highlifers," who lean toward imports but are knowledgeable and try anything; "insecure social drinkers" and "cautious conservatives," the former of which drink most anything but wine, while the latter, low-educated females, are just uninterested; lastly come the "disaffected wine drinkers," who are careful with a buck, and don't like wine ritual or think it's fun.

The study concluded that wine drinkers are a reluctant audience for the message the industry is currently sending, and rely more on friends and liquor store employees for suggestions. Most who do drink wine regularly stick with a few brands. Oxtoby-Smith recommended ignoring the mass media, developing more restaurant programs, retail trade programs and other channels. Curiously, the survey didn't deal with those Americans who don't drink wine, which suggests giving up on a rather large segment of the population.

From his own perspective, Payne believes that it would be almost impossible to catalyze the entire industry to cooperate in a mass campaign. "You've got a lot of relatively small players, with budgets that are very modest, and who wouldn't really get the benefits of a big program. It's the giants who tend to dominate advertising that would benefit most." And as the marketing order that funded the Oxtoby-

Smith study and the abortive Julia Child campaign came up for a renewal vote in 1987, it fell apart and expired. The Wine Institute took no position on the matter.

Like most trade organizations, the Wine Institute essentially lobbies governments and conducts public relations work. Under Director John DeLuca, the emphasis has been placed more on the former than the latter. Much dissatisfaction is expressed within the industry about the Institute's priorities, particularly among its smaller members. "The Institute gets its money from wine assessments," says one vintner. "And who has the most wine to assess? Gallo, of course. So what it all boils down to is Gallo controlling the Wine Institute. When Gallo says frog, the Institute jumps. They're essentially a marketing arm of Gallo, and they just throw sop to the rest of us. That's why we have to form our own organizations based on viticultural areas to get our story across."

Gallo, says the clearly agitated vintner, doesn't care about promotion. "They can afford to do their own promotion and PR, and plenty of it," he adds. "What they want are basic changes in state laws that will allow them to sell more of their product, and protection from higher taxes."

The Agitated Vinter feels it isn't fair that the Wine Institute's money often goes mainly to what the Gallos want. "There isn't diddly left over for the kind of programs that would help small premium wineries," he growls. "We don't move hundreds of thousands or millions of cases, so lobbying isn't a crucial issue for us. What we need are good, upscale promotional programs that tell the story about premium wine and good food. We don't get that from the Institute. Their educational programs are a joke."

"Education" is a word that comes up over and over when winegrowers and wine writers talk about the public. They surely mean well, but it's an odious word in this context. It implies that consumers must learn to pick up on the nose in a glass of wine, describe the length and sensory qualities in its finish. It implies that consumers just don't know enough to serve white wine with fish, and red with meat and cheese. It implies that while an individual may be smart enough to choose a prime filet mignon for the barbecue, he or she

71

needs eight weeks in an enological boot camp to be able to buy the correct wine. The word "education" smacks of arrogance, and as long as wine promotion suggests that it's trying to teach the great unwashed anything, the great unwashed will recoil.

Gerald Asher feels that most of the industry's efforts are "aimed at those persons who are already buying." Marketing managers are more concerned with protecting their brand and holding market share than "civilizing the savages," as he facetiously adds. But he also believes that if many of the barriers to wine-buying were simply removed, its popularity would take care of itself.

"In large portions of this country," he says, "people can buy wine in grocery stores, or state liquor stores, and most of what they find is Gallo. But the problem is that the ordinary person in these areas would try other wines. If you go to Kansas and Oklahoma, and see the things that are on sale in supermarkets, it's readily apparent that these people are very savvy and sophisticated about food. They'll pick something up and try it. What they don't pick up is a bottle of wine, because it's not there. So they have to make a conscious decision that 'I am a person who drinks wine,' and go get it at a state store. If it's not a habit, it's not going to happen that often."

Louis Gomberg thinks the industry should go all out to put that thought into the public mindset, but he doesn't see it as education, which is intimidating and patronizing. "I've thought about this quite a bit over the years," says the venerable statistician, "and I'd rather call it 'wine awareness.' It would consist of images, as much as anything, that link wine to family and food throughout history. Start with Rome, tastefully done of course. But they would be common, familiar settings to which people can relate, and show wine as an integral and enhancing part of the settings."

The milk and cheese industries have done this. The California raisin industry and an almond growers co-op have pulled off exceptional institutional advertising campaigns that have juiced public awareness of their products. Even orthodontists have done this, in a manner of speaking, and lured in many new clients, both children and adults.

The real challenge of Vintage 2000 isn't to make some super Cabernet, Merlot or the next sweet and fizzy concoction to capture the fancy of young drinkers. It's to get the public to think of Wine, with a capital W, or even better, to grab a bottle in the grocery or liquor store, any bottle, without even thinking.

In August 1989, Buena Vista hosted another industry symposium. An advertising executive advised the wine-growers to throw away their fancy phrases and gold medals and reach out to new markets such as the elderly as minorities. In talk after talk, these people exhorted each other to quit snubbing potential customers. But, alas, the time to do that had been two years before, when labeling wasn't that real an issue. Today, going after new markets—as much as they're needed—is almost chimeric, an opportunity lost. Growing anti-alcohol sentiments are the industry's biggest current nightmare. And it's compounding a long-standing problem.

The American public, if they're only goosed right, will buy practically anything. Except more wine.

Section Two

A
Ripening
Industry

5

ELUSIVE PROMISE, PATRIARCHS AND PROHIBITION

At an annual convention of California grape growers and winemakers, one of the state's most prominent vintners stood before his fellow businessmen and bluntly laid out some of the problems facing the industry. "Let us see to the making of better wine, and more of it," he said. "However, I must caution against our over-sanguine producers not to expect too great a return for their products until the market has been firmly established, and to those who are about entering upon the seductive pursuit of raising grapes, I must caution against paying an extravagant price for vineyard land. That is an important factor in your profit."

These and other cautions came from Arpad Haraszthy, the

first president of California's State Board of Viticultural Commissioners, and a son of Agoston Haraszthy, about one hundred years ago. The problems and promises of today are, as his talk suggests, nothing new.

As Frona Eunice Wait wrote in her chatty 1889 book, *Wines and Vines of California, a Treatise on the Ethics of Wine-Drinking*, a tome officially endorsed by the Viticultural Commissioners no less: "At this stage of our viticultural progress, I consider it more important to teach the people the proper use of wine as a daily beverage than the extension of our vineyards, or any other viticultural work that the Commission can enter upon. At this critical moment our future success depends upon the immediate popular increased consumption of our wines more than greater production."

To the vintners who made it and the pundits who wrote about the beverage, American wine, a 400-year saga, has always been on the verge. While their optimism was bred by no small measure of self-interest, the North American landscape itself seemed to hold a Manifest Destiny for the vine.

So suggested one Edward R. Emerson, in his 1902 book, *The Story of the Vine*. "America with her many climes and her different soils, her growing population, and her liberal mode of government," he wrote, "is sure to be the land of destiny for the wine. Her progress in this branch of industry has already created a feeling of apprehension in the breasts of the thinking people of Europe and the rapid strides she has made in the last twenty-five years would have been called simply marvelous had they occurred in any other land but America. This is not written in the spirit of boastfulness, neither do I wish to be taken as a prophet. . . . After all, time alone can prove the assertion that America will in time be the leading wine-producing country of the world."

At least Emerson demurred on his prophetic skills. However, this author trumpeted America's wine future at a time when the industry started to soar, before hopes were ultimately dashed by Prohibition.

However, long before 1920, forces worked against the wine trade. Kansas went dry in 1880 and by World War I, thirty-two of the forty-eight states followed, seriously cutting into the wine trade. And yet, for decades the industry did a fine job of cutting its own throat. Brutal competition and nefarious acts of sabotage by vintners in rival American wine regions created internecine warfare that drove the public to drink; to drink almost anything but wine.

Above all, wine is a product that has never quite caught on with the general American public, at least when compared to the volume of beer that's consumed. No one knows why, but it all could have been quite different.

From the very start, the New World had all the fixings to make wine the national drink. It was not for nothing that the Norse Viking explorer Leif Eriksson, who upon landing on the North American continent in the year 1,000—likely in present-day Nova Scotia—proclaimed the area Vinland. Whether the ancient Icelandic sagas accurately reflect the events of that time, or whether "Lucky" Eriksson really found squashberries instead of wild grapes (both are matters that continue to keep academics gainfully employed writing papers), it's a fact that grapes are native to America.

Most of the native grapes were of the *Vitis labrusca* variety, a sturdier "slip-skin" fruit somewhat different from the *Vitis vinifera* of European vineyards. They were wild grapes that could survive the harsh climate of New England and the Midwest. These yielded a wine with a strong grape flavor, which wine experts call foxy. Yet another native variety is the *Vitis rotundifolia*, also known as the Muscadines, which give fruit similar to cherries.

It was a Muscadine grape, the Scuppernong, that was turned into America's first wine by French Huguenots who had set up camp in Florida in 1564. In 1609, at Jamestown in Virginia, colonists fermented wine from native grapes. So did the *Mayflower*'s passengers; in 1623, three years after driving ashore at Plymouth, Massachusetts, the Pilgrims had made enough progress to serve native wine with their first Thanksgiving feast.

This was for entertainment. Commercial ventures were already underway. On July 7, 1616, Lord Delaware dispatched a report to the London Company, a commercial trading company chartered by King James I in 1606, to colonize the eastern American coast in the vicinity of Virginia. "In every boske and hedge, and not farr from our pallisade gates we have thousands of goodly vines running along and cleaveing to every tree, which yields a plentiful grape in their kinde," he wrote. "Let me appeale, then, to knowledge if these naturall vines were planted, dressed and ordered by skilfull vinearoons, whether we might not make a perfect grape and fruitfull vintage in short time?"

What Lord Baltimore meant, in the colorful argot of the day, was that the grapes were growing like weeds in the New World and if the Company would just send some capital and skilled labor, he thought he could make the London-based investors some serious money. The shareholders agreed, and in 1619 supplied Delaware with a large collection of French vines and a legion of French vignerons to plant and tend them.

In recruiting the vignerons for the New World venture, the London Company granted the French émigrés exceptional terms. The French, of course, promptly took advantage of the situation. In 1623, the Virginia Colonial Assembly passed a law requiring each householder to plant ten vines; the vignerons, in theory, were supposed to help get this industry off the ground. For about a decade they didn't, growing tobacco on their leases, withholding viticultural advice and in general ticking off the Brits. Their behavior eventually inspired a damning popular resolution.

It said: "That the frenchmen transported into this country for the plantinge and dressinge of vynes and to instruct others in the same, have willinglie concealed the skill, and not only neglected to plant any vynes themselves, but have spoyled and ruinated the vyniard which was, with great cost, planted by the charge of the late company, and yet receaved all favour and encouragement thereunto, which has dishartened all the inhabitants." Insults weren't enough.

80

The colony also levied a punishment, restraining the vignerons from planting tobacco "upon penaltie to forfeit their leases and imprisonment until they depart out of this Colony."

In addition to sticking it to the French in this act, the colony ruled that all corn and tobacco workers must plant five more vines, or lose a barrel of corn in revenues for failing. Thanks to its stronger wine or dine policy, Virginia was able to ship a small quantity of its wine to England, but musty casks and the long voyage more or less wrecked the vintage. For a time, a Virginia law prohibited the import of wines; like much protectionist legislation, it hurt as much as it helped and in 1639 was repealed.

Meanwhile, other colonies also gave winemaking a try. In 1632, for the express purpose of planting wine grapes, Massachusetts Governor John Winthrop was given Governor's Island in Boston Harbor. Eleven years later, Sweden's Queen Christina ordered the governor of New Sweden, John Printz, to urge the colonists to plant vines. In wine, these leaders saw a beverage that for an alcoholic product was rather temperate; those European wine-drinking nations had a relatively low incidence of public drunkenness. It was also a product that helped diversify agriculture.

Just as important, wine could be easily taxed at each stage of its manufacture and sale. For example, while advocating its use, the Massachusetts Puritans placed downright biblical fire and brimstone levies on the product; for every dollar's worth of wine sold in the colony, duties, licensing fees and other taxes put about fifty-three cents into government coffers.

Consequently, Puritan fathers actually encouraged wine-drinking, although unlike some other colonies, put forth no formal government effort to plant or control vineyards. The sale of "good wine" to Indians was even recommended, although selling "strong waters" to Native Americans would bring severe penalties. By 1680, Boston had six wine taverns, four retailers of wine and spirits and the public complained this wasn't enough. Four years later, the General Court, which regulated licenses, allowed five more establishments to open. But wine was soon to fall to other alcohols.

For one thing, the Colonial vintners who planted the Vinifera varieties from Europe generally failed. Just when these species would begin producing, cruel winters killed the immigrant vines. Likewise, disease and pests took their toll. In the Eastern regions, only the native grapes, and later hybrids of Vinifera and domestic stock, thrived without modern pest controls.

Poor wine, moreover, had much to do with retarding the drink's colonial popularity. During the last half of the seventeenth century, Virginia offered prizes for the best colonist wine, and had not a winner. Thus, the stuff simply couldn't compete with hard apple cider, later whiskey and in particular, the cheap demon, rum. More than anything else, rum dampened viticulture in the colonies. Easy to make, inexpensive and a most highly effective mind-numbing agent, rum besotted the colonies, which led to restrictive laws on public drunkenness and in some ways started what wasn't yet even a nation on the road to national Prohibition.

Colonial leaders wanted the revenues generated by alcohol, but not the social problems associated with overuse. Massachusetts went to considerable length to shame drunkards such as one Robert Coles, a backsliding church member who in 1633 was ordered to wear a large letter D on his clothing for an entire year. Other drunks were fined, banished from inns and taverns or simply whipped like dogs.

Rum and wine, of course, are quite different beverages. Moderate use of the latter has almost universally been considered healthful; despite the hysteria of modern-day neoprohibitionists, medical evidence tends to support a couple of thousand years of folk wisdom, which shouldn't be surprising. (Peter Stuyvesant, who governed New Netherland—where vineyards were planted on Manhattan Island not long after the Indians accepted the beads and left— once wrote an ordinance that required sailors to be issued a daily wine ration as a health measure.) And yet, intemperate rum quaffing clearly disrupted society and demolished health.

Wine, however, was seen as a boon by many influential early Americans, Thomas Jefferson among them. In *The Memoirs of Thomas Jefferson*, the President wrote: "I rejoice, as a moralist, at a prospect of a reduction of the duties on wine by our national legislature. It is an error to view a tax on that liquor as merely a tax on the rich. It is prohibition of its use to the middling classes of our citizens, and a condemnation of them to the poisons of spirits, which is desolating their homes. No nation is drunken where wine is cheap; and none sober where the dearness of wine substitutes ardent spirits as its common beverage."

For roughly thirty years, Jefferson tried to make uncommonly good wine at Monticello. In 1773, most of the 10,000 European vine cuttings brought to the New World by Dr. Flippo Mazzei of Tuscany, and tended by skilled Italian winegrowers, were planted on Jefferson's estate. He ostensibly even tried importing soil and vines from Château d'Yquem in France. Such desperation is ample evidence of the results. Again, European vines didn't particularly hold with the immigrant experience. Jefferson didn't cave in on Vinifera until 1809, when he reluctantly concluded that native vines would best suffice in America.

However, in 1769, on the other side of the continent, vines of European origin were making their way north from Mexico, after originally landing with the conquistadors some 200 years before. Credit for planting wine grapes in California is often given to Father Junipero Serra, the spiritual leader of Gaspar de Portola's expedition. The popular tale is replete with warm fuzzies; the padre, needing wine for mass at California's first mission in San Diego, plants vines of a species known as the Mission grape. The vines follow the missions north, and winemaking—after frightening the Indians into professing Christianic conversion—becomes the state's second-oldest profession.

Thus, the California missions and grape vines virtually sprouted together. When a Spanish priest sat at a dinner table, wine was his usual drink. Moreover, mass celebrations demanded the fluid. But the original plan of the Franciscans who established California's mission system was to supply wine from Mexico. Had Serra actually planted vines in 1769—the date California's wine industry used as an excuse to hold a bicentennial promotional bash—he'd have had a crop and some raw wine within a few years. But only when the supply lines from Mexico broke once too often did California have its first indigenous vintage— perhaps as late as 1781 or 1782.

In *The Book of California Wine*, published by the University of California Press and Sotheby Publications in 1984, a clinical dissection by Roy Brady discounts Serra's influence. Using the padre's diary from 1769, Brady points out that it took Serra four and a half months to walk from a mission at Loreto far down on the south coast of the Baja peninsula to San Diego.

Hobbled by a chronic infection in a foot and leg, the fifty-five-year-old Franciscan had to cover the thousand-plus miles over rugged and hot country. His mule, according to his diary, was a broken beast. Since moisture and low temperature is necessary to preserve cuttings from dormant vines—and it's unlikely that either Serra, the mule or anyone else could have lugged a big Coleman cooler on the rough journey—the priest couldn't have arrived with healthy cuttings.

In addition, he didn't pick a site for the San Diego mission until mid-July, too late for planting. And as Brady explains, all manner of hell had broken loose for Portola on land and sea; Serra's party fared well, but five members of another land group starved to death. One of Portola's ships disappeared, while scurvy incapacitated or killed the crews of two more. Indians raided and attacked the nascent settlement. Since the surviving ships had brought plenty of mass wine anyway, the notion of the gentle father planting vines is, considering the circumstances, nonsense.

However, as the twenty-one missions rose between San Diego and Sonoma, so did the vine around most of them, although the origin of the Mission grape is quite unclear. It is clearly a *Vitis vinifera* variety, probably from Spain, but has no counterparts there today. Flourishing in southern California's hot climate, it dominated California winemaking until the mid-nineteenth century. While acclaimed by travelers—whose opinions were obviously influenced by long-denied quenching of thirst—the Mission wines made by the padres were like Mission grape wine produced today; flat, dull and totally unremarkable.

When the Mexican government took away what power the Franciscans had in 1833, the missions and their wines were doomed. But while wine had never played a great economic role in the missions, others in Southern California saw the potential of the vine. That same year, Jean Louis Vignes, a Frenchman born in the Bordeaux region, purchased land in east Los Angeles and planted a vineyard of Mission grapes. Within seven years, after success with local sales, he'd started shipping wine to Santa Barbara and Monterey.

Other vintners followed his lead, including a pair of German musicians who in 1854 were living in San Francisco, Charles Kohler and John Frohling. With no experience or training in any facet of the wine business, the men purchased a Los Angeles vineyard and rented a cellar. Frohling handled the wine production in the southland while Kohler pushed the sales side in San Francisco. Highly successful, the men even began selling wine in Manhattan before Frohling died in 1862. A decade later, Kohler claimed that his wines were available in every major metropolis in the nation; in this sense, Kohler and Frohling were the prototype for Ernest and Julio Gallo.

Sophisticated wine scholars can argue endlessly on whether Junipero Serra or another priest planted the first vines, or whether Jean Louis Vignes was the true father of the California wine industry. But another man took credit, became recognized as such, and despite the bogus claim probably did more for the business—through sheer self-promotion—than anyone until Robert Mondavi.

A Hungarian born in 1812, in what is today part of Yugoslavia, Agoston Haraszthy de Mokesa was the scion of an aristocratic family with court connections. Before the age of thirty, he had been an imperial bodyguard, a public official, silkworm producer and a member of the Hungarian parliament. He and his equally aristocratic Polish wife had produced three sons, including the aforementioned Arpad. And the Pride of the Balkans was only getting started.

Indeed, Haraszthy came to the United States in 1840, a political fugitive who had turned against his former imperial employers by helping an anti-government separatist to escape from prison. Hunkering down in Wisconsin, he named a town after himself. Along with a partner, Haraszthy started a steamship line, brickyard, a sawmill and a gristmill. Hearing of the 1848 gold strike at Sutter's Mill, Haraszthy struck out for California; only, instead of heading for the gold fields, he settled in San Diego. He proceeded, as usual, to make things happen.

For all his Wisconsin enterprises, Haraszthy arrived in San Diego broke. The man to whom he'd given power of attorney back in Wisconsin—believing a slim rumor that the Count and family had died en route—sold all the businesses and took off with the cash. The Hungarian started over, farming fruit and vegetables, starting new business partnerships and founding a place called Middletown, today a part of San Diego, where the original Haraszthy Street still exists. His enterprises included a butcher shop, livery stable, and a contracting operation that built the city jail. Haraszthy, perhaps because of his Imperial Guard background, became San Diego County's first sheriff. His father, who'd come along for the ride, served as a judge and city councilman. Agoston got himself elected to the new state's Assembly.

This took all of three years. In 1852, Haraszthy bought land in San Francisco and moved north. For whatever reasons, he got involved in the viticultural business, and planted *Vitis vinifera* vines in what is today the heart of San Francisco, and others in San Mateo County on the San Francisco peninsula. The grapes failed to grow in the foggy coastal climate. Moreover, Haraszthy got himself in trouble with the United States mint, where his father and then Agoston himself served as smelter. Indicted for embezzlement, his property confiscated, it took three years for Haraszthy to clear his name.

In 1856 or 1857, Haraszthy and family moved to Sonoma, where he purchased 560 acres of land. A small portion of the land already had grape vines, and there were remains of an old winery on the property. Haraszthy now placed his often diffused energy into the wine business. Within eight years, he had grabbed 6,000 more acres of prime land, put grape vines on 400 of them, and built a magnificent and elaborate winery. He had Chinese laborers carve storage tunnels into the hillsides. Haraszthy called the place Buena Vista.

The existing vineyards had been planted by the brother of General Mariano Guadalupe Vallejo. A native Californian, Vallejo, ironically enough, started the legend of Padre Serra and the vines; his father had known the Franciscan. A couple of budding legends themselves, Haraszthy and the General—who had hired a French vintner to make wine from his own grapes—intertwined throughout the 1860s, their wines going head to head at state fair competitions. Arpad and Attila Haraszthy married Vallejo daughters.

The Count, however, was not satisfied with Mission grapes. He put Attila in charge of Buena Vista and immediately imported cuttings from some 165 grape varieties. As he'd done with other businesses, Haraszthy kindled enthusiasm in others; he urged friends and neighbors to invest in more land and vineyards. He wrote pamphlets and courted newspaper publicity, in which he touted California's wine-growing potential and promoted the use of Vinifera varieties. Sonoma became the center of viticultural knowledge in the state; Haraszthy sent letters, papers and cuttings to vineyardists throughout California.

In 1858, allegedly at the request of the State Agricultural Society, Haraszthy wrote a long paper describing every detail of a winemaking operation, a primer that started with advice on laying out a vineyard, how to dig holes for planting vines, how and when to pick, crush and ferment the juice. Three years later, thanks to his stature in the business, Haraszthy was appointed by California

Governor John G. Downey—backed by the state's legislature—to visit Europe, learn more about winemaking on the Continent, and bring back a report and perhaps more grape varieties.

Haraszthy traveled through France, Spain, Italy, Switzerland and Germany in 1861, taking voluminous notes, interviewing hundreds of grape growers and vintners and purchasing thousands of grapevines; 100,000 vines, reportedly, from 300 varieties. Along with his report to the legislature, the energetic Haraszthy polished off a then-definitive book in 1862, *Grape Culture, Wines, and Wine Making*. The trip and its publicity again elevated Haraszthy's acclaim, although it was not without one sour note.

Haraszthy had fronted all his expenses for the European sojourn, with the idea that the state would cover the tab and farm out most of the vines he'd sent back to other California winegrowers. He asked for $12,000, saying it covered only a third of the value of the plants, not to mention his other expenses. The state stiffed him; in part, history suggests, because Haraszthy had voiced support for the Confederate side in the Civil War. Many of the cuttings went to waste. Worse, the phylloxera vine louse, which destroyed Buena Vista's vineyards among others in the 1870s, may have come into California on Haraszthy's imported vines.

Despite the California legislature's heavy-handed treatment, Haraszthy continued to promote winegrowing in the state. In 1863, with nine backers, he started the Buena Vista Agricultural Society. Overloaded with debt on his acreage and facilities, Haraszthy's society was a way to get around a state law prohibiting corporations from owning more than a certain amount of farmland. The backing also promised financing to plant 6,000 new acres of vines within a decade; and to produce 2.6 million gallons of wine annually, mostly champagne made by the European-trained Arpad.

Haraszthy's star, however, began to decline rapidly at that point. He had always lived at the edge with his ventures, and this one was no different. A San Francisco newspaper called Buena Vista "the largest winegrowing estate in the world, and also the most unprofitable." Banker William C. Ralston and the other backers squeezed Haraszthy out in 1866.

A veritable multi-lived cat, Haraszthy simply moved to Nicaragua and started a host of new ventures. However, while crossing a flooding stream in 1869, the Count finally failed to land on his feet. He fell in and either drowned, or, as more befits a legend, was eaten by crocodiles. While his fame lingered throughout the nineteenth century, Haraszthy was eventually forgotten; his legend wasn't revived until long after Prohibition ended.

Meanwhile, the wine industry had picked up in other states. In the early 1800s, Alexander grape vineyards were planted in Indiana, Ohio and Pennsylvania. Concord grapes were planted in Massachusetts. And other domesticated native varieties—along with hybrids of American and Vinifera—began appearing around the country. During this century, winegrowing ventures also started in Georgia, Iowa, Kansas, Illinois, Mississippi, Michigan, West Virginia, Tennessee, Virginia, New Jersey, Kentucky, Alabama, New Mexico, North Carolina, Maryland and South Carolina.

In fact, just as Agoston Haraszthy started to make a name for the California wine industry and himself at Buena Vista, Ohio became the nation's top wine producer. In 1859, producing about 570,000 gallons annually, the land along the Ohio River was being called "the Rhine of America." Like California, Ohio also had legendary wine characters, including Nicholas Longworth, who in 1823 planted a vineyard overlooking the river near Cincinnati.

The Vinifera tried and died. But Longworth then learned of a grape called the pink Catawba, replanted in 1825, and less than two decades later had 1,200 acres of vineyard. His wine and champagnes were sold in the East and even in California. Wine made him a millionaire, but by 1860 a plague had hit his vineyards and others in the Cincinnati area. However, the business continued elsewhere in the state until Prohibition; some Ohio wines even won medals in international competitions.

In 1866, Missouri passed Ohio in wine production, while the Finger Lakes region of New York began producing considerable quantities, despite the fact that the temperance movement was born in Saratoga County, a fervor that did much to temper winemaking progress. By this time, the Eastern wine markets were largely controlled by producers in Ohio, Missouri and New York. Upon the completion of the transcontinental railroad in 1869, a virtual war broke out among vintners in the East, California and Europe. And it was one of the most dirty wars imaginable.

At first, the Eastern winemakers simply accused Californians of putting European labels on California wines, a charge that in certain instances was accurate. They also claimed that the Westerners slapped California labels on the Eastern wines. In response, finally, New York and New England wine merchants took some of the most wretched, adulterated wine that could be found, spoiled rotgut from Europe and unknown origin, and brazenly sold it as California wine.

Shady winemakers used sugar and water to stretch their products, or all manner of adulteration to mimic a wine's coloring in liquids that were probably ciders. Pure wine laws were a pressing matter, but this too created conflict between the two coasts. Californians saw sugar as an adulterating agent, but Eastern vintners needed to add some sugar to their wines because their shorter growing seasons yielded grapes with too much acid.

Frona Wait explained some of the other techniques used to deacidify wine, which was "usually done with chalk, plaster of Paris or gypsum, air-slacked lime, neutral tartrate of potash, marble dust or other similar materials." A federal law was finally passed prohibiting the sale of wine not made from pure grape juices or that included chemical antiseptics and dyes. A limited use of sugar—of relief to Eastern winemakers—was allowed by Congress in 1894.

In the midst of the bicoastal competition and the growing production from more and more wineries in the United States, the basic economic forces of simple supply and demand torpedoed many operations. Three years after the global economic depression of 1873, the bottom fell out of the grape and wine markets. The fruit sold for less than the cost of picking it, and two out of three wineries in California folded. In 1870, there had been about 140 in the state; a decade later, only forty-five remained.

Violent fluctuations in wholesale wine and grape values persisted after the turn of the century, making stability—particularly for small vintners—impossible. Bumper grape crops were followed by low harvests. More significant was the fact that while American wine was holding its own in competitions with the best of France and Germany at this time—both prime Eastern and California vintages—the United States public still preferred beer and spirits. Prior to Prohibition in 1920, few brands, except for Captain Paul Garrett's Scuppernong-flavored wine, Virginia Dare, were nationally recognized. And though some vintners recognized the need for an industry-wide promotional campaign to encourage wine as a daily beverage, consensus and funding could not be generated.

It wouldn't have mattered anyway, for Prohibition almost wiped out the art of quality winemaking. Grape growers ripped out their vineyards and many vintners moved on to other means of making a living. However, those who continued to grow grapes did well, for a loophole in the Volstead Act allowed citizens to make 200 gallons a year of "nonintoxicating cider and fruit juices exclusively for use in the home." Juice grapes were suddenly a hot property, their price soaring from $10 a ton to more than $100.

Moreover, about a hundred wineries in California, Missouri, Ohio and New Jersey survived Prohibition by making sacramental and medicinal wines. The latter wasn't that tasty except when refrigerated, a process that forced the medical ingredients to settle at the bottle's bottom. Grapes pressed into packages called bricks were sold and used by home winemakers. These came with a yeast pill and a warning not to use it, for it would make wine, which, stressed the caution, is illegal. Hypocrisy, more than temperance, flourished.

On Repeal in 1934, it was time to start all over, to relearn what grapes grew best in a particular location and produced a superior wine. It was time to relearn how to make superior wine. And it was time to once again confront the same problems outlined by Arpad Haraszthy and Frona Wait nearly fifty years before. America was still not a nation of wine drinkers.

6

THE OLD GUARD

Superficially, it seems that doctors, lawyers and a bunch of other enological upstarts created the modern premium wine industry. However, there was an old guard in place long before the nouveau riche moved in. They rebuilt the staggering industry in the wake of Prohibition, and controlled it before the boom of the 1970s. Their influence remains a factor, and some of these patrones are still around.

Italian for the most part, they preserved ideals brought from the Old Country, by themselves or their forebears. They believed in the transcendent importance of family. They loved good food and a genteel agrarian environment, although it's doubtful they'd ever articulate it in such terms.

Their views on wine were radically different from those of the newer interlopers. To the old guard, wine was nothing more nor less than a part of the daily diet; to sit

93

down to a meal without wine was inconceivable, for it was and is as much a part of daily Italian cuisine as bread. To them, wine was "good" or "bad." Not surprisingly, they viewed it as an agricultural commodity. Their definition of a good winemaker was a guy who moved a great deal of product through his cellar and sold it at a good price. Quality was incidental; it mattered only inasmuch as it helped sell wine.

But most of all, the old guard that made it through the 1930s, 1940s and 1950s were survivors. The wine business in the wake of Prohibition was rougher than it is even today, although an awful lot of folks gave it a try. It's not a widely known fact, or at least a well-remembered one, but in the 1930s, California alone had more than 700 wineries. The vast majority were family-owned, "Mom and Pop" establishments.

Lou Gomberg remembers them well. "They were a unique outgrowth of Prohibition," he explains, once again growing animated in his San Francisco office, "and were mostly small grape growers who were looking for a second profit center." The operations were extremely small, says Gomberg, and usually served their local community. Customers, just as in many places in France, would bring their own jugs to Ma and Pa and have them filled with a puppy-age wine that was most often red, occasionally white or a rich gold. Questions on grape varieties would draw an uninterested shrug.

"For a time these little wineries could sustain themselves at a minimum profit level," says Gomberg. "But they eventually found that the wine business requires technical skills, management skills and marketing skills." Even on a small-scale basis, the operations demanded maintenance, inventory build-up and, above all, capital investment.

Small farmers in the 1930s, suggests Gomberg, simply weren't accustomed or amenable to heavy outlays of capital. "All but a handful of these Mom and Pop operations, and there were at least 500 of them in the state at one time, went out of business or were taken over by a larger concern," he notes. More than 90 percent just disappeared.

Between the end of Prohibition and the boom of the

1970s, about 150 somewhat larger family-owned wineries entered the business. "Most of these sold their wine in bulk," Gomberg says. "They loaded it into railroad tank cars and shipped it elsewhere for bottling, often to the East." These family wineries had even less direct consumer contact than the Mom and Pop businesses. By concentrating on bulk production, they avoided spending money for bottles, bottling equipment, marketing and so on, things which Gomberg says leads to "extremely retarded return on investment capital." Most of these wineries folded, sold out or merged with others, although when compared to Mom and Pops, a slightly higher percentage survived.

Problems also plagued California's winery co-ops, which did just about as poorly as Mom and Pop and small family operations. Gomberg once compiled a business history of the forty-four cooperative wineries that had been established in the state from 1944 to 1975. "Only eight of them made it," he says, "and only two or three of those had any kind of brand in the market; the rest were bulk producers."

However, there were also larger operations, family enterprises or corporations that had invested capital, weathered the five to fifteen years until positive cash flow commenced, and kept going. While the others dropped out, says Gomberg, "the successful few were doing good business or extremely good business." It was, he claims, a classic example of the concentration of economic power, "where more and more revenues find their way into fewer and fewer hands."

Of course, in the 1970s the business did an about turn and went in the opposite direction, with more and more producers grabbing a piece of the market. This suggests that given the current state of the industry, concentration could evolve once again; business and economic cycles are powerful things. But in any event, the same kind of businessmen and women who survived before will do so again. They will be like today's old guard.

The roster is fairly short, but includes winery names such as Italian Swiss Colony, Charles Krug, Inglenook, Beringer, the Concannon Vineyard in the Livermore Valley, Paul Masson, Mirassou and Beaulieu Vineyard. The latter was aided by André Tchelistcheff, a man who has been almost unanimously acclaimed as the definitive winemaking genius. He served as Beaulieu's enologist and winemaster from the late 1930s until 1973, and made its reputation. But Tchelistcheff also provided guidance to literally dozens of other wineries in the U.S., and continues to do so in the eighth decade of his life. Spreading out his time and advice, he's still a consultant to such major operations as Buena Vista and Château Ste. Michelle, as well as many, many smaller wineries.

Some of the old guard wineries and players operate in the limelight; Tchelistcheff, for example, gets around and is bestowed with constant praise and honors. The Gallos are known because of the sheer size of their operations, the Sebastianis because of their messy and public family feuds and the Mondavis because of constant promotion. But there are other First Families in the wine business who have made the transition from post-Prohibition era to today without as much publicity, and who prefer it that way. In a sense, they have remained truer to the ideals of their fathers than their headline-grabbing compatriots.

However, their resistance to altering their lifestyles has not meant they are inflexible. They have responded to the marketplace as the marketplace changed; sometimes they refined what they did best, and sometimes tried completely new courses. They always tried to give people what they wanted, as long as it didn't eat into profit margins.

Perhaps no winery personifies this image of the long-term survivor more precisely than the Louis Martini Winery. It's a landmark in the Napa Valley, albeit an unprepossessing one. Located south of St. Helena on Highway 29, it is a sprawling, slightly seedy complex framed by scraggly sycamores and a dusty parking lot. The Louis Martini Winery is about as far from the ideal of a typical tourist winery as you can get.

There are no meticulously cultivated flower beds, expansive executive offices or vaulted tasting rooms paneled in blond wood. Everything is strictly business here—but business with a distinct farming tenor, business as it used to be in the Napa Valley. That was low-key business, conducted by men who indeed viewed themselves more as farmers than winemakers, whose word was their bond and who concluded deals with a handshake instead of attorneys. They were men whose idea of a good time was a game of boccie ball or jump-shooting mallards from Napa Creek, not hosting seven-course sit-down dinners or playing a few chukkers of polo.

The family that runs this particular winery is much like the structures they work in. Patriarch Louis P. Martini is an amiable bear of a man who ambles around the winery in work-boots and blue jeans. Wry humored and laconic, little irritates him save pretension and wine doubletalk. His daughter, Carolyn, is the winery's president. Plainspoken and forthright, she shares her father's sense of humor and pronounced lack of pomposity. Winemaker and winery vice president Michael Martini is Carolyn's younger brother. Like his father, he is large and ruggedly built. When not overseeing operations at the winery of the family's vineyard holdings, he favors motorcycle racing.

The winery was founded by Louis M. Martini—Louis P.'s father—in the early 1920s. It began to come into its own after Prohibition, when Louis M. purchased a 1,000-acre vineyard in the Mayacamas Mountains above the Napa Valley floor, in 1937. Born in 1887 at Pietra Ligure on the Italian Riviera, the senior Martini died in 1974.

Martini felt strongly about quality, and the family's red wines have long enjoyed a reputation for being well made and moderately priced. Earned by his father, the reputation was maintained and enhanced by Louis P. At the 1983 Napa Valley Wine Auction, auctioneer Michael Broadbent—a renowned British wine critic, writer and principal in the international auction firm of Christie's—lauded the history and wares of the Martini Winery. "The wines of Louis Martini are some of the most underrated wines in the country," he told the assemblage of vintners, bidders and wine groupies. "His lovely Cabernets are some of the best values in wine."

Indeed, Louis Martini Winery continues to produce exceptionally fine red wines at modest prices—usually around $6 to $8 for the Cabernets. At the same time, the winery maintains what is at best a casual advertising and public relations program. Yet it prospers, mainly because the family has been at it a long time, nearly seventy years. It's generally assumed that they can produce all the cash they need internally.

Those years also assure them a good market share, because of brand recognition and loyalty. Generations of enophiles, in fact, cut their teeth on Martini wine while in the process of upgrading their tastes from sweet, pink and cheap liquids. But while Martini wines were not only good wines, they were bottles that students, law clerks and medical interns on the way up could afford.

The extravagant praise for the Martini red wines has a corollary, of course: the whites have never been all that swell. Often flat and insipid, they've been at times downright terrible, stinky, oxidized or grotesquely out of balance. In the past, that never bothered the Martinis much. Business was still good.

But the Martini family recognized that their whites were being knocked in the wine press and out of the market. When he took over the head winemaker job from his father, Michael Martini decided to do something about this.

Making excellent white wine is, of course, more difficult and expensive than producing excellent reds. The latter is a relatively straightforward process, assuming that grape quality is high. Depending on the variety of grape and the style of wine preferred, white wines may require capital-intensive equipment such as must chillers, decanters and centrifuges. Whites usually require more labor and skill. The equipment at Martini, while certainly adequate, was not up to the high standards used to make the Chardonnays and Sauvignon Blancs that emerged and won such a big piece of the market by the early 1980s. Michael Martini wanted to upgrade equipment and cooperage; his father and sister agreed.

Yet it was important to the family that their basic wine-making philosophical cornerstones remain in place. They did not want to make an extremely complex, powerful $20 Chardonnay. They wanted Chardonnays that were medium-bodied, subtle and well balanced, easy and enjoyable to drink and that went well with food, but which would not cost consumers an arm, leg or any other favorite extremity. So at Michael's behest, the family began investing in new equipment; he installed refrigerated fermenting vats in 1981, eventually doubling the winery's temperature-controlled fermentation capacity. While he also upgraded some of the Martini vineyards, perhaps more significantly he purchased new French oak cooperage to replace the old American oak barrels upon which the winery had previously relied.

Michael Martini had absorbed the family tradition of making well-balanced, well-made wines from his father. "My dad taught me the virtues of judicious blending," he says. "He showed me how to structure a wine by identifying and fine-tuning its components." Yet Michael differed in some respects. While he learned much from his father, Michael also picked up a few ideas at the University of California at Davis, where he obtained a fermentation science degree in 1977. He also traveled to Burgundy and Bordeaux, where he studied such typically Gallic applications as barrel fermentation of white wines, stem retention in Pinot Noirs, and extended maceration, or skin contact, with newly fermented red wine. By applying his own ideas back at Martini, Michael has made wines that are much more complex and varietally intense than those produced under his father's and grandfather's regimens.

But his white wines still aren't getting breathless reviews in the wine press—they probably never will. The wines of Louis Martini aren't likely to be considered in the same company as those of a fellow Italian and industry peer, Robert Mondavi. Unlike Mondavi, the Martinis aren't obsessed with the idea of being "the best." Martini's best wines are not the equivalent of Mondavi's top releases, but then, they don't sell for nearly as much money. Frankly, Martini's reds are probably better values.

Where Bob Mondavi reigns, he also pours—money. Money gushes into his winery and floods right back out. The Robert Mondavi Winery is a heavily leveraged firm. But the Martinis ostensibly paid off their debts long ago. They sit on pure equity, and there's a lot of it; the winery, inventory, thousands of acres of prime vineyard and ranch land. They sell a tenth as much wine as Mondavi, 250,000 cases versus 2.5 million, and not for as much money. But without steep advertising, public relations and promotional expenses, the Martini net profit is certainly substantial.

Profit seemingly runs against the vows of poverty, chastity and obedience taken by the Brothers of the Christian Schools, a lay religious teaching order of the Roman Catholic Church. But there was a time, a few decades ago, when Brother Timothy Diener was one of the best-known money-making vintners in the nation. In certain parts of the country, if folks drank wine or brandy, it was Timothy's Christian Brothers wine and brandy from the order's Mont La Salle Vineyards, or nothing else. Since 1935, Brother Timothy, who is now in his late seventies, has stood as an emblem for this operation.

During the 1980s, however, time started to forget this once-important, old guard player. Brother Timothy's good name was no longer enough to move products. Without the hard business acumen of a Louis Martini, the Christian Brothers were getting torn apart by the lions and jackals of the modern wine business. Within the span of eight years, their wine sales dropped nearly 60 percent, while brandy sales slumped from 1.9 million cases annually to 1.2 million cases in 1986. They had been California's leading brandy producer; their prominence fell, not surprisingly, to Ernest and Julio Gallo, who in the marketplace clobber the heathen and heavenly blessed alike.

But Fratres Scholarum Christianarum haven't been around since 1680 for nothing. They know how to pray and are acutely aware that God will help those Brothers who help themselves. In recent years, this order has accepted some fundamental changes in how they do business, and accepted the help of non-Brothers who have played a major role in bringing the tax-paying, privately owned corporation back from the near dead. To the Brothers, the wine business is a means to a divine end—education.

Founded in Rheims, France, by nobleman and priest Saint Jean Baptiste de la Salle, the Christian Brothers today have about 9,000 members worldwide, working in eighty nations. They teach in, operate and support more than 1,000 schools around the globe, about 105 of which are in the U.S. The Brothers started their first American school in Baltimore in 1848, came to California twenty years later and opened a novitiate, or training school, at Martinez in 1879. The land there happened to contain twelve acres of vineyards.

At first, the Brothers in Martinez just ate the grapes. But by 1882 they began crushing them, making sacramental wine and saving some for their dinner table. It was pretty good stuff, relatively speaking, and people in the neighborhood started purchasing the excess quantities. The cash helped support their schools, until Prohibition wiped out their commercial business. But as Christians, at least the Brothers could continue making altar wine.

As they started to support more schools in California and Oregon, the Brothers outgrew their Martinez home and in 1932 moved to the Napa Valley and a new novitiate. However, when Prohibition ended, the Brothers' wine operation, Mont La Salle Vineyards, wasn't suddenly in fat city. In fact, it nearly went bankrupt before they linked their fortunes to those of one Alfred Fromm, whose marketing skills helped make the Christian Brothers brand—it was he who suggested changing the name from Mont La Salle—one of the best known in America.

The Brothers expanded and now hold more Napa Valley vineyard acreage than any other grower. In 1950 they purchased the Greystone Cellars, a massive stone winery that sits at the north edge of St. Helena. Built in the late 1880s by William Bowers Bourn, at the time reputedly the richest man in the West, Greystone has a history as checkered as the wine industry's. A rancher, financier and owner of one of California's most productive gold mines, Bourn figured Greystone could serve Napa Valley growers who were getting gouged by San Francisco wine merchants.

After Bourn, it had numerous owners, many of whom leased out wine storage space to the Christian Brothers, who in 1950 eventually bought Greystone for themselves. That same year, Seagram purchased a controlling interest in Fromm & Sichel, the company that marketed the Brothers' wines. Things were fine until the late 1970s, when the big distiller became more interested in promoting Taylor California Cellars and Paul Masson, its own brands.

Like the Brothers, these wineries made low-priced wines and not vintage-dated varietals. Brother Timothy did a fine job of making consistently good ordinary wine, a kind of art in itself. But at the time, growth in the business rested with vintage-dated varietals. Moreover, Seagram obviously had little incentive to push Christian Brothers wines, in that they competed directly against Seagram's own labels. And as if this bad combination weren't enough, engineers declared Greystone structurally unsafe; it had survived the Great Quake of 1906, but a much lesser shake could now bring it to the ground.

The Brothers prayed, as usual. And they also took action in 1982, turning loose chipmunk-cheeked thirty-eight-year-old Brother David, an aptly named soul, considering he'd be taking on the industry's Goliaths. As president and chairman of the board, Brother David Brennan authorized millions of dollars for new winemaking equipment, ordered up a vintage-dated varietal program and combined four wineries into one state-of-the-art facility. He engineered the purchase of controlling interest in Fromm & Sichel from Seagram in 1983, called it the Christian Brothers Sales Co., and bought the remainder of it in 1986. Brother Timothy is still around, as a vice president and cellarmaster. But Brother David hired a mustachioed thirty-five-year-old "civilian" to be head winemaker: Tom Eddy, a headstrong U.C. Davis graduate.

Along with Eddy, he hired Richard Maher to be president of the Christian Brothers Sales Co. A former president of Seagram Wine Co. and the man responsible for reviving the moribund Beringer winery, this ex-marine is about as tough and volatile an hombre as one finds in the wine business. But Brother David went another step and, in 1987, appointed the first external board of directors in the Christian Brothers winery's one-hundred-year history. Brennan wanted a board "of Fortune 500 caliber," and he got it; the external list includes Fernando Gumucio, president of Del Monte USA; Dale Lynch, retired chairman of Safeway Stores; James

Miscoll, an executive VP of the Bank of America; Raymond O'Brien, chairman and CEO of Consolidated Freightways; and Donley Ritchey, retired CEO of Lucky Stores.

The sales slump has stopped, and wine and brandy volumes have slowly started to creep upward.

"It's vital that the winery turn a profit," says Brennan. "There might be those who would question the motives of the Christian Brothers winery becoming competitive and aggressive in today's market. But if that's what it takes to provide an excellent education to young people, then that's the future as we see it."

However, during the summer of 1989, with the recovery well underway, the Brothers concluded on a different future and bailed out of wine. For an estimated $100 million to $150 million, the operations became the property of Heublein Inc., a division of Grand Metropolitan PLC's International Distillers and Vinters Ltd. in London. The sale stunned the wine industry. For one thing, the price was high. But for another, the Brothers seemed to have caved in to pressure from anti-alcoholic activists and charges that they were "making money selling alcohol." For an order that withstood Prohibition, the capitulation appeared chilling.

Bob Trinchero's family had not taken a vow of poverty when they came to the Napa Valley from Manhattan, but that's the state in which they arrived. One finds Trinchero today at a winery just across Highway 29 from the Martini joint, where his family owns the Sutter Home Winery. Until the early 1970s, this Italian clan's business was modest in the most literal sense of the word. The winery produced about 25,000 cases a year, the return on which barely kept the family fed.

Trinchero is now the CEO and chairman of Sutter Home. In his early fifties, he's a fleshy, avuncular man of medium stature who looks vaguely professorial. "It was 1949 and I was thirteen," he says of the move from New York. "Talk about culture shock. My father bought the place with my uncle Mario. We lived in a little house the first winter without heat. Things gradually got better, but they were never really fat. When I took over as winemaker in 1958, we made fifty-two different wines. Our motto was, 'If you can get it through the door, we'll fill it up for you.' I cut down the number of wines we made, and concentrated on producing sound varietal wines. We did okay, but we still didn't have that particular identification, that special brand awareness that I knew we needed.''

During the late 1960s, Trinchero expanded his search for grape sources beyond the Napa Valley. His quest eventually took him to the Sierra Nevada foothills in Amador County. This inland area is rolling, open country, studded with oak and digger pine forests. Summers here are marked by very warm days and crisp nights: perfect for the cultivation of Zinfandel grapes.

Zinfandel is America's mystery grape. It is true *Vitis vinifera*, so it originated in the Old World. But it is a cultivar which was first recognized in California. Throughout the early part of this century, Zinfandel was the red variety preferred by most of the state's grape growers. The vines were hardy and fecund, and produced well under dry-land farming conditions. Its fruit yielded fresh, rich and tasty red wines and vintners later found that the grape was amenable to a variety of vinification styles. It could make crisp, simple rosés, complex, elegant dry red wines similar in character to Cabernet, or deep, powerful dessert wines similar to ports.

While the grape had legions of faithful devotees, no one knew where it came from. Current research indicates that it's a clone of an obscure, pedestrian grape grown in southern Italy, called the Primitivo. In Italy, Primitivo produces coarse, all too powerful wines of no particular virtue. The clone that somehow found its way to California, however, blossomed in unexpected ways.

Zinfandel has been grown in Amador County since the mid-1850s, and in fact this was one of the first wine regions in the state. There are still a few vineyards in the county that support 120-year-old Zinfandel vines; gnarled, beautifully weathered relics that look more like bonsai oak trees than grapevines. Such venerable vines produce especially intense, flavorful fruit, grapes highly prized by winemakers.

When Bob Trinchero was exploring the Amador foothills, he found just such a vineyard on the Deaver Ranch. He was so impressed with it that he bought the entire crop of 1968, and made a premium, oak-aged table wine from it. Prior to this purchase, the Deaver Ranch grapes had gone to bulk producers in the San Joaquin Valley, dumped into cheap rosés and bogus burgundies. The Deavers had never really thought of their grapes as a premium product.

But Trinchero's first Amador County Zinfandel received glowing reviews. It was compared in quality to the finest California Cabernet Sauvignons, although that particular spicy essence of the best Zinfandels was noted with appreciation. So effusive was the praise, in fact, and so great the demand for the wine that Trinchero decided to restrict the repertoire of Sutter Home even further; from that point on, he concluded, Sutter Home would make only Zinfandels.

"It was a radical marketing decision, especially for that time," Trinchero concedes. "Virtually all the California wineries were making several different wines. But that Amador Zinfandel really put us on the map. It gave us that identity we lacked. I somehow felt that our future was tied to that variety. We decided to go with it."

Trinchero conducted extensive experiments with the grape, and was impressed with its malleability. "You can make any type of wine you want with Zinfandel," he says. "It's the most versatile grape there is. I started tinkering with the idea of making a white wine from it. If you pick Zinfandel at relatively low sugars and press it as soon as you crush it, you have very little color pick-up. I made a very small amount of this in 1972, just a few hundred cases. And I made it along the lines of a Chardonnay—dry, oak-aged, fairly complex."

Trinchero thought of this wine—a white made from a red grape—as more a novelty item than a mainstay, and initial sales confirmed his inclination. It sold, but didn't fly off the shelves. However, he tinkered with the style some more, and finally ended up with a White Zinfandel radically different from the first. It was crisp, simple and fruity. It had some residual sugar in it, to emphasize the fresh, natural grape flavors.

The wine sold out almost immediately. Trinchero made more the next year; again the sales were phenomenally brisk. Distributors and accounts screamed for more. Sutter Home quadrupled production, and it still wasn't enough. In

1980, Sutter Home made 47,000 cases of wine, most of it White Zinfandel. In 1987, production had climbed to almost three million cases. Bob Trinchero became rich.

Along the way he also popularized a seemingly new variety of wine, and made his brand the best-selling varietal wine in America. It was, he admits, a scenario he never expected and which Trinchero attributes as much to luck as anything else. "We were there with the right product at the right time," he says. "White Zinfandel is popular because it's easy to like. It tastes good, and you don't have to have a degree in enology to enjoy it. It's reasonably priced and it goes with anything. What I find amusing is the industry's reaction to it; at first, a lot of winemakers dismissed it. They called it soda pop. Now, more than fifty wineries make White Zinfandel. Suddenly, it's become a respectable variety, since it can make people a lot of money. White Zinfandel proves that if you give people what they want, you'll be successful. That's a lesson a lot of people still haven't learned in this industry."

The success of White Zinfandel turned the varietal demographics of the entire wine industry askew. As more and more wineries made it, the demand for the grape skyrocketed. Growers stopped ripping out their Zinfandel grapes, or budding them to Cabernet or Chardonnay. New Zinfandel vineyards started going in, slow at first, then with alacrity. Within three short years, this grape went from being a stepchild to a star.

"It became apparent that we were going to have to do something to secure our grape sources if we were going to continue to make money from it," Trinchero explains. "There weren't enough grapes out there—people were fighting for them. So we decided to plant our own."

White Zinfandel sells, at the most, for $5 a bottle. That means that the grapes can be purchased for no more than $450 to $500 a ton if the winery wants to make a profit. It's not fiscally possible to grow $450 grapes for $5 wine on raw land that costs $25,000 an acre, and which requires even more investment to bring it into production. So Trinchero looked in places other than the Napa and Sonoma Valleys for his vineyard land. In fact, he looked so far afield that his final choice made seasoned viticulturalists blink in disbelief.

Trinchero chose the northern Sacramento Valley near the town of Artois for his 2,000-acre planting. This valley is considered fine land for rice and corn, but not grapes. The days are hot. So are the nights, for that matter, or very warm in any event. Good wine grapes, it is generally thought, need cool nights to preserve their natural acids. Trinchero concedes that this is generally true for most wine grapes, but not for Zinfandel grown specifically for blush wine.

"The best White Zinfandel is quite low in alcohol, which means that the grapes don't have to be very ripe when you pick them," he notes. "We pick at 17 to 18 percent sugar, and there's plenty of acid left in the grapes at that level, even in the Sacramento Valley. It's true the grapes wouldn't be that good if you left them on the vine until they hit 22 to 24 degrees Brix, which is the level you need for dry, full-bodied table wines. But those aren't the kinds of wines we make with these grapes. For simple, crisp, fruity wines, Artois is actually superior to prime viticultural areas."

None of the wineries in this old-guard trio are big medal winners. But it's a safe bet that they'll be around long after many of today's hot medal-winning wineries are bankrupt, dissolved or sold off to conglomerates or foreign investors. Unlike many others, they simply sell good wine at a fair price.

7

U.C. DAVIS— THE HARVARD OF ENOLOGY

Padding about in a pair of hiking shorts and wearing a casual shirt with a couple of pens tucked into the pocket, Dr. Ralph Kunkee leads a visitor on a whirlwind, back-room tour of wine academe. A professor in the Department of Viticulture and Enology at the University of California Davis (U.C.D.), Kunkee moves quickly past the school's crusher-stemmers, fermentation tanks and through a pair of rooms full of large jugs and plastic buckets. One of the rooms is devoted to jugs and buckets full of white wine in progress, the other, reds; each batch represents an experiment.

Down some stairs, through several heavy doors and into a cool cellar, Kunkee shows his guest a massive display of bottled and tagged wines. There are more than 250,000 bottles here in all, in racks from the floor to a high ceiling. It is the proof of U.C. Davis research on thousands of types of grapes and fermenting processes, experimental vintages of years gone by, for better or worse.

A broad-faced, outgoing man whose bushy moustache gives him a resemblance to comedian Rip Taylor, Kunkee is a microbiologist by trade. Born in California, he studied biochemistry at U.C. Berkeley and did his graduation work in DNA research, about the time British biophysicist Francis Crick and American biologist James Watson were unraveling the mysteries of the double helix. Kunkee knew these Nobel Prize winners and once had "a marvelous opportunity to go into the field." And yet, fearing he'd always be a step behind the leading edge of research, he opted instead for applied science, taking a job with the DuPont Corporation in Delaware. He spent five years there before eventually coming back to California and the U.C. system. Kunkee has been a fixture at Davis since 1963.

His bent for applied science is most evident when his tour finds its way to the Viticulture and Enology research labs, scattered over three floors in Wickson Hall. It is here where the groundwork that leads to those experimental wines is conducted, where ideas are developed that often make their way into the vineyards and wineries of California, Oregon, New York, Australia, South America and even Europe.

It is a quiet Saturday and though few colleagues are working, the professor pulls forth a ring of keys from his hiking shorts and enthusiastically leads his guest through a series of cramped quarters, a journey not unlike an enological-technological Outward Bound. He shows the visitor where Associate Professor Carole Meredith is trying to regenerate grapevines from cells genetically engineered or picked for desired qualities, such as resistance to disease and pests, extreme temperatures or poor soil. Kunkee goes through the lab of Dr. Ann Noble, who developed the Davis Wine Wheel.

He then moves on to where Associate Professor Roger Boulton is studying the "kinetics of sulfide oxidation and reduction reactions," a mouthful that is significant to someone in the winemaking trade. Boulton is also known for his work in developing a computer program to help winemakers take on-line measurements of fermentation rates. The professor envisions a system in which real-time measurements, so to speak, would be compared with an ideal computerized fermentation model; the vintner, or even an automated system, could adjust refrigeration units.

Not far from here is where Professor Vernon Singleton is investigating ways to speed the aging process of wine, which isn't quite as oxymoronic as it sounds. The flavors, aromas and qualities in aged wine aren't the product of romance, but are basically chemical reactions. Finding a means to juice the reactions so that they occur quicker, and yet produce the same properties as slow aging, is a potential financial boon. Singleton also developed the technique of using wood chips instead of oak barrels to impart certain wine characteristics.

"Storing wine is very expensive, just in accounting for the loss of interest on a valuable commodity alone," says Singleton, who has been at Davis for more than twenty-eight years. He realizes, of course, that premium wineries will keep oak barrels for the public relations and marketing value, even should the chips do the same job, which they don't entirely. Still, if Singleton can better understand the intricacies of the aging process, he says, "it then can be managed and controlled and the costs reduced."

While Kunkee didn't chase the leading edge of DNA research, he's right there in the study of yeast and wine. Faster fermentation through the use of new yeasts and bacterial strains, while maintaining and controlling quality, are among his major fields of study. He's also trying to identify yeasts that are more tolerant to higher levels of alcohol. "Alcohol is toxic to yeast," Kunkee explains. "A yeast that better tolerates the alcohol will carry out fermentation faster."

Few institutions in the world contribute so much to any business or industry as U.C. Davis does to wine. In 1980, Professor Singleton and recently retired Department Chairman Cornelius Ough tried to figure the value of the school's contribution to American winemaking. It was a pretty wild stab, going through several thousand books and technical articles; but the pair guessed that the business would be 10 percent smaller without the studies, science and techniques developed at Davis. This is probably conservative.

Indeed, the only other schools with staffs as respected and adept is at Montpellier in France and Geisenheim in Germany. Perhaps feeling left behind by U.C.D.'s growing technical acumen in the 1970s—as Professor Kunkee suggests—European governments began pouring money into university wine research efforts. In the early 1980s, Montpellier doubled the size of its faculty and facilities. Kunkee actually fears that the Europeans now have much more modern and better equipment, in what passes for an enological arms race.

Still, there are Europeans who still feel the Americans are leading. Francisco Monteiro, whose family owns a vineyard in Portugal, considered the big-time schools of France and Germany. He wanted to earn a doctorate in applied microbiology, focusing on enology, and return home to manage the family vineyard and teach winemaking. He chose America instead. "The feeling in the wine industry is that California has the edge," he explains. "In California, you can still experiment, try new paths. In France and Germany, the teaching is good, but they use methods from the past." Monteiro chose to attend California State University, Fresno.

In the U.S., only Fresno's enology and viticulture program begins to compare with Davis, mainly because students there are taught to make wine. The thirteen professors at Davis also teach, albeit wearily. Student demand to get into introductory classes for non-majors has at times been simply overwhelming.

Davis offers bachelor's degrees in Viticulture, a specialization in the Plant Science major, and Enology, a Fermentation Science specialization. Master's degrees in Viticulture and Enology are, respectively, part of the school's Horticulture and Food Science programs. Each year, U.C.D. sends about thirty to forty new winemakers and vineyard tenders, armed with bachelor's degrees, into the real world.

Some go into management in family operations. Others land jobs as assistants at wineries, where they drive tractors, clean tanks, hold tastings and muck about doing the hardest chores the cellars have to offer. Davis grads may comprise a set of the best-educated winery tour guides in the world.

Most of the new graduates don't make much more than $12,000 to $20,000 a year. Phil Woodward, president of Chalone Inc., one of the few publicly owned winemaking businesses in the nation, says, only somewhat in jest: "We hire Davis graduates despite the fact that they're Davis graduates."

What Woodward means is that Davis does a marvelous job of technical training in the Davis way of doing things. Practical winemaking is another matter. "But what I think the Viticulture and Enology faculty at Davis does best," says a current student, just a bit ruefully, "is train undergrads to be graduate students." Adds a Davis graduate who has gone on to become one of America's leading winemakers: "It's almost like they don't want to let you out to work in the industry."

It's said that Davis grads can tell you all about how to make a wine. Enology grads from Cal State Fresno can actually do it. Says Willy Joslin, winemaker for Wente Brothers in California's Livermore Valley: "What it comes down to is you can't be a vineyard manager if you can't speak Spanish and get a tractor to run."

Davis doesn't offer John Deere 101, and helpful graduate students, the arms, legs and backbone of a professor's research projects, are a prize commodity. But it's never been crystal clear whether U.C.D.'s Department of Viticulture and Enology is around for teaching or research.

The program was established in 1880. Phylloxera infestations were menacing all of California's vineyards. And though grape growers and winemakers in California had been trying their damnedest since the 1850s to get the industry going, failure after failure mounted. Basically, few knew what they were doing.

Wrote an author of the era: "We have thousands—perhaps the large majority of our wine growers—who are comparatively poor men, many of whom have to plant their vineyards, nay, even clear the land for them with their hands, make their first wine in a wooden shanty with a rough lever press, and work their way up by slow degrees, to that competence which they hope to gain by the sweat of their brow and many bring but a scanty knowledge to their task."

The university first started enological and viticultural study at the U.C. Berkeley campus, a pleasant, urbane atmosphere that had a climate unsuited to grape growing. But the school still had to deal with phylloxera. A proposal emerged to kill the grapevine louse by inundating vineyards with mercury compounds, a system tried in Europe, and which is highly toxic. A German geneticist, Eugene Woldemar Hilgard, who headed the U.C. Viticulture department, opposed this wretched plan. Instead, phylloxera was stayed by grafting *Vitis vinifera* vines onto domestic American rootstocks, which were resistant to the pest.

Despite Hilgard's efforts, California farmers complained that the program didn't provide much in the way of practical training. Thus, when the system acquired land at Davis, in the flatlands of central California not far from Sacramento, things began to change. While headquarters remained at Berkeley for a time, Davis had room for vineyards.

Hilgard was replaced in 1906 by the small, slender and fragile-looking Frederic Bioletti, who had been on the Berkeley faculty. Two years later, Bioletti engineered the move of the Viticulture and Enology work to the new Davis campus. It was then a true cow college, not much more than a vocational institution where Berkeley agriculture majors could go to make the mistakes and return to their homesteads properly broken-in. Under Bioletti, the department made strides in the understanding of winemaking yeasts, only to be derailed by the looming Prohibition movement. As Prohibitionists applied pressure, the U.C. Board of Regents caved in, halting all fermentation work in 1916. The Davis enology section was renamed the Department of Fruit Studies.

Bioletti concentrated on table grape and raisin research. He also hired a crack researcher named William Cruess in 1912, and another, Albert Winkler in the 1920s. It's said that Cruess, an expert in yeast studies, ignored the Regents' ban, if not the spirit of the Eighteenth Amendment to the Constitution, by continuing his investigations off-campus.

113

Winkler, who'd pioneered the development of sulfur dioxide treatment to retard spoilage of grapes shipped east, took over the department in 1935. He faced a brutally tough road, and was fortunate to have Cruess around, since his background and sub-rosa work were a foundation from which the Davis enology department could begin rebuilding its research and advisory resources. And yet, as Winkler looked at the ruinous state of California's vineyards—Napa Valley, for example, had only five remaining acres planted in Cabernet Sauvignon—it was clear that Davis and the industry would have to start from scratch. He hired a bright researcher for the faculty, one Harold Olmo. He also took under his wing a young enologist named Maynard Amerine. The team of Winkler and Amerine then launched one of the most ambitious projects in the history of viticulture.

While most of the state's wine vineyards had been converted to table and raisin grapes, small pockets of wine grapes were left. But few landowners even knew precisely what varieties were growing. Moreover, Winkler and Amerine still didn't have the slightest idea of what kinds of grapes might grow best in California's various climates and soils. So, in the summer and fall of 1935, the pair began driving throughout the state, picking grapes wherever they could find them and each day hauling the load back to Davis.

In that year alone they collected some 600 different batches of grapes. If the identities were unclear, they brought cuttings back to campus for analysis. There, in a shed that passed for a winery, Winkler and Amerine crushed each lot, set the juice to fermenting and put it up in five-gallon bottles. They also logged data on the temperatures of the areas from whence the grapes came. Then, often with only a few hours of sleep, they'd head out for more grapes.

In the spring of 1936, Winkler and Amerine began tasting, assessing the quality of each wine as it matured. During that summer, as grapes around the state ripened once again, they covered still more territory. Winkler and Amerine repeated that pattern through 1939, eventually creating more than 4,000 wines. By tasting each variety and matching its origin to climate conditions, Winkler divided the state into five viticultural regions.

In cool, coastal areas and in the northern reaches of the state—including the Napa and Sonoma valleys—he found that Cabernet, Chardonnay and Gewürztraminer produced the best wines; just as these grapes do in similar climates in France and Germany. In the state's hot inland areas, Colombard and Thompson Seedless grapes yielded the better vintages. Armed with a growing bank of information, the work of Cruess and their own winemaking knowledge, Winkler and Amerine again hit the road, this time to do some educating.

Funds, however, were tight. The box-shed winery limited what Winkler and Amerine could do, and their five-gallon bottles had pretty much filled the available space beneath the school's field house. Winkler then approached A. P. Giannini, a member of the U.C. Board of Regents, requesting $100,000 to construct an enology building and a pilot winery.

Of course Giannini engineered the appropriation, for Winkler must have known that he was approaching the Regent most likely to accede. The founder and president of the Bank of America, Giannini may have had some altruistic motives for supporting the Davis enology department; after all, long before Prohibition, California's legislators had believed that a strong wine industry was important to the state's economy. Then again, he was known for offering liberal credit terms to small businessmen and farmers, as the "little guy's" banker. Most winemakers would be his type of customer. And in fact, the Bank of America did become the financial institution of choice for much of the industry, and to a large degree still is today.

Invigorated by the cash and facilities, the Davis researchers concentrated on expanding their knowledge of wine and grapes. However, not content with merely figuring out which grape grew best where, Harold Olmo began creating new ones. In fact, over a fifty-year career of painstakingly slow and meticulous grape breeding, Olmo has introduced some two dozen varieties of table and wine grapes, vines now planted in South Africa, South America, Italy, Hawaii, California and many other places.

While Dr. Carole Meredith's 1980s approach to new grape strains involves genetic slicing and dicing, Olmo did it the hard way. To build a hybrid grape, one cuts open the buds from one variety and dusts them with pollen from another. Once the pollinated seed begins to grow, it takes four years for the vine to produce fruit. In addition, more vines, taken from the seed plant, must be grafted onto rootstocks and allowed to mature. With enough grapes in hand, a test wine can finally be made. It can take a decade just to get the hybrid ready for commercial planting, and of course, at least four to five more to get a product on the market.

Such techniques lead a researcher to more dead ends than successful products. While both parents of the hybrid may be great grapes, the progeny can be downright dour. Genes contain such variables that latent characteristics, entirely bad, could spring forth. In any event, the hybrid will be quite different from the two. Meredith's approach, using cells, is an attempt to cut down on guesswork and chance, to extract only the best traits of each parent vine. Still, she must go a long way in her research to even begin to match Dr. Olmo's contributions.

At the age of seventy-six, Olmo is still at it, and he's a man who is accustomed to the fact that some things just plain take a lot of time. Indeed, shortly after joining the Davis faculty, he found a Muscadine vine growing in one of the school's experimental fields. It was the rootstocks of such hardy American natives that saved both California's and Europe's vineyards from phylloxera. Olmo decided to try and breed some of these pest-resistant genes into *Vitis vinifera* varieties.

In 1935 he ordered graduate students to work on the matter, and the students ultimately planted roughly 1,000 hybrid vines, which unfortunately proved sterile. Although told by the Department of Viticulture and Enology chairman to get rid of the embarrassing things, Olmo kept the vines around for more than forty years. In the late 1970s, the United States Environmental Protection Agency began to restrict or ban the use of several chemical pesticides that

116

had helped keep *Vitis vinifera* from being eaten alive. Phylloxera was making a comeback, and while it took a good five years to develop from Olmo's vines a hybrid, pest-resistant Muscadine rootstock, the biological bulwark is now a part of many vineyards.

Olmo, who worked on the project with others, considers the sturdy hybrid perhaps the greatest achievement of all his viticultural research. And yet, one cannot ignore the school's Foundation Plant Vineyard, a living museum of roughly 5,000 different vine varieties; a certified, disease-free bank of wine grape stock taken from all over the world. Most were collected by Olmo.

The Foundation Vineyard contains some vines acquired a century ago, and includes plants from Asia, South Africa, South America, the Soviet Union, a large number of French hybrids and Mediterranean varieties. Isolated from other vineyards and possibly contaminating influences, each variety is represented by a pair of vines. Nurseries get their cuttings from this resource; the variety is certain, and the plants carry neither disease nor pest. In turn, the nurseries that receive the plants have agreed to carefully control and maintain such status, so when the cuttings are promulgated into more vines, these too contain no diseases and are infested with no pests. Vineyard owners pay a premium for such guarantees.

Then there is Professor Mark Kliewer, a balding graduate of Cornell University, who did post-grad research at Oregon State University before joining Davis in 1963. An expert in plant biochemistry and plant physiology, he is investigating a rather obvious, but generally overlooked, component in how grapes grow—sunlight. Concerned with soils, temperatures, irrigation, rain, frost and pests, most growers really haven't pondered how light and the shading influence of leaves affect the berries.

Indeed, vineyards with cuttings from the same foundation stock, planted in nearly identical soil—in fact, these vineyards may be right next to each other—can produce wine with different qualities that have nothing to do with winemaking style. Kliewer figures it has something to do with the duration of sunlight exposure and the spectrum of light clumps of grapes receive. Some clusters are subject to direct sun, while others on lower portions of the vines or back among the foliage receive filtered light. Red and blue light, Kliewer has noted, is absorbed by the leaves, while the wavelengths in the yellow spectrum pass through.

He also noticed that the grapes that came from vineyards with fewer leaves were often better than those with a heavy covering. This led him to believe that the full spectrum of light, particularly during the last month or two of ripening, was a critical factor in wine grape development. He has also looked at other environmental factors, including humidity, wind and temperature, and, as his biography in the Viticulture and Enology department's directory says, how these things "influence growth, bud fruitfulness, productivity and the composition of grapevines and their fruits."

Consequently, Kliewer has developed "canopy management practices," systems of plant spacing and techniques for training growing vines, and sculpting the density of the leaves, essentially, to take advantage of available light. Some of his results have been dramatic, boosting Cabernet Sauvignon production from some acreage by 60 percent.

Davis certainly has its critics. To them, the Davis style of wine—if there even is such a thing—seems to suggest something cold, mechanical, scientific. But this could also again be a product of folks with romantic notions about wine rebelling against the fact that the fermentation and aging process is fundamentally a chemical reaction. The Davis scientists who remind romantics of reality are thus easy targets.

But if this school does deserve some harpoons, it is for weaknesses in teaching, since science is emphasized far more than practical vineyard and cellar skills. And yet, many undergrad and graduate students who have entered the Viticulture and Enology programs have had goals other than becoming scientists.

Take the case of Dave Barnes, who came to Davis from Orange County in 1976 looking for some kind of agricultural education. He took some introductory viticulture and enology courses, graduated with a degree in agriculture science and then went after a masters in viticulture. He considered

118

a doctorate and an academic career, but became less and less enchanted with research. On trips to the Napa Valley, however, he did become enthused with the business side of wine.

Barnes then went to U.C. Berkeley for a second masters, this time in Business Administration, and since 1984 has worked for the Bank of America. He's in the bank's St. Helena office, right in the midst of Napa Valley's action. He makes and manages loans to an awful lot of vineyard and winery owners. From whatever purgatory holds dead banking magnates, A. P. Giannini must ponder Dave Barnes and chortle with delight.

Jill McGillivray Davis, though, had the concrete goal of becoming a winemaker when she transferred to U.C. Davis after two and a half years at Yuba College. From Yuba City, California, the daughter of a small businessman, Davis joined her father in an invitation to pick some grapes at a nursery, just before the start of her senior year in high school. Jill and her father tried to make some wine, the first vintage from a woman who went on to become the head winemaker at Buena Vista Winery and Vineyards, the business operation founded by Count Agostin Haraszthy more than 130 years ago.

At first, she found herself somewhat intimidated by the dominance of the graduate students at the school. She didn't know many people on campus, and few of her high school friends even attended college. Moreover, since Davis concentrated heavily on her schoolwork, she didn't even notice that most of the Viticulture and Enology students were considerably older than she. "I was very determined to do well and didn't spend a lot of time socializing," she now says. "And that's something I look back on with regret."

Davis also discovered that the basic groundwork classes, in math and biochemistry, were anything but a snap. Whether she wanted it or not, U.C. Davis was going to give her a hard science background. But one thing she doesn't view with retrospective regrets is the quarter she took off and the summers she spent working at wineries. After being exposed to the real world, "all of the core classes became very vocational. It all clicked together."

Jill Davis was thus something of a rarity in the U.C. Davis Viticulture and Enology department—a student the same age as most of the other juniors and seniors. Most wine students are in their late twenties to mid-thirties, and are either enthralled with the idea of being in the wine business or unhappy with their current vocation.

Canadian Dave Hulley was working toward a degree in Chemical Engineering at McMaster University in Hamilton, Ontario. With a year to go he switched majors and earned a bachelor's degree in Political Science. Meanwhile, however, he began making wine, entered amateur contests and won a few. (Competitive amateur winemaking, along with curling, is big in Ontario.) Like most poli-sci majors, Hulley wasn't quite sure of what to do with the degree, but one day his wife said simply: "Dave, why don't you be a winemaker? You get more excited about it than any other topic. You're doing it already. So be a winemaker."

Hulley looked into European schools, Cal State Fresno and Davis. He picked the latter because it was more management and science oriented. "I was also told that people from Davis move up into management faster, and that people from Fresno work for people from Davis." He's found the school's alumni to be very open. "They have no hidden secrets," he says. "They'll tell you about their mistakes and victories." The process of learning about wine at the school probably teaches the benefits of sharing.

"As a student you have a responsibility to taste as many different wines as possible and learn their sensory qualities," Hulley explains. "Forget the classwork. It's your mouth that will make money for you. But good wine is expensive, so groups of 10 to 15 students get together, pool their cash and put out a series of 30 to 35 wines that we couldn't otherwise afford."

Hulley was slightly shaken, but not daunted, when he also heard from recent grads who were earning $12,000 a year and doing every dirty job a vineyard and winery had to offer. "But I've been told that if you're good, within six to ten years your salary will triple," he says. But money doesn't matter all that much to this Canadian. "I just like the idea that a winemaker is a person who can be up to his neck in shit all day, wearing his coveralls, and then that night has to be in a tuxedo."

By his senior year, Hulley was on his way to the alternately crappy and classy lifestyle, having signed a contract to work for the Hillebrand Estates Winery in Ontario, a 150,000-case-per-year operation that's not far from Niagara Falls and which is owned by a German company. He's the first Davis graduate ever to work in Ontario. And after a few years, Hulley can probably hire a former Fresno student, just for sport.

8

BETWEEN THE STATES— A MOSTLY CIVIL WAR

In 1981, Allen Shoup walked back to his office in the enormous, Bordeaux-style Château Ste. Michelle headquarters building, feeling a bit dazed. Set in the midst of eighty-seven acres of landscaped splendor in Woodinville, a small town north of Seattle, this winery had generated tremendous sales growth since being purchased by the United States Tobacco Co. in 1974. The only operation in Washington producing significant volumes of wine, this was a business headed toward major league status, with markets in all fifty states. Since Shoup had come on board in 1980 as vice president of marketing and corporate planning, the ambition in Ste. Michelle's plans had grown, too.

Indeed, its officers had just asked U.S. Tobacco's board of directors for something like $26 million and change to buy land in southern Washington's Columbia Valley. There were plans to plant about 2,000 acres of vineyards and build one of the biggest wineries north of the Federal Republic of Gallo right in the middle. And somewhat to Shoup's surprise, the U.S. Tobacco directors had given their answer—an unqualified yes.

Shoup figured the investment was good for UST and Ste. Michelle for a number of reasons. The Columbia Valley's soil is a rich sandy loam that vines like. It's a region that's blessed with cool evenings and consistently sunny summers; though it only gets seven to eight inches of rain each year, it is well supplied by irrigation systems. Thus, a winegrower there has considerable control over the elements. Because new premium varietals had been selling like crazy since the mid-1970s, Shoup felt the big new venture could help the UST subsidiary control its marketplace destiny.

The U.S. Tobacco board's easy acquiescence, however, left the thirty-nine-year-old Shoup slightly dazed; pleased, but surprised. Despite his relative youth, he'd been around enough corporate power—at E. & J. Gallo, in the cosmetics industry as director of marketing for Max Factor, and as director of corporate communications for Boise Cascade Lumber Products Corp—to know this was unusual. An open-faced, amiable man with a balding pate and a shock of frizzy hair, Shoup knew that the UST directors were either foolish or awfully brilliant. While cash-rich, UST could buy a lot of other things for $26 million. And despite the growth in varietal sales, this was, after all, still the wine business.

Followed to his office by one of the directors, Shoup shook his head and asked why it was that U.S. Tobacco seemed so willing, even eager, to invest so much in an industry so capital intensive, and that takes so long to give returns. "You'd do better if you just put the money in the bank and drew simple interest," said Shoup. Stockholders and securities analysts, he knew, grow visibly edgy when large publicly traded corporations plow money into ventures that don't yield rapid dividends.

The director nodded. "The way I look at it," he said quietly, "is that any prudent businessman would be out of his mind to do what we just did." He then gave Shoup a wry grin. "But twenty or thirty years from now, they're going to wonder how we had the genius and foresight to do this."

Shoup also knew that UST's directors had done similar things in the past; the company had a track record of foresighted, long-range investments, and patience in awaiting returns. And Shoup, whose drive and talent has made him slightly less patient, is now president and CEO of Stimson Lane Wine & Spirits Ltd., which manages Château Ste. Michelle, the new operation (called Columbia Crest), and several other small wineries and related enterprises.

The $26 million vineyard and winery has not been quite as successful as the corporation probably would have liked, considering that growth in wine sales started slowing before the whopping winemaking complex, much of it underground, was even finished. But from the moment Columbia Crest released its first vintages in July 1987, it succeeded, more than anything, as a concept.

Columbia Crest immediately became the second-largest selling winery in Washington state, after Château Ste. Michelle. But it wasn't just a second label for Stimson Lane. No, it became an "adversary," so to speak, to the older, established operation, a challenger that tests it in the market and in the process heightens the public appeal of both. More important, it helps convey the perception to the wine world that there is more to this sometimes soggy Pacific Northwest state than the anomalous Château Ste. Michelle. Columbia Crest was and is a concept to market the notion of Washington wines, plural.

"Say there's a shop in Chicago that wants to feature wines from this state," says Château Ste. Michelle's marketing director Bob Betz. "Before, he could get plenty of our wine, and just a few bottles from some of the small wineries in the state. Now, with Columbia Crest, he's got two major labels, can fill in with the others, and do a big promotional on the Wines of Washington." It's such thinking that is turning the region into a wine industry force.

Indeed, Washington has roared out of a stagnant enological backwater like one of the hydroplanes that race on Lake Washington during Seattle's annual Seafair celebration. The residents here largely eschewed wine in favor of locally brewed Rainier and Olympia beer, and Washington has always been a great tavern state. Of the forty-two wineries that sprang up in the state after Prohibition ended, only three survived into the 1970s; two were progenitors of Ste. Michelle, which can trace its roots to 1934. Only a quarter of a century ago, Washington's handful of wineries made either no or very bad use of *Vitis vinifera* grapes. On a 1966 trip through the Yakima Valley, fabled wine writer Leon "Wines of America" Adams was astonished to see Cabernet Sauvignon and Pinot Noir grapes blended with Concord grapes "in nondescript ports and burgundy blends."

Washington's latitudes, however, encompass the same swath of the globe as most of the Bordeaux, the Loire and Burgundy regions of France. In the past couple of decades, Washington winegrowers have tumbled to this fact, and its borders now contain at least sixty-two wineries. It is the nation's No. 2 premium wine producer, with about 11,000 acres of producing grapes. The state's annual output is now in excess of a million cases of table wine.

While this isn't much of a threat to California, which produces more than 400 million gallons annually, it's clear that the Golden State has no monopoly on making fine wines. But threat isn't even an appropriate word, for the success of Château Ste. Michelle has turned Washington into a state of zealous wine drinkers. Sometimes, a few individuals among the fairly new crop of consumers will try something other than an indigenous release, although drinking California products is perceived as being somewhat disloyal in what even Washington natives agree is a highly provincial state.

But drink they do, having climbed to fourth place in the national wine consumption rankings, approaching four gallons per capita. Ahead of Washington are only the District of Columbia, Nevada and California. (D.C. and Nevada, however, levy lower taxes on wine than their neighbors; the per capita figure is thus skewed by visitors who buy an unknown but considerable volume of wine and take it home.)

Washingtonians who ten or fifteen years ago drank wine only during Communion now attend tastings, pay $30 apiece to try samples at the Northwest Enological Festival, visit the burgeoning number of wineries, and earnestly study restaurant wine lists.

Washington wines are favored, and about 80 percent of the time that means Ste. Michelle, although Shoup often encourages people to try some of the state's other wines. In fact, he's become something of a spokesman for all Washington vintners. He has also served as chairman of the Washington Wine Marketing Advisory Board, which was created and funded by the state to push its wines. As for Ste. Michelle, Shoup's involvement is a policy of enlightened self-interest as much as generosity. Small winegrowers feel less threatened by this relative leviathan, and their presence in the national market helps Stimson Lane project an identity for Washington wines, which has long been a problem.

Bob Betz has a favorite story about this, which he often tells. Several years ago, while touring the country to promote Washington and Château Ste. Michelle wines, he gave a presentation in Washington, D.C. "I was up there in front of a very socially important women's group," he explains, "and really selling it. I talked about the warm days and cool nights in the Columbia Valley, the good soil, the latitude being the same as Burgundy and Bordeaux. I had their complete, rapt attention. And then, when I stopped and asked if there were any questions, a lady in the back of the room raised her hand. 'Can you tell us on which side of the Potomac the vineyards are located?' "

In any event, Washington has certainly embraced its wine industry, and it's a model for what other states might consider encouraging. As Allen Shoup explained when he sat on the panel at the Buena Vista Vintage 2000 affair in 1987: "Our industry is a very popular industry. It's sexy. It's attractive. It's non-polluting. It stimulates other things like tourism and agriculture."

Oregon is also up-and-coming, with a Wine Advisory Board and more than fifty wineries, most of which concentrate on producing Pinot Noir, Chardonnay and Riesling.

Moreover, although Washington has staked a claim to those French latitudes, Oregon may correspond to more of Bordeaux than its northern neighbor. In addition, Oregon's climate east of the Cascade range is probably more like the traditional European wine grape regions than the temperatures and rainfall of eastern Washington.

Its vintners are now producing roughly 600,000 gallons of wine each year, most of it super-premium varietals. Most of it is consumed in Oregon, which is in seventh place in national per capita wine consumption. Because the wine is in such demand, and the wineries are small, the prices range from at least $10 to $15 per bottle. But the cases that do make it out of state sell in an instant, for Oregon wines are still a novelty and there are always wine fanciers who will snap up anything unusual, however priced.

In this sense, Oregon wines have not yet been forced to worry about identity in the national market, for they appeal to a thin slice of consumers. Its wines fit comfortably in a tiny niche that is for now self-sustaining. No Oregon vintner has even started to approach the size of Château Ste. Michelle. But should this ever happen, it would be forced to aggressively build and maintain a significantly larger niche; easy sales would be history.

For all his kind words about competitors in Washington, Allen Shoup is not so sanguine about Oregon wineries, which he has suggested are trying to trade on Washington's more advanced reputation by talking about "wineries of the Pacific Northwest." Shoup pretty much draws the line in the middle of the Columbia River, and has charged that "all the major Oregon wineries have bought Washington grapes from day one."

In a 1985 interview with *The Wine Spectator*, he derided Oregon vintners for choosing to grow Pinot Noir, quoting a California winegrower who once said, "you have to be a masochist to grow that grape in the first place." Shoup also pointed out that Washington wineries don't buy Oregon grapes. "You never catch butter trying to sell itself as margarine, but quite the opposite is true." Shoup clearly and quite simply doesn't want Oregon stealing any of

Washington's hard-earned thunder, although comparing its wines to imposter margarine is a bit specious.

Oregon's Chardonnay wines have, however, been justly criticized as being a bit "thin." (In this sense, it does mean a lack of buttery richness; give Shoup a half-point.) This is due to the fact, no doubt, that Oregon's climate, cooler than California's, produces more "delicate" Chardonnay grapes. Vintners have modified some enological techniques to put more richness and fullness in the wines, but the rap lingers.

On the other hand, *The Wine Spectator*, which closely follows and hangs on such things, has done the Dance of Joy over Oregon "Pinot Noir That the Experts Mistake for Burgundy." The state's frequent cloud cover and cool weather make for better Pinot Noir than does California's climate. Experts have rated the Oregon reds from superb to outstanding, if expensive. The masochists of Pinot Noir are apparently happy in their pain.

Texas is the home of what's been called "Château Bubba," the house of Redneck Reds and Oil Baron Whites. But it's too easy to make fun of Lone Star wine, too mean, and not entirely accurate. Texas winegrowing generated about $21 million in 1986, and wines from a trio of vintners—Fall Creek, Pheasant Ridge and Llano Estacado—are developing reputations for quality. Texas wines, like those of Oregon, are still in their new and trendy phase.

Nevertheless, Texas actually produced wine long before California. In 1662, Franciscan priests founded the Ysleta Mission in the El Paso Valley and, as the padres so often did, planted vines. This area had a number of wineries up until Prohibition, but afterwards the industry didn't start to make a comeback until the 1970s. Horticulture professors from Texas A&M University surveyed the state and found its soils and climates were amenable to several kinds of wine grapes.

However, just as the Texas wine industry got rolling, it got smacked like an armadillo crossing a farm-to-market road. In April of 1987, a big freeze wiped out most of the vine buds in the state, knocking down grape production in some areas by nearly 70 percent. The High Plains of West Texas were largely spared by the cold, but a month later a drenching rain led to bunch rot in about 20 percent of that area's vines. Moreover, Texas bankers view wine as even more risky than oil. And these days, an oilman's credit rating is somewhere above that of Bangladesh, but not as good as Brazil's. Wineries here simply cannot borrow cash to expand, and thus must use private funds or miss an opportunity.

Ste. Genevieve Vineyards, which was started in 1985, quickly became the biggest vintner and then just as swiftly ran into financial difficulties. Started as a limited partnership between Texas natives Dick Gill and the family of A. R. Sanchez, and a pair of French companies, Richter Inc. and the Bordeaux wine company Cordier SA, Ste. Genevieve's major problems stemmed from virulent disagreements between the partners.

After the Bank of America foreclosed on it, Cordier SA paid $9 million to lease Ste. Genevieve's vineyards and winery. But there's a law here that requires 51 percent Texas ownership of such companies. Cordier seemed to satisfy this when one John Collet, a San Antonio resident and president of the company, showed that he held majority ownership. But other wineries in the state challenged the new deal, claiming that Collet was a front, that it was foreign interests that truly controlled Ste. Genevieve.

Given the history of the Texas Railroad Commission, Lyndon Johnson's early elections and the very social fiber of this singular state, this was a penny-ante beef. The Texas Alcoholic Beverage Commission granted Ste. Genevieve its new license, and the joint's back in business, with plans to begin marketing outside the state.

While the banks aren't helping fuel new Texas wineries, private financiers are trying. A partnership of well-heeled investors has formed what's become known as the West Texas Project. With $2.2 million gathered to buy Cabernet Sauvignon and Chardonnay vineyards near Lubbock and to build a winery, the group has touted the fact that this area, west of the Texas High Plains, has a climate more like that of France than does California.

Texas has high hopes for winegrowing. With its petroleum-based economy battered, and its traditional cotton crop evolving into an agricultural loser, grapes, of all things, are a bright spot. Wine, of course, doesn't dovetail with this state's chili, Willie Nelson and beer image. But then, most Texas cowboys are of the urban variety; the beds of their pickups never carry a blade of straw, their boots a pungent whiff of eau de manure. Texans are more like Californians and New Yorkers than they dare think. And in the next decade they'll become just as provincial as Washingtonians over their state wine, believing that it's somehow different because the grapes spring from Texas dirt.

Before Washington state passed it, New York was the nation's second-leading wine-producing state. From 1981 to 1985, its vintners fermented the state's grapes into an annual average of some twenty-eight million gallons of wine. (The state's total wine output, however, is greater, due to bulk juice imports from the West.) But while a venerable and well-developed state industry, New York's winegrowers have been going through hard changes. Grape acreage and the number of producers are in decline, even in prime vineyard areas such as the Finger Lakes region and the Chautauqua-Erie area. Average prices earned by these growers have declined from more than $300 a ton in 1981 to $180 and less just five years later.

Wineries have also suffered, primarily because New York consumers are partial to imported European wines when the price is right. The strong dollar in the mid-1980s and the slowing in premium wine sales growth put the squeeze to New York vintners.

The state's grape industry produces between 150,000 and 200,000 tons each year, a combination of native Labrusca varieties, hybrids and *Vitis vinifera*. Concords are the predominant native grape, although 75 percent of that goes to juice and jelly, and the rest to foxy wine. But the recent problems experienced by growers are not the first. Indeed, New York wines started to gain favor with Eastern consumers in the mid-1970s when Empire State vintners started blending more bulk California wine into their vintages, cutting down on the Labrusca flavor. Winemakers cut their purchase of these grapes, which left the growers in the lurch. Moreover, at the time, New York law made it prohibitively expensive for growers to start wineries.

In 1976, reacting to complaints from farmers, Governor Hugh Carey started a state-sponsored program to promote New York wines. In addition, a new law made it easier for farm-wineries to get started. "Immediately scores of farmers banded together to build wineries," wrote Leon Adams in *Wines of America*. "Within a year, twelve new cellars were opened for business or were under construction, increasing the state total from thirty-nine wineries to fifty-one." New York today has about seventy farm wineries, but most produce less than 20,000 gallons annually.

Growers are having a difficult time covering costs. Most of these farmers are dependent on a handful of big companies for up to 90 percent of their sales. (These include Canandaigua Wine Co.; Taylor Wine Co. Inc., which controls the Great Western Winery and Gold Seal Vineyards; the Brooklyn kosher outfit of Kedem; and the Hammondsport winery, Bully Hill.) But with jug wine sales declining, their future isn't looking much better.

Seagram, moreover, has reportedly been unhappy with the returns of its Taylor-Great Western-Gold Seal holdings. It's become clear that New York growers have higher production costs than counterparts in California, and while the state does produce some well-received Long Island Chardonnays and sparkling wines, New Yorkers simply do not feel that great a passion for local wine, at least not to the degree consumers do in other states. With a choice between a comparably priced French, California or Washington wine, the Empire is out.

A number of Southern states have been active in new winegrowing ventures. In the past decade, Alabama, Mississippi, Florida and Georgia have quadrupled their number of bonded wineries, from ten to about forty. From 1976 to 1986, Missouri, Minnesota, Illinois and Iowa saw the winery count in those states jump 77 percent, from fifty-two to ninety-two. Indeed, a recent statewide promotion of Missouri wineries has increased public awareness and boosted sales of its wines. Once a major player in the American wine industry, this state is attempting a comeback.

From a business standpoint, of all the efforts by wine-producing states over the past decade—outside of California—none is more compelling than the successes of Washington, and its leading light, Château Ste. Michelle. "In the early 1980s," says Bob Betz, "about 70 percent of the wine we sold was in Washington. Today, about 30 percent of our wine is sold here, and we haven't lost a bit of market share in the state."

Ste. Michelle does it by using about 300 different distributors throughout the U.S., and highly paid divisional sales managers who can pull down $60,000 to $80,000 a year. That's no great shakes considering a parent company like U.S. Tobacco, but heady wages for a wine hustler, the kind of money that attracts a good pool of talent.

The visibility of Ste. Michelle in Washington sometimes puts Shoup in a difficult position. "After people go to Boeing and the major banks, they come to us for contributions," he explains. "We aren't a fraction as large, financially speaking, as Boeing or the others."

And it is now trying to strengthen itself by projecting the concept of Washington wine throughout the U.S., with the Columbia Crest label. "I really hate to call it a second label," says Shoup, "because it's a winery that essentially stands on its own."

Columbia Crest moved out of the box a bit slower than expected. Only half of the twenty-acre, underground facility is in use, and while "constructed for growth," as Shoup explains, the dormant half is a non-producing asset. Its first release, in 1985, sold about 25,000 cases, and the following year Columbia Crest produced and sold 70,000 cases. By 1987, it had leaped to nearly 135,000 cases. "In 1988," he adds, "we hope to sell about 250,000. But I'll admit that when we started, I thought we'd be up to 350,000 by now. The sales force, however, is moving fast up the learning curve, and most people would be ecstatic with the kind of success Columbia Crest has had."

More than a few states would like to have the success of Washington's wine industry. And to a degree this is possible, for Ste. Michelle started making its reputation around the Puget Sound before branching out. It started by kissing individual bottles, as Betz says, to give its customers the warm fuzzies when they bought this real-life Washington wine, which was, after all, much less "mysterious" than French and California products.

California, obviously, is the state with the greatest national marketing presence. And while the Golden State is its own best customer, it still depends on the rest of the country for most of its revenue. Over 32 percent of California wine is sold inside its borders; some 65 percent goes to other states. Between 2 percent and 3 percent is sold internationally.

As more states develop their industries, there will be more wineries vying for the dollars of that limited pool of novelty buyers. But on the whole, a growing wine business within any state is good for the American wine business. Ste. Michelle turned Washington residents into wine drinkers, and if Texans, Hoosiers or Georgians grow accustomed to their own wines, and it becomes a frequent beverage, they're more likely to be interested in wines from other locales.

Trade barriers and boneheaded liquor laws still cause friction between states. But the business war is highly civil, for winegrowers know they must cultivate consumers everywhere. Appealing to provincialism is a fine way to start. It's nothing more than states' rights.

Section Three

STRONG BACKS, ALCHEMIC MINDS AND THE PLAYERS WHO COUNT THE BEANS

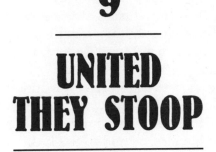

9

UNITED
THEY STOOP

Valente Calderon's opinions on the progress of the up-coming grape harvest aren't sought out by journalists preparing features on the vines and wines of Sonoma County, although he's right in the middle of the action. A short and slight man with a wry disposition, Calderon doesn't attend tastings; to him, enophiles might as well be aliens from the planet Mongo, although they probably wouldn't care much about what he has to say, either. In fact, since his responsibilities consist of hoeing weeds, driving a tractor, pruning vines and picking grapes, he simply doesn't count for much on the public side of the wine business. But the wine business depends on Valente Calderon, and tens of thousands of people like him.

Workers such as Calderon are the flip side of the glitter and gloss; without their backs and hands, there wouldn't be affordable premium wine. While the wine business is capital intensive, it's also highly labor intensive. By and large, many things are still done as they've always been done—by hand.

Most premium wine grapes are hand picked; all of those grown on hillside vineyards must be harvested this way, since machine harvesters can't work on a slope. Pruning and vine training perforce must also be done by hand, a very time-consuming process. And no cybernetic marvel has yet been created that will disc between the vine rows or administer a spray of sulphur or herbicides by itself. This still calls for a man on a tractor—a man willing to work for $5 to $7 an hour, and sometimes less.

It is not the easiest or most rewarding of careers. But Calderon has gladly taken the work, for it beats the alternative he faced. His story reflects a side of the industry that folks sipping wine rarely ponder. Such thoughts just might take the bloom off their pleasure.

Calderon was born in the mountainous, rural state of Michoacán in western Mexico twenty-five years ago, in a small village of campesinos who worked the fields of a local landowner. He was one of nine children. Their diet consisted of tortillas, rice, beans and chiles, and rare pieces of meat, fruit or vegetables. Over the years, the family saved a small amount of money which they used to buy a minuscule plot of land. They built a dwelling out of adobe blocks made with clay, straw and manure. They planted corn, cabbage, chiles and a few fruit trees. They kept some chickens.

Valente worked as a goatherd for the resident landowner until he was fifteen. He spent every spare moment hanging around local shadetree mechanics, and demonstrated a natural aptitude for such work. At sixteen, he landed a job as an auto mechanic in Acapulco. Since he sent a good deal of his earnings home to help support his brothers and sisters, Valente still lived in grinding poverty.

Throughout his life, though, young Calderon had heard about life in El Norte: of the money, the grand houses, the highways filled with new cars. He took it all with a grain of salt. Still, it was apparent to him that the United States did offer opportunity. Acquaintances in Acapulco had come back from there, some with thousands of dollars in their pockets. Thousands. Valente decided to try his luck.

From Acapulco he hitched rides north until he came to the border at Tijuana. He'd heard many dire tales about the town and attempted crossings: coyotes who ripped off their clients, cholos (American-born Latins) who lurked on the north side of the border, ready to beat, rob—even kill—the naive and gullible Mexicans. Corrupt cops on both sides of the wire, he'd been told. Danger at every turn. But he found a coyote who took only $100 and smuggled him across without incident.

Once in California, Valente teamed up with a quartet of Mexicans from his native Michoacán who had a beat-up 1968 Olds Cutlass. Calderon's skills as a mechanic were enough to secure a ride north. They drove straight up Interstate 5, then cut over at Highway 680, near Fremont, a city on the southern fringes of the San Francisco Bay. The youth was taken with both the wealth of the country and the frenetic pace of its inhabitants. He suddenly felt lonely, despite the others: the displacement of being a stranger in a strange land. Valente's friends, who had worked in the North before, told him to cheer up.

"It's not paradise," one of them told him. "The gringos are generally pricks. But we can get work here. You can stay with us. You'll make good money, and you can send most of it back home. It beats starving in the pueblo, waiting for something to happen."

His new-found friends drove to the house of the driver's cousin, in the town of Windsor. It had only three rooms. It was dilapidated. But it had indoor plumbing, electricity, and a strange assortment of amenities that its residents had collected over time; two televisions, a VCR, several radios and various electric kitchen appliances. Valente found the juxtaposition between squalor and what would constitute the trappings of wealth in his Mexican village perplexing. But he didn't have much time to dwell on it.

The next day the six men who shared the house took him to work with them, stringing deer fencing for a grower in the Alexander Valley. For six months Calderon picked grapes, pruned vines and drove tractors for a number of growers in

Sonoma County. One of them learned of Calderon's skills with internal combustion engines, an asset that elevated his worth beyond that of casual labor. The grower offered Calderon a full-time job. He took it, and has been there ever since.

Valente Calderon has been in the U.S. for seven years now. He earns $6.50 an hour, and commonly works fifty to sixty hours a week. About half his money is still sent back home to Mexico.

Calderon and his fellow working poor are the bottom link in the wine labor chain, but the industry couldn't get along without these Mexicans who are willing to toil hard for a better life. "I get so tired of hearing people claim that these workers are taking jobs away from Americans," says Patrick Campbell of Laurel Glen Vineyards. "The fact is that Americans won't do this kind of work. The only workers you can get who are American citizens are derelicts, drunks or the incorrigibly unemployed. And they're totally unsatisfactory. The Latins need the work, and we need them to work for us. And people who like to drink decent wine without paying an arm and a leg for it need them, too."

Abuses of this labor pool were once fairly common, but Campbell claims this is rarely true today. "These guys aren't going to work for anybody who's taking advantage of them. They're too smart, and the competition for their labor is too keen."

There are growers who have established good relationships with laborers, and who are generally acknowledged as equitable and fair. Most premium wineries have been able to escape the bitter strife which has characterized relations between laborers and large grape growers in the Central Valley. Most, but not all.

Beaulieu Vineyards has had some particularly severe labor relations problems. Visitors to the Napa Valley are apt to see ranks of farm workers arrayed by the road outside of Beaulieu, waving red flags emblazoned with the UFW (United Farm Workers) logo. The union has prosecuted a boycott against the winery.

"Beaulieu had a contract with the United Farm Workers," explains one Napa Valley insider. "Or, that is to say,

Heublein, which owns Beaulieu, had a contract. Then a few years ago, they divested themselves of their vineyard operations and contracted their vineyard work out to a guy named Andy Beckstoffer. Beckstoffer chose to use non-union labor, and the UFW claimed that Beaulieu's divestment comprised a cynical and calculated design to bust the union. I'm inclined to agree with the UFW—in spite of Beaulieu's protestations to the contrary."

In any event, Beaulieu's relations with the union deteriorated. In 1985, a nocturnal raid on one of its vineyards by persons unknown resulted in the destruction of several hundred vines, at a cost of thousands of dollars. The UFW denied all responsibility, and Beaulieu blustered and howled, decrying the act as wanton and heinous vandalism. Since that nadir, no similar acts of property destruction have been leveled against Beaulieu. But the strikers continue to picket, Beaulieu's management blandly denies any culpability in the farm workers' problem, and the winery continues to sell wine without any seeming impact from the UFW sanctions.

"If this was 1968, then the UFW actions would be having a lot more effect than it does," says *The Napa Insider*. "But it's 1988, and people don't care much about Cesar Chavez these days; at least those who know and buy good Cabernet Sauvignon don't care enough about him to give it up. And Beaulieu makes dynamite Cabernets. They're selling them without any difficulty. Good wine means a lot more to people these days than 'correct' politics."

Good wine also takes more human hands. Unlike most industries, the premium wine industry seems to make advances by adding labor, rather than reducing it. Viticultural research has suggested that closely spaced vines on intensive trellis systems produce fruit of higher quality than widely spaced vines on one- or two-wire systems. Closely spaced vineyards, however, require more labor; there are more rootstocks to plant, more buds to be grafted to the rootstocks, more grapestakes to be pounded, and more wires to string to the stakes. Such vineyards do not lend themselves to mechanical harvesting, so nearly all the new closely spaced vineyards must be harvested by hand.

The demand for imported labor isn't new. A century ago, the wine industry relied heavily on an earlier group of migrant workers—the Chinese.

When Agoston Haraszthy returned from Europe in 1861 with all his new vine cuttings to try out in California soil—he clearly needed immediate help. But California's labor pool wasn't particularly attuned to this type of employment. The Gold Country contained men who would work very hard, but only on their own claims, not for wages. In a chapter on this labor situation, published in the University of California Press's *Book of California Wine*, Jack Chen noted that in the labor-short state, those who even entertained the thought "demanded a minimum wage of thirty dollars a month, with board, for vineyard work that they did not want anyway—two or three times the eastern states' wage rate." Haraszthy, observes Chen, would have instantly gone bankrupt trying to pay this scale.

The Hungarian entrepreneur turned to another enterprising immigrant, a man named Ho Po. A Chinese labor contractor, Ho Po had several hundred men in Haraszthy's fields within days. Many had been farmers in China. Most had left spouses and families behind in the years following 1849, hoping to earn a relative fortune in North America before returning home. Cut out of major gold prospecting, they gladly accepted the eight dollars a month, plus board, that Haraszthy offered.

Other winegrowers contracted with Ho Po for the use of Chinese labor. In the fields of Northern California, Chinese made up more than 80 percent of the vineyard workforce, diligent and reliable. Some helped out in the winemaking, and a few started their own enterprises. However, the Chinese were never truly accepted or appreciated, and given what they were paid and the living conditions, their existence was only a cut above slavery. In fact, says Sue Eileen Hayes, who contributed a short essay in *The Book of California Wine*, black slave labor was advocated for the larger farms in the state during the 1850s. A spokesman for agricultural interests wrote in the May 25, 1854, issue of *California Farmer* that the Chinese should "be to California what the African has been to the South."

Antislavery sentiments quieted such talk. But in practice, Ho Po kept delivering motivated workers who didn't cost much more to employ than real slaves. Racist hate also boiled near the surface, and began to bubble up and over in the mid-1870s, when California's gold and silver industries declined and a recession created widespread unemployment. The Chinese, the Mexicans of the late 1800s, were accused of stealing jobs. The United States Congress passed the Chinese Exclusion Act in 1882, halting the influx of Chinese.

For all the bitter invective they aroused, these Chinese workers were largely unobtrusive. Not so with the Mexicans a century later. The thousands of Latin laborers who support the premium industry have formed a subterranean but highly visible society in the wine country. Their presence has not come without tension, and a certain undercurrent of racism pervades white consciousness in the wine regions.

"All you have to do is read *The Santa Rosa Press Democrat* to see what's going on," fumes a Sonoma County resident. "Look at the arrests for drunk driving and hit and run. Most of them involve people with Spanish surnames. None of them have insurance. They're always stabbing and killing each other. The crime rate in this area would drop tremendously if we didn't have them around."

Dan Weinberg, an emergency physician who rotates between Sonoma County's Palm Drive Hospital in Sebastapol and Community Hospital in Santa Rosa, sees it a little differently. "I patch up quite a few guys with Spanish surnames who have been stabbed and shot," he says. "And it's probably true that Latin workers are involved in a disproportionate number of drunken driving arrests. I certainly have no use for people who drive drunk. But these guys are facing two things up here—their own cultural imperatives and the stress that comes out of loneliness and deprivation. They're either breaking their backs, or desperately seeking work."

Dr. Weinberg explains that up to a dozen Latins are often crammed into a two- or three-room house. "They're living in one of the most affluent areas of the country, but they don't have the money or cultural tools—even the language—

143

to be part of the society. So they drink to handle the stress. And when they drink they get into disagreements, and when they get into disagreements, they're likely to resolve them in much more violent ways than North Americans do. It's part of machismo, the Latin code of masculinity. Their culture almost requires them to resolve their problems violently when their pride is at stake."

That pride is easily injured in the States, says Weinberg, "where they're treated as menial nonentities. They can't take out their frustrations on their employers or the white power structure," says the physician, "so they take them out on each other. I certainly don't condone the situation, but I can understand the problems they face. They don't have an easy time of it up here."

Not all Latins share common backgrounds and cultures, so the Latin community is considerably more heterogeneous than might be immediately apparent to Anglos. Mexicans identify closely to their regions of origin, identifications strengthened by ties of kin and compadrazgo, the Latin concept of intense friendships that are considered as strong as blood relationships. This, coupled with the fact that the market for seasonal labor can at times be competitive, translates into considerable tension between Mexicans from different states. Even more pronounced is hostility between Latins from different countries.

"One of the first jobs I ever had in this industry was driving a tractor during the crush for one of the largest grape growers in the Sonoma Valley," recalls a vineyardist for a large Napa winery. "This was a big operation, hundreds of acres of grapes, and they sold all their fruit to Sebastiani. The ranchers had a compound where they housed all the crews. It was in pretty shitty shape, and there wasn't much in the way of amenities.

"The workers were crowded in there," he continues, "and things were pretty tense. All the workers were from Michoacán or Guerrero, except for one crew of Cubans. They were Marielitos, part of the bunch of misfits and criminals that Castro shipped over here, and they were a raving bunch of assholes. They constantly bullied the other crews, and one of them hit me in the back with a rock once when I was driving a tractor. I just blew up. He was on the other side of the vine row from me, and I grabbed him and damn near pulled him through the trellis wires. It took the whole crew to pull me off him, and the Marielitos left me alone after that.

"But they were always terrorizing the other Latins, until one night the Mexicans couldn't take it any longer; they all ganged up on the Cubans and beat the shit out of them, and sent two to the hospital. Really, the Cubans were lucky they weren't all killed. Mexicans just hate Cubans. They think Cubans are liars, and that they're always scheming on their women."

The United States has reached a certain degree of affluence, and its citizens have cultivated a certain attitude about agricultural labor that's not at all positive. Domestic agricultural jobs go begging, and the only folks who will take them are the dispossessed and disenfranchised, the abysmally poor and desperate. In short, the landless, workless campesino and urban dwellers from Mexico or Central America.

However, not everyone considers the flood of immigrants pouring across the southern border of the U.S. salutary for the country. In response to the years of wild and unmitigated immigration, legal and otherwise, Congress passed the Immigration Reform and Control Act of 1986. The legislation sent a frisson of foreboding down the wine industry's spine.

The Act required all employers to verify and document the residence or citizenship of all newly hired employees. U.S. passports, certificates of U.S. citizenship, certificates of naturalization, foreign passports with employment authorization endorsements, or green cards are required from potential employees. Naturally, the Act has resulted in selective enforcement. In California, the only potential employees who are really subjected to genuine scrutiny are those of Latin extraction. They are visibly and linguistically different; they are the ones whom officers of the Immigration Service—or "migra" as it's known by Latins—search out, interrogate, detain and deport.

Since previous immigration statutes made no provision for the punishment of those who knowingly hire illegal aliens, growers simply signed on Latins as needed, and with impunity. The new Immigration Act, however, carries stiff fines and imprisonment for those who don't bother to verify the legality of workers.

However, no matter how the Immigration Act is enforced, the domestic wine industry is dependent on cheap agricultural labor, workers who must inevitably come from south of the border. There is no alternative, save wine that would be prohibitively expensive. The higher-priced wine would languish on shelves, beaten by cheaper products from Europe and Australia. This would devastate an already stumbling wine industry, not to mention many other sectors of U.S. agriculture, including orchard fruits, vegetables and greenhouse operations.

When all is said and done, immigration policy will have little effect on the flux of migrant workers coming into the U.S. Everything abhors a vacuum, and that includes an economic system. As long as there is lousy work that no one else wants in the North, and poor people like Valente Calderon in the South, the two will find a way to get together.

10

CELLAR RATS

It was speed, relentless speed that most impressed Cathy Dalsis when she first appeared for work at the E. & J. Gallo Winery in Modesto, California, in 1977. The massive, 400-acre facility includes dozens and dozens of clean white storage tanks that would be the envy of any petroleum refinery. It includes a twenty-seven-acre warehouse, a glass factory, research labs and an underground aging cellar. She left seven years later. But even today, it is still the speed—bottle after bottle and jug after jug of wine rushing pell-mell through the plant—that sticks in her mind.

She started out in the bottling room, checking labels and putting foil over the tops of bottles that whipped by on one of fourteen lines, at least six of which run at all times. Shifts keep the plant going around the clock, and if a line breaks down, the crew moves to another.

On an eight-hour Gallo shift, workers get two ten-minute breaks and a twenty-minute paid lunch. The worst job, recalls Dalsis, is "dumping glass," standing face-to-face with other workers across a high-speed line, pulling off cases and piling them on pallets. The atmosphere calls to mind Laverne and Shirley at the Schotz Brewery, only the winery moves too quick to be funny. The plant rules say you can't leave your assigned spot. The owners are going to get a full $12 worth of work for every sixty minutes an employee is there. The clock is always ticking. Relentlessly.

But Dalsis actually liked it, although when her fellow workers found that this young woman from upstate New York, the daughter of a Lincoln Mercury dealer, was a real live college graduate, they initially thought her daft. Most of them hold a fairly low opinion of their employment. It's a job, but no place for someone with the options of the higher educated.

Dalsis just laughed, and explained that she thought they were making darn good money and had great benefits, especially compared to a junior high teacher in Florida, a position she'd left behind along with a bad marriage. The work at the winery ended after eight hours, not with late night calls from troubled parents. She didn't have to deal with school administrators, teacher politics and junior high students.

Today, Dalsis is the business representative for Local 186 of the Winery, Distillery and Allied Workers Union (WDAWU), based in Modesto. Between the nearly 1,900 members she represents and the management at the dozen wineries that employ them, Dalsis is strangely enough back in the middle of an atmosphere not unlike junior high. Discipline problems, petty contentions and hot emotions are part of a routine week. But the students are adults; the administrators play very rough and instead of bad grades and detentions, money and livelihoods are at stake.

All wineries need manpower during the crush, human labor to shovel the detritus of vines, haul hose, move product around in barrels, bottle wine and so on. In small, premium businesses, the winemaker, an assistant and maybe a couple of hired hands can do the chores. But while more automated, the larger outfits still need winery workers, in particular the jug wine producers. It is blue-collar labor, and in most cases not all that skilled. They're called cellar rats, and they are largely hands and backs; management at the big operations does the thinking.

"A monkey can do most bottling room jobs," says a former cellar rat. "But then, if you screw up on a high-speed line, it does cost 'em a lot to fix it. The people who work in the cellars, helping to blend wine, are probably the smartest; they probably have to be to survive. The dumb ones don't make it there, so they're sent to the warehouse."

More than 2,200 winery workers belong to WDAWU locals 186 and 45. Nearly half the total work for E. & J. Gallo. The union represents workers at large bulk wineries such as Franzia Bros., Vie-Del, Sierra, Alamadén, Bronco, Lamont, and Gibson, as well as at premium houses such as Christian Brothers, Charles Krug and Beaulieu Vineyards. Typical of union and management relations, the cellar rats and the winery employers are not the best of friends.

"Most of the personnel managers are very hard-line," says one union official who requested anonymity. "Much more so than they could or should be. If they were just a little less tight-assed, we'd have a lot less problems. And some of the winery owners, especially the Italian owners, are real jerks. I think it's an Old World, medieval thing. 'I own the company, it's mine, mine, mine, and no one is going to tell me what to do.' "

Dalsis feels an affinity for the underdog, which the winery worker is indeed. She takes their side and fights hard on their grievances, something that comprises about 80 percent of her job. But she also has a pretty solid and pragmatic perspective on her clients. "Workers get reprimands, and if they don't like it they file a grievance to get it removed from their record," she explains. "Or they're terminated for absenteeism. About 90 percent of all reprimands are justified. But if a person wants to file a grievance, we have to if they're insistent."

Problems often arise, however, when employers are inconsistent, or have done a poor job of articulating their policy, Dalsis says. She describes the case of a seasonal worker who'd been issued a written warning over a minor

149

transgression about ten months prior to a second warning. The second one, however, was given orally and only in passing by his supervisor. The man didn't even really know it was a formal warning. But a month later, after a new plant manager had come in, he got a third warning, was suspended and then discharged.

What most aggravates Dalsis is when employers get greedy over what by any definition are token sums of money. Days of union-management meetings and reams of paperwork have been filed over attempts by wineries to save $24 in wages. When a dispute can set a precedent under a contract, such contention is understandable. But the staff time needed to deal with even a small grievance is astonishing.

There are three steps to a grievance, leading from the shop steward to a supervisor and then the winery's personnel manager. If it's not resolved, the grievance triggers a labor-management hearing at the plant where the problem occurs. Two shop stewards from different plants, and two personnel managers from other WEA (Winery Employers Association) wineries attend. "The case is presented just like a trial," says Dalsis. "There are opening statements, rebuttals, cross examinations and closing statements. We all leave and the four vote and 90 percent of the time it's a two-two split. Then it may go to arbitration and it's the same thing all over, only instead of me, the attorney for the local handles it."

Matters that go to arbitration usually involve terminations. "Somebody's job is at stake," Dalsis explains. "Say the person was fired for drinking, and the person claims he or she wasn't. By the time you go through all this, months and maybe a year have gone by since the person was fired. I think the American system says a person is innocent until proven guilty, but labor relations is slanted in favor of the employer."

But in a curious way, WDAWU almost makes things easier for wineries, and perhaps cheaper. We live in an era when firing a worker can lead to enormous wrongful-termination lawsuits, which discharged employees quite frequently win. "But if a winery worker calls the state and claims they've been a victim of harassment," says Dalsis, "the first two questions the state asks are 'Do you have a union?' and if so, 'Have you pursued this all the way through union channels?' " The union provides employers with a well-defined and well-established "door" out which to boot employees who truly deserve it; cleanly and legally, if not always as expeditiously as they might wish.

The WDAWU almost got the boot in 1986, after it launched a major strike against California wineries and came close to suffering the fate of a champagne glass at a Jewish wedding. The WEA members turn out between 40 percent and 50 percent of all the wine produced in the U.S. But pressure had been building for years on this segment of the business, as jug wine sales declined and foreign brands like Riunite cut into the shrinking share. On top of the $12 per-hour average wage, WDAWU members received about $3.50 an hour worth of benefits. Add in taxes, and these wineries were paying roughly $20 an hour for labor.

The union's officials and membership knew they'd have to give up something, and claimed to prefer wage reductions rather than benefit cuts. "You can always get increases in wages over the years, but you can't build up benefit packages," said Jerry Davis, a union executive board member from Napa. The winery employers suggested that slashing benefits would enable workers to maintain their current standards of living. Talks stumbled along through the spring of 1986, and the contract expired on July 31. The union offered to take a seventy-five-cent-per-hour wage reduction the first year, a freeze the second year and a seventy-five-cent-per-hour increase the third. The WEA said it wanted a pay cut in one job classification, and reductions in pension and health benefits. But what the employers most wanted, and didn't really care in what way, shape or form they got it, was a 5 percent reduction in labor costs.

On August 18, fifty Christian Brothers employees, including warehousemen, bottlers and equipment operators, walked off the job at noon and started a picket line in front of the winery, just as the grape crush was starting and the workers were most needed. The next week, picket lines spread to several big Central Valley wineries, and on September 16, about 1,000 workers at Gallo took a hike. Less than 3 percent of Locals 186 and 45 remained on the job. By overwhelming votes, the union rejected WEA offers, including a "final offer" on September 24.

At one point, Local 186 president Robert Fogg threatened to "shut down the California wine industry." It was then, however, that he ran smack into Robert Lieber.

After eighteen years with the San Francisco management law firm of Littler, Mendelson, Fastiff and Tichy, Lieber has handled labor and employee relations matters for such firms as Safeway, General Foods, Pan American and American Airlines. His firm has a reputation in organized labor as union busters.

When the union walked during the crush, employers were a bit harried. "There are certain jobs in wineries that take skill," explains Lieber. "The mechanics are critical, and a process operator A is working with sophisticated machinery. Rackers and blenders need a combination of skill and physical strength. But beyond that, most jobs require only a little dexterity and watchfulness."

Non-union employees and management took over in the wineries, and though volumes were reportedly down in some wineries, costs were considerably lower. Because California weather remained fairly cool that summer, the grapes didn't ripen all at once and the fruit came in at an even pace. Wine quality didn't suffer noticeably, since this is always under the control of management, the winemakers and staff.

After the winery workers had been out for about six weeks, "a confluence of events," as Lieber calls it, brought the strike to a crashing halt and revealed the weakness in the union's strategy and tactics. With the talks stalled, the WDAWU called for a boycott of the WEA wineries' products. They published a newspaper ad in Modesto announcing the boycott, and passed handbills throughout the San Joaquin Valley. Given the dynamics of the wine business, this was a self-destructive proposal in more ways than one.

Assuming that wine drinkers went along with the boycott, switching to different brands could have led to a permanent shift in buying patterns. A switch to foreign wines, it could be argued, would be disastrous. Thus, the union was fouling its own nest, although the WEA didn't really think the boycott would appreciably hurt sales. But the folly of it opened a large wedge to use against the WDAWU.

Lieber had carefully orchestrated all the WEA moves, including the various offers. He had a pretty good idea of how the union would react, although didn't expect them to go this far. But it was just what he was waiting for. "A boycott," Lieber explains, "is the industrial equivalent of nuclear war. So we dropped a bomb of our own."

The WEA announced that if workers were not back on the job by October 6, they would be permanently replaced and, even if rehired, would lose all seniority. The tactic was sanctioned by the Taft-Hartley Act in 1947, is increasingly being used by management during protracted strikes, and the legality of it has been upheld by the court system. Lieber naturally dances around this point, since negotiators loathe to give too much information to their opponents, but the WEA clearly had the lid off the silo before the strike even started. The boycott simply gave them a needed excuse to launch, and the union took a direct hit.

Some 300 workers almost immediately broke ranks and went back to work. On October 2, the WDAWU membership voted two-to-one to accept an offer they'd rejected by a three-to-one margin about two weeks before. The package amounted to a fifty-cent reduction in hourly wages, cuts in benefits and the loss of Veterans Day as a holiday. The total whack came to about $1 an hour. That's five percent. Just what the WEA wanted.

Some wineries that employ union members either rescinded or didn't institute the wage cuts that were allowed. But under a tier system in the contract, new winery employees are paid about $8 an hour. And that's not enough, says Tim Allen, a sub-foreman and union shop steward at Beaulieu Vineyard, to attract and keep good cellar rats.

Tim Allen, thirty-six, is a thinking man's cellar rat. Proud and perhaps a bit stubborn, he's earned his stripes at

Beaulieu Vineyard over the last thirteen years, a winery not nearly so mechanized as Gallo. His work allows him to feed his family, but it's clear that he values what he does. While no management toady, Allen seems to truly care about BV and its products.

Allen grew up watching the Italian Swiss Colony Little Old Winemaker commercials on television, and despite being raised in Napa the ads formed his major image of the business. During summers he fried burgers at an A&W Root Beer stand, went into the Marine Corps for a while, and drove a truck for a sheetrock outfit. A buddy of his had started work at BV, and got him a job interview. He started in January of 1975, and for the first eight months felt like an outsider.

"The staff was made up mostly of older men who were about ready to retire," Allen recalls. "Most of them had been there for twenty or thirty years. After the Little Old Winemaker stuff, I was disappointed at first. They had me washing barrels, tanks and mostly cleaning." Allen didn't know it then, but he would not and could not be accepted as a true cellar rat until he'd gone through a harvest. He remembers the summer of 1975 well, of shoveling pomace into screw augers for sixteen, eighteen hours a day. From 7:30 in the morning until 2:00 the next morning, for two weeks straight, he shoveled, and scrambled, and swept and cleaned.

As Allen was given more responsibility, he began to realize the value of the products with which he worked, "especially compared to what it costs the winery to have me or anyone else there. I was pretty nervous in the beginning. Once, before my boss went on vacation, he handed me a work order worth, conservatively, about $6 million."

Allen has become increasingly conscientious over time. For example, he didn't like the BV rule that prohibits radios in the cellar, but understands that a cellar rat's ears are tools. "We listen for things that aren't right," he says. "You can hear when a barrel is pumped dry, even if eight pumps are going at the same time. You can also hear leaks."

With a self-deprecating laugh, Allen admits that, "We're

154

still sniveling about the radio, but a cellar is different from other departments in a winery. The others just don't have the risks of serious mistakes. You can contaminate fine old wine in seconds by doing the wrong thing with a tool, say a hose that's just been used for new wine. When you're working with reserve Cabernet that goes for $20 a bottle, $100 a gallon, a year's wages could go down the drain in seconds. Drains are unforgiving. And it's somebody else's money."

But it's a cellar rat's life and the job is not without hazards. Perhaps the greatest irritant they face is being exposed to sulfur dioxide gas. The sulfur is used to sterilize cooperage and stabilize wine, and the workers wear respirators to protect themselves from fumes. There are also fumes from using chlorine to clean floors, and carbon dioxide to clean tanks. Any time Allen goes into a large vessel, he dons an air mask. "People have died in the tanks," he says, "and the carbon dioxide is everywhere during the harvest. We're constantly kicking the tourists out during those times, because you can never get overconfident around gas. The carbon dioxide collects in low areas, and you've got to be aware of it. Otherwise, you'll feel like you're breathing down a long garden hose, and you're out." Caustic cleaning agents like soda ash can also burn the skin or eyes.

Tim Allen wants in on more of the action at BV. He doesn't want to stagnate in his job. He explained this to the shop steward and general manager, and has since been cross-trained for many winery jobs, where he frequently serves as a relief worker. When he discovered that coopers were charging $15 a stave to repair a barrel—and there are fifty staves on one of these items—he learned how to do the work himself. He likes the idea of management thinking: "If we go to a cooper it will cost this much, but if we ask Tim . . ."

The garden variety winery worker may be fairly easy to replace. If push had come to shove after the 1986 strike went briefly thermonuclear, "the employers would have had to do some training and things might have been a little rough," admits Lieber, but bringing new workers to a marginal level of competence would have been well within the art of the possible. Losing the best ones, however, is a different matter. Tim Allen is a cellar rat, but a motivated cellar rat, and he clearly deserves a fair share of cheese.

11

GROWING PAINS

In the European château system, premium wineries make wines that can only come, by law, from vineyards on château property. Many American wineries also grow their own fruit, to one degree or another, and sell their wines as "estate-bottled" releases. These usually command higher prices than wines made from grapes purchased off the winery property, although the term "estate-bottled" may not represent greater quality. However, most of the wines made by the nation's vintners come from fruit grown by professional grape growers.

This fact creates the industry's most significant bifurcation, a divergence of thought, spirit and economic interest. It is the source of contentious battles that are generally kept from public view. The conflicts are often painful, with an intensity that's clearly growing.

Grape growers are farmers, and they tend to have the perspective most farmers have. They look upon their crop as an agricultural commodity, not the raw material from which deathless works of fluid art are fashioned. Like farmers everywhere, they want to get as much money as possible from the crop. And the vintners, in spite of their desire to craft gold medal–winning wine that sends dinner party guests into gibbering rapture, are unspeakably shrewd and determined to get the grapes as cheaply as possible. Growers and vintners need each other. But they don't necessarily love each other.

There is only a certain amount of profit to be made on each bottle of wine. Both a grower and vintner want that wine to earn the greatest possible profit. Depending on which one you ask, an equitable split can mean quite different things. In fact, growers and vintners even have different ideas on the definition of the term "wine industry." In no locale is this more apparent than the Napa Valley, where feuds between growers and winemakers are perennial.

There, growers have petitioned the Napa County Planning Commission to require all new wineries to use at least 75 percent Napa Valley grapes in their releases. Andy Beckstoffer, a prominent Napa grape grower who has recently begun releasing his own line of estate-bottled wines, is particularly incensed by a trend toward crushing grapes from outside the area. "Does the processing of Sonoma or Monterey grapes serve to preserve Napa Valley agriculture any more than the processing of wheat from Montana?" he rhetorically posited during one commission meeting. Like many of his grape-growing brethren, this Dartmouth MBA fears that the valley will end up wall-to-wall wineries— establishments that make wine fermented from cheap, out-of-area grapes and sell it to throngs of besotted tourists.

Vintners, on the other hand, counter that their primary obligation is to produce wine profitably, not subsidize local growers. "Since the growers are asking for an economic home for 75 percent of their grapes, maybe you should consider guaranteeing us an economic home for 75 percent of our wine," replied Louis Martini president Carolyn Martini, acidly, at the same planning commission meeting.

Growers and vintners must remain bedfellows, but while sparking and spooning, they frequently close their eyes and pretend to be somewhere and with someone else. Dave

Steiner, a Sonoma Mountain grower, is considerably disillusioned by many of his past dealings with vintners.

"Sure, we're in this together, but we each have our own perspectives," says the articulate, muscular U.C. Berkeley graduate. Steiner took his degree in literature, but moved to Sonoma Mountain shortly thereafter and abandoned forever a life of letters. He grows twenty-three acres of Cabernet vines on a southwesterly exposed slope of Sonoma Mountain. In the thirteen years since he planted his vineyard, his fruit has gained a following among area vintners for its richness and complexity.

Steiner notes that he had hard years working to establish his reputation, and that the vintners were less than sympathetic. "You're on friendly terms with these guys, and you work hard to give them fruit that's the best you can grow, fruit that will do justice to their wineries," he explains. "Some appreciate that, and pay fair prices on time. But I've had some terribly unpleasant encounters with certain wineries. Some of them have been months late in payment, which made it really difficult to cover my own financial obligations. Others didn't market the wine like they said they would; to give it vineyard designation, or put it in a reserve bottling. All that doesn't necessarily constitute bad faith, but it can lead to strained relations."

Steiner recalls some wineries that led him to believe that a kind of partnership was contemplated. "Often in the early stages of a relationship between a grower and vintner, there's a lot of honeyed words and oaths about fealty and loyalty and all that crap," he observes wryly. "Some vintners get very carried away about their sentiments on soil, microclimates and the fact that wines are grown, not made. They can do and promise you all kinds of things. But I've learned not to believe anything if it isn't spelled out in the contract. When it comes down to the crush, and they find they're short on fermenter space or some other grapes that they really wanted become available, you may find yourself with nothing more than a weak smile on your face, a winemaker who won't return your calls and a whole load of fruit on your hands."

Since vintners put the screws to growers whenever the

opportunity arose, it's not surprising that many growers are just as quick to exploit an opportunity at a winemaker's expense. Now that good grapes are in short supply, some growers have gotten a little creative—or even larcenous—when it comes to selling their fruit. Sometimes the tricks take the form of a "top dressing," covering a load of mediocre fruit with a layer of cream-of-the-crop grapes. Sometimes, it involves even more duplicity.

"It seems like a lot of Grenache has been turning into Zinfandel between the vineyard and the crush pad for the past couple of years," says a Robert Mondavi viticulturalist who prefers anonymity. "I mean, you have Zinfandel bringing up to $600 a ton and Grenache down there at $200 or $300, so it makes sense that people would want to sell Zinfandel more than Grenache. Trouble is, they're selling Zinfandel that isn't Zinfandel. Grenache grapes just happen to look an awful lot like Zinfandel grapes when they're in the gondola."

Kelly Krug, an employee of the California Department of Agriculture Statistics, has arrived at a similar conclusion. "Zinfandel tonnage has gone up tremendously in the past couple of years, and Grenache tonnage has gone down to an almost parallel degree," he says. "The funny thing is, though, the amount of producing Zinfandel acreage and producing Grenache acreage has remained about the same. You don't have to be Sherlock Holmes to make some educated guesses about what's going on."

"What's going on," says the Mondavi viticulturalist, "is that a lot of the White Zinfandel people are drinking is really White Grenache."

The supply and demand crunch on wineries is one factor. So is the growing recognition among premium wine consumers that grapes are the primary factor in wine quality. This puts pressure on vintners to develop, consolidate and secure sources of premium fruit. Growers who own such vineyards are finally getting their due. Winemakers aren't all that happy about the additional costs of greasing growers. Farmers have long memories, and can vividly recall each and every time they were screwed.

The animosities are a backdrop for periodic efforts by the

industry to bring growers and vintners together in a kind of unified field theory; to build a united front, if not a cooperative atmosphere, that could help both groups sell more wine for greater profits. The last major push in this direction was the Grape Marketing Order of 1984. The project consisted of an assessment by the industry for every gallon of wine produced and every ton of grapes grown. The monies raised were to be used for promotional and lobbying activities. A similar assessment in the 1940s and 1950s helped to popularize basic dry table wines in America, and industry heavyweights felt another order could prod the industry out of the doldrums in which it found itself in the 1980s. Growers and vintners expressed optimism, and viewed the new attempt as a peace pipe.

By 1987, however, the order had dissolved. "What went wrong?" asks California Winegrowers of California Executive Director Bob Reynolds. He sighs. "Basically, it was simple enough. There were profound personality conflicts. And because there were personality conflicts, there were terrible difficulties in organization. The entire project eventually pulled itself apart." Reynolds notes that there was no basic disagreement on what had to be done; the problems cropped up in priorities and implementation.

"First, you had the major brand wineries—no point in naming them," he explains. "They felt that money would best be spent promoting specific brands—especially their own. On the other hand, you had smaller wineries who wanted to promote the California wine industry as a whole, rather than specific brands. Then you had another split, between the growers and vintners. Historically, the vintners have been much more sophisticated than the growers. They're better organized and better funded. The growers have always chafed about this. Plus, California's vintners grow about 15 percent of the grapes produced in the state, so they've also had leverage within the growers' sector. The growers just felt that their interests weren't adequately represented within the framework of the order. There were a lot of nasty comments bandied back and forth—when you're talking $19 million, people tend to take the gloves off."

The marketing order led to some success. "We did best with domestic trade barrier activity," Reynolds recalls. "We funded a lot of aggressive lobbying in Washington, based on personal appeals by the vintners and a well-funded letter-writing campaign. As a result, we avoided an excise tax in 1986. That helped a lot."

Another satisfactory effort was a trade education campaign. "We conducted some marketing analysis and found that people relied on waiters and retail salespeople to tell them about wine, most of whom were abysmally ignorant about the subject," says Reynolds. "So we put together print and video packages aimed at retailers and distributors, the thrust being that they could increase profits by educating their staffs with the materials we provided. The program met with a lot of enthusiasm, and it's just getting off the ground now—just as the order is being killed. We hope it can be continued and funded in one form or another under the aegis of another organization."

Then there was the Julia Child Project. It led to terrible squabbles, and few among the growers or vintners were happy with the way the commercials looked. The growers in particular felt that Child was preaching only to the converted, that the message, as Reynolds says, "was too narrow and sophisticated from the beginning." There was nothing in it for them, no return on the levy against their grape production. Dissension and dissatisfaction ripped the order to pieces.

The fact is, growing grapes is damn near as risky as making wine. While unsold cases of wine can sit around in warehouses and eventually be remaindered out for a few bucks, grapes that don't sell instantly go to rot. Only financial masochists who like to eat dust and chemicals while riding tractors should consider this game. This is especially so for newcomers, who must post higher returns on each acre than established growers, so increased debt loads may be addressed.

According to Kirby Moulton and Gino Zepponi in *Economics of Food Processing in the United States*, established growers who don't have to account for imputed interest or changes in replacement values are able to accept lower prices than new growers, who have to pay current interest and asset costs. What this means is that a grower with no interest and no set-aside for amortization can survive with revenues of $1,500 per acre in Napa and Sonoma Counties, while a new, highly leveraged grower would require close to $4,000 an acre in return. Such a figure is almost impossible to achieve in many North Coast growing regions, since it requires both higher than average yield and grape prices that are from 25 percent to 75 percent higher than the North Coast average.

However, new or old, the growers who consistently shine are those who play the vintners' game. That is, they promote themselves and their product heavily to whoever will listen. Robert Young is one such grower.

A robust septuagenarian with hands that are as cracked and fissured as Sierra mountain granite, Young is considered the grower emeritus in Sonoma County. He lives in a vast, antebellum-style house on an agricultural estate that is more than a little reminiscent of Tara. Young grows mostly Chardonnay, Cabernet, Pinot Noir and Sauvignon Blanc on his ancestral family ranch, which is located in the foothills bordering the Alexander Valley in the northern portion of the county.

Young planted his first vines in 1963. "This area was all prunes back then," reflects Young as he sits under the shade of a redwood tree in his backyard. "The Alexander Valley was once a major production area for table fruits. It grew a lot of the prunes consumed in the U.S., since prunes need the same conditions as fine wine grapes: relatively warm days and cool nights. The director of the farm extension service came around my place in 1962 and tried to convince me to grow some wine grapes. I was a little dubious, because a lot of grape varieties ripen at the same time prunes do, and I didn't want to be distracted from the prune harvest. But he pointed out that I could plant some Cabernet, which ripens later than prunes, so there wouldn't be any problems."

Young began cautiously, with a hillside planting of four acres. "We got budwood from the U.C. Davis station at Oakville, and it turned out to be a very nice clone," he remembers. The grower soon found that Mayacamas, Simi,

Windsor and Sebastiani wineries were all interested in his fruit. "From the beginning, I had a sense that the best way to market my grapes was to spread them around, rather than tie my fortunes to a single winery," says Young. "I always have been leery about putting all my eggs in one basket. And I think a grower loses some of this autonomy when he sells to only one winery. He may have a sense of security—he doesn't have to do any legwork or worry about whether he'll find a home for the fruit—but he won't be able to get the best deal possible."

Young's Cabernet Sauvignon proved so popular that he soon put in more acreage. By the late 1960s, the California premium wine boom began in earnest, and he planted a few acres of Chardonnay on some alluvial valley land near his house. As the demand for the fruit increased, Young turned more of his energy toward grapes and away from prunes. Ultimately, he abandoned prunes altogether. "At a certain point, it became evident that the future of the entire area was in wine grapes," he says. Today, of his 300 acres, more than 50 percent of it is in Chardonnay, the varietal for which he is most noted.

Demand for his grapes far outstrips supply, and Young is sitting pretty. Alexander Valley soils typically produce five tons of fruit per acre, so Young's holdings usually yield around 1,500 tons annually. Since the average price per ton for his grapes exceeds $1,000, the grower's gross income probably weighs in at roughly $1.5 million. That's a comfortable margin for a rancher whose land was paid off long ago, and who does not carry a heavy debt load. "We're comfortable," Young admits with a gentle smile. "Grapes have been good to us. Then again, we've worked for it, and not just in the vineyards."

What he means is that grape growing involves more than growing grapes. "I realized early on that winemakers needed to see the grower's face as much as retailers need to see the winemaker's face," he says. "By that I mean you have to sell yourself as much as the grapes. You need to get out to see the vintner, get to know him. The vintner has to have faith in you and your operation. Of course, the most important thing is grape quality. But given that, given that two people have grapes of excellent quality, the one who will make the sale is the one who's taken the time talking with the vintner, getting to know his requirements and problems. Growers have typically been pretty unsophisticated about marketing. I don't blame them; I'd rather stay on the ranch myself. But this is a people business, and you've got to play by the rules."

Young has some very good relationships with the winemakers he works with. "I really owe the popularization of my Chardonnay to Château St. Jean, which gave us vineyard designation and pushed it right from the start," he says. But Young feels that growers and vintners have such different perspectives that tensions and conflict are inevitable.

"What gets me about the marketing order is the fact that it was the growers' idea in the first place," he explains. "We wanted to do it way back in 1980. Then the vintners jumped on the bandwagon, and asked if they could join us. We went for it, but then they more or less took the whole thing in their own hands, or tried to. A lot of them wanted to promote specific brands—their brands, as opposed to California wine in general. That kind of approach didn't sit too well with us."

Young believes that some growers are more aware of the need to market themselves, but the nature of their breed works against them. "I think the grower who understands marketing enough to get out on the road once in a while will remain the exception," he sighs. "Either they're too individualistic, or they're apathetic, or both. And that's too bad. Some concerted efforts by growers at this point could do a lot to stabilize the industry."

Like Robert Young, Rene di Rosa has enjoyed great success as a grower. Beyond that, the two men are as dissimilar as fish and fowl. Di Rosa recently sold his holdings, Winery Lake Vineyard, located in the Carneros region of the southern Napa Valley, to Seagram-owned Sterling Vineyards, for a reported $8.5 million. This coup gives Sterling exclusive access to 250 acres of some of the best Pinot Noir and Chardonnay in the state. It also gave di Rosa the leisure and financial latitude requisite for pursuing his most consuming passion—the patronage of Northern California artists.

Di Rosa kept his houses and 250 acres of raw land when he sold Winery Lake to Sterling. The structures were built in the late nineteenth century. Di Rosa and his wife, Veronica, have refurbished them to express their exotic tastes in both art and lifestyle. "I got into art when I was in Paris after the war, trying to write novels," di Rosa says, walking along a grassy knoll that overlooks the lake that the estate was named after. Peacocks and Chinese geese accompany him like favored dogs, the former venting bloodcurdling screams on occasion, the latter picking at the herbage. Large sculptures are scattered throughout the property; here a ceramic rendering of a grotesquely comic family portrait, there a sheet-metal angel of sinister mien, bearing a scythe.

Di Rosa says he realized that he didn't have talent in the arts, "so I started supporting people who did. I made some very good purchases early on that have appreciated tremendously as the artists have gained in renown." After leaving Paris, he worked for several years as reporter on *The San Francisco Chronicle*. The opportunity to buy Winery Lake, then a derelict and nondescript property that was used as dry-land pasturage for sheep and cattle, came up in 1962, and he took it. "I'd made the circuits of the Frisco fleshpots a sufficient number of times," he says dryly. "I was ready to rusticate for a while."

Once on the property, di Rosa decided to try agriculture. He did not favor livestock like most of his neighbors, so he opted for viticulture. "My neighbors thought me eccentric, to say the least," he recalls. "And I guess I was. All I had was a copy of Maynard Amerine's *Viticulture*, and a sporadic crew of sailors on shore leave from the Mare Island Naval Station to help me. The farm advisor came by and told me I'd be better off operating a trailer park, because people could use the lake for swimming and water skiing. Louis Martini thought it was a mistake too, since we didn't have any markets for the fruit lined up. Bob Mondavi came by as well. He was interested, but not particularly encouraging. I always liked swimming against the tide, so we just kept at it."

Winery Lake's cool microclimate makes it ideal for Pinot Noir and Chardonnay, and it's on these two varieties that di

Rosa based his reputation and fortune. "The funny thing is, though, we didn't really realize how suited to Burgundian varieties the Carneros was in the beginning," he says. "We planted the vines we planted because they were the vines we were able to plant that were certified disease free. I got some good Chardonnay and Pinot Noir budwood, so we went with it."

Like Young, di Rosa preferred to spread his grapes around a number of vintners. "I did that more out of instinct than anything else," he explains. "In fact, I never really had a marketing strategy to speak of. I had a sense for the underdog, though, and I liked dealing with the smaller wineries. They liked dealing with me, too, so were more inclined to give Winery Lake recognition on the label than some of the larger wineries." Di Rosa credits his success to quality fruit, which he admits was an outgrowth of luck, and to his insistence on dealing only with people he liked.

"Winery Lake grapes are among the most expensive in the country, no doubt about it," he acknowledges. "What's ironic is that other people recognized their value before I did. Gino Zepponi was an old friend of mine, and the winemaker at ZD Winery—he was killed in a car accident not long ago. One day he came by and checked my grapes out, and said they were the best he'd ever seen, that we ought to charge more. So I did."

Di Rosa enjoys the pose of ingenuous naif; and the fact is that he did approach his business more as a series of interpersonal relationships than mere commerce. But that in itself is good business. "It's much better to deal with people who are your friends, if you have the opportunity," he observes. "They're much less likely to disappoint you." Still, he's had his share of disappointments. He sold grapes for several years to a winery which had been founded by one of his good friends, who also served as winemaker. The winery had financial difficulties, and new partners came in. The new investors implied that they would set things straight with both the winery and the creditors. Instead, they promptly went into Chapter 11, leaving di Rosa's friend with neither equity or a livelihood. Di Rosa himself was stiffed for a sum that ran into six figures. "They're reprobates and thieves," di Rosa still fumes. "They're no better than criminals. It was just as much theft as if they'd put guns to our heads. Both the winemaker and I were victimized."

Notwithstanding di Rosa's claims that luck and amity between friends with mutual interests are most responsible for success, a firm—if subconscious and osmotic—understanding of the industry has helped him along. He comprehends very well indeed that he is a dream merchant as much as a grape farmer. "The fact that I'm of an artistic bent, that my wife's an artist, that I'm a patron of the arts, have given me an advantage over some of my fellow growers," he admits. "I know that wine is really more an idea than a product, you see. We sell rainbows in this business. At least, winemakers sell rainbows. And if the growers want to prosper along with winemakers, they have to sell their share of rainbows, too. We have to be part of the process. That's the main reason Sterling retained me as a consultant when they bought Winery Lake. My technical advice is valued, I'm sure, to a certain extent. But when they bring writers and key account people out here, they bring people who know the history of the place and my name. They bring people who want to associate the name and face with the grapes. So Sterling actually values me more for my name than for what I know."

Winery Lake must produce rainbows out of necessity, since the shallow, spare soils of the Carneros District produce very little in the way of fruit. Where Robert Young can expect yields of five tons or more per Alexander Valley acre, Winery Lake averages two and a half tons to an acre. "And it was a lot less before we put in drip irrigation systems," says di Rosa. "Water has made all the difference here. But the very fact that Winery Lake grapes are rare no doubt contributes in large part to the price they can command on the open market—up to $2,500 a ton."

Di Rosa believes that Sterling will make the most of his old vineyards, and will add to their prestige. Although out of the grape game, he still laments the tendency for internecine warfare between growers and vintners. "We could achieve so much more if we could just quit the bickering and work together. We're all involved in selling labels—just like Calvin Klein sells labels, not jeans. I sold Winery Lake labels. People buy labels more than they buy products; people seem to need labels to define the relative worth of their lives. Maybe that's too bad, but that's the way it is. If we could focus on that simple fact and capitalize on it, we wouldn't need to be cannibalizing each other."

Other growers are not so gracious in their assessment of the situation. "I've had some pretty tough years during this past decade," says Dave Steiner, "and I saw damn little in the way of sympathy or understanding from some of my buyers. When some of them could squeeze me, they squeezed me. I have twenty-three acres of grapes. I plan to plant maybe seven or eight more. That's how I make my living. I do all the work myself. This isn't a game for me. And well, the market has changed in the past year or so. There's a shortage of good Cabernet, and it looks like that's going to be the case for a while. Guys who wouldn't give me the time of day two years ago are calling me up like we're old friends."

Standing amid his Sonoma Mountain vines, Steiner takes a deep breath and continues: "Lots of people want my fruit now. And that's fine. I'll give it to them. But they'll have to pay for it and it'll have to be cash up front. I'm a farmer, and I have to make money when I can. Because when the market goes against you, winemakers don't seem to care too much about whether or not you can keep your act together. I can live with that. But it cuts both ways."

12

BANKING ON THE STARS

Paul Draper calls it "a mask," a persona that he adopts and role he plays. The head winemaker of Ridge Vineyard, who prepped at Choate, earned a bachelor's degree in Philosophy at Stanford and later studied at the Sorbonne, long enjoyed the part. Unattached, and with his life devoted to his work, Draper didn't even realize that he had donned a kind of psychic shroud. He became accustomed to projecting the persona that appealed to those who were either seeking insight into the magic of wine, or who simply wanted to experience the presence of a highly regarded winemaker.

Draper married late, in his forties, and now has a young daughter. A trim man whose beard has largely given way to salt, leaving only a sprinkling of the original pepper, Draper

170

explains that his family has given him a new perspective. He travels less, goes to fewer winemaker dinners and is more selective about making himself available to journalists. He wears "the mask" of the winemaker less often, for it sometimes conflicts with his new life. "I've learned to step back," he explains, "because to paraphrase Thoreau, I wished to live deliberately, learn what life had to teach and not, when I came to die, discover that I had not lived. I'm trying to be much more conscious of just 'who is this guy?' Of who is the real Paul Draper?"

Thus, he "went to the woods" after concluding that living the winemaker role exclusively is a spiritually confining thing, no matter its appreciable rewards. Perhaps only the Existential Enologist could put it this way. Then again, he still occasionally puts on "the mask," because Draper, as well as Otsuka, the Japanese pharmaceutical company that purchased Ridge in late 1986, knows that superstar winemakers indisputably sell wine.

On behalf of Buena Vista, which is helping to culture and promote her reputation, Jill Davis handles the role with enthusiasm. Energetic and forthright, she can talk tannins with the most knowledgeable of wine freaks, or for novices keep it as light and unintimidating as a new release of White Zinfandel. While Davis may rue some of the time away from the winery, playing star winemaker is still a fresh and heady experience; she hasn't been around the track near as often as Draper. But she does it very well indeed.

"Jill has personality in caps," says Rick Raymond, Buena Vista's vice president of sales. "In 1983 and 1984 she did a lot of traveling, talking to restaurant groups, retailers, at dinners and to the media. At first we worried that maybe we were spinning our wheels, touching on only a very small segment of the wine-drinking population, and not making efficient use of her time. But with Jill's presence in a market, say for a week-long visit, we've learned that we easily expect a 10 percent sales increase for the year in that area, something we hope sticks."

Who better can speak for a winery than a superstar winemaker? A public relations rep can provide information to journalists, but what publication wants to carry lengthy profiles and descriptions of a flack? Winemakers actually do something productive—as if public relations pros don't— and are artisans to boot, or so the perception goes. If they are a good winemaker, and if they look good and speak well, the superstar, real or manufactured, can be a winery's primary marketing tool.

Relatively few producers can afford a national advertising campaign, much less a paid spokesperson who registers instant recognition among the public. There are dangers, moreover, that a wine company will pick the wrong mouth-piece. For example, America dearly remembers the late Orson Welles, and the way he intoned: "We will sell no wine, before its time." The line was memorable, to the degree that it became a cultural icon. And yet Paul Masson fired Citizen Welles, because the sheer magnitude of his screen presence—in size and personality—overwhelmed the product. As Michael Cliff, CEO of Vintners International, which now owns Paul Masson, told *The Wall Street Journal*, "Mr. Welles was a 'video vampire'—he stole the show. The product was secondary to the man."

Ed Bartles and Frank Jaymes are phenomenal pitchmen for Gallo's wine cooler. But these fictional characters are inseparable from what they're selling. So are winemakers, who can speak to potential consumers with authority, convey that there's a human touch behind the wine, and don't command fees for doing so. When U.C. Davis graduate Dave Hulley was hired by Hillebrand Estates Winery in Ontario, Canada, his boss told him, "I want you to be our star," even though Hulley joined them as an assistant winemaker.

"The winemaker we've got is good, very good in the cellar," says Hulley. "But he's not very good with or comfortable around lots of people. So they got me to be in the front lines, going to parties, meeting with people, the social thing."

"The winemaker is an excellent liaison with the public, perhaps the best," says Beringer's Tor Kenward. Beringer would like to put its Ed Sbragia out in front of the public more. A bearish thirty-nine-year-old, Sbragia is getting more visibility as a winemaker, but is reluctant to take the time

away from his post. "I'd love to get Ed at more tastings,"
says Kenward, "but he's a hands-on winemaker, and we
keep getting bigger, which makes it hard for him to get
away. So we've taken to using him on radio ads. Radio
reaches a lot of people who might look at wine as something
mysterious. The ads are very casual, down to earth, and it
puts Ed before the public."

So what's a star winemaker worth to a winery? It's a
formula that's as complex as the weird and myriad elements
that go into the pricing of a bottle of wine, including
dubious economics. When Rutherford Hill hired esteemed
winemaker Jerry Luper away from Château Bouchaine in
1985, he was reportedly paid $100,000 a year. "But you
can't buy the kind of publicity Rutherford Hill got when
Luper first arrived," says one wine journalist, although the
stir has since quieted.

A few other top enologists who are strictly salaried—and
don't have a piece of the company's action—have com-
manded $125,000 and perhaps more, although those making
$100K are a rare breed. Wine companies are not Fortune 500
industrials, and consequently don't pay professionals and
executives nearly as well as automakers, computer firms
and conglomerates. "Competent enologists," says one winery owner, "are a dime a dozen." Most are paid accordingly.

A winemaker's worth depends first and foremost upon
the product that's turned out. The ability to speak to various
audiences with different levels of wine knowledge—
including the media—is almost a bonus, although it's a
quality winery owners are now looking for. The true superstar, however, is a multifaceted player, an enologist and
public spokesperson who also understands marketing, business plans, trends and personnel management; what goes on
in the cellar can tremendously influence business decisions
down the line.

However, a winery may face certain dangers when it
overly promotes a winemaker as superstar. "Putting a winemaker on a pedestal is one of the greatest mistakes you can
make," says Dennis Marion. "I put my guy out there, for
marketing purposes, but not on a pedestal. The winemaker
doesn't direct the company, management does. And a big

problem can come if you build up a winemaker and he suddenly leaves, taking your investment in building his image with him.''

Moreover, the superstar winemaker image, suggests Gerald Asher, is going out of date. There was a time not long ago when winemakers were viewed much the same way as chefs; ingredients available to anyone else came in the back door of the restaurant and the kitchen wizard, through culinary prestidigitation, would send magic plates of comestibles to the tables. ''Not many people really believe that about wine anymore,'' says Asher. ''The importance of grapes is realized. Serious wineries are seriously involved in vineyards, and know that winemaking begins with the growing.''

There are numerous ways in which wineries use their enologists to market product. Most winemakers understand that like professional athletes, public appearances for the team are part of the job. In fact, the winery's economic fortunes, and in turn their salary, can often depend on how well one executes such a public role. Moreover, although grapes are the most important factor in a wine's quality, winemaking techniques have reached a level of sophistication so that enologists can now create distinctive styles. Over time, a certain style—such as Paul Draper's powerful, signature Zinfandels—becomes identified as their own. When that wine fetches high prices, the enologist represents a high rate of return on investment.

One such winemaker is Zelma Long of Simi Winery. Formerly the head enologist at Robert Mondavi, Long was induced to leave by a Simi offer that would make her winemaker, a senior vice president and, presumably, provide a shot at equity in the firm. Zelma Long was, and is, one of the top enologists in the U.S., and this is certainly the primary reason she was hired. But it wasn't the only reason. Right from the start, Simi promoted Long almost as assiduously as they promoted their Cabernets.

A statuesque and long-legged blonde in her mid-forties, she cuts an attractive figure whether in work-boots and jeans or an evening dress. But Long, who graduated from the University of Oregon with a degree in chemistry, microbiology and nutrition, and did some graduate study in enology at Davis, is also articulate. A talented winemaker who is well-spoken, energetic, outgoing, knowledgeable and just happens to be an aesthetically-pleasing-to-look-at female— well, it's a most felicitous blend. The way Simi projects her, Long doesn't just make the product; she is part of the product.

In 1979, Moët-Hennessy, the French wine and spirits company that owns Simi, planned to spend about $5.5 million to upgrade the winery. They were also looking for someone to replace the former winemaker, Mary Ann Graf. "We interviewed every upcoming winemaker in the business," says Simi President Michael Dixon. "Finally, we narrowed it down to five; four men and Zelma Long. I must say that the board of directors was not too keen on hiring another woman, but Zelma was just the most qualified, so she naturally got the position." Dixon calls the decision to hire her "one of the most important I have made at Simi."

Long was one of the first winemakers to attempt to find a new definition for the concept of grape ripeness, specifically in terms of Cabernet Sauvignon. She didn't want to rely strictly on the old measure of high sugars, which produced Cabs which to Long had too much alcohol. She also realized that the "taste test" method favored by winemakers of past generations had limitations.

"What we needed were quantitative methods for determining the optimum time for harvesting grapes, that would use criteria other than sugar and acid," says Long. "In some years, grapes may be ripe at 23 degrees Brix, in others, it may be 21 degrees Brix. It will fluctuate from year to year, and if you don't harvest at precisely the right time, you lose flavor and aromatic intensity." Long and her staff experimented with a variety of methods to help in their quest, and found themselves relying heavily on sensory observation; how easily the grapes came off the stem, the amount of varietal intensity in the fruit, and whether or not the vines were "shutting down," or losing their foliage.

Long finally focused on the transitional point when the flavors in Cabernet grapes subtly change. As Cabernet fruit matures, it goes from tasting "juicy" to tasting "jammy," she says. "We felt this was caused by a change in the molecular structure in grape pectins, and it seemed to us that this shift could mark the point of optimum grape maturity." The cell walls of grapes break down as they ripen, which converts large pectin molecules in the fruit to small molecules, which are more water soluble, and make the juice more viscous. "The grapes become softer," says Long, "and flavor and color compounds are more easily extracted during the fermentation process."

Through constant tests and note-taking, Long and her staff discovered the minute break-point in grape ripeness that they feel produces the best Cabernets. Moreover, of late she is investigating another factor, the point at which tannins in the grape begin to shift and soften. A willingness to develop and employ new concepts is the mark of a cerebral wine-maker, a fact that reflects Long's cool and somewhat detached intellectual bent.

Long's complex wines are widely respected in the industry, but paradoxically, she is even more respected than her wines. Simi wines invariably evoke kind words from the press, but seldom receive the effusive encomia that wines from the top smaller, more specialized wineries enjoy. Long's winemaking style produces Chardonnays and Cabernets that are subdued and restrained—the type of wines, in short, that don't win many medals. However, Long herself commands near adulation.

Indeed, any symposium on wine gains immediate credibility if she's seated on the panel. Long serves on the National Committee for Grape Stock, is associated with the Foundation Plants service at Davis and, diverging from wine and into community service, sits on California's North Coast Water Quality Control Board. All this gives her political juice inside and outside the industry.

In addition, her intelligence, encyclopedic knowledge of both viticulture and enology, good looks and charming disposition win new converts for Simi and solidify old friendships wherever she goes. When Dixon hired Zelma Long, he got the one thing the winery desperately needed to go along with that $5.5 million investment: a face. A recognizable face that just happened to look a helluva lot more attractive, for example, than Ed Sbragia's bearded mug. Her skills on the promotion circuit, in fact, have helped Simi's fortunes as much as her abilities in the vineyards and cellars.

There's but a handful of true enological superstars, names and faces that would eventually help a winery's bottom line, as much for their presence as winemaking skill. Jerry Luper is one, Dick Arrowood of Chateau St. Jean, another. One might include the late Myron Nightingale of Beringer, a wizened presence who guided his protégé, Ed Sbragia. Buena Vista's Jill Davis hasn't reached such stature, or even that of Zelma Long and Sonoma Cutrer's Bill Bonetti. But at the age of thirty-two, her star is decidedly ascendant.

Some observers feel that Davis's wines reflect uneven quality; that Buena Vista's Cabernets are outstanding, but other varietals sometimes aren't as good. The criticism is rather limp, given that she presides over the making of more than a dozen different wines, from eight or nine varietals and permutations and variations on their themes. Bonetti just does Chardonnay; Davis puts out a complete product line. And no matter what's said about contests, Buena Vista takes home more medals than the female athletes of the German Democratic Republic. Davis joined the Buena Vista staff as assistant winemaker in 1982, and from the time she became head winemaker the following year through June of 1987, she'd picked off twenty-seven gold medals, twenty silver and seventy-one bronze in various contests.

This, of course, means that Buena Vista enters a lot of competitions, figuring medals boost marketing efforts. It also means that Davis' wines stand out in a crowd. This isn't always a hallmark of superior quality, but Davis insists: "We don't make wine for contests."

Her status in the industry still surprises the woman behind Buena Vista's wines. When Davis left U.C. Davis in 1978, she didn't feel qualified to be a winemaker, despite the summer internships that had layered practical training on top of the university's scientific curriculum. "I really needed someone to work under," she now explains, "whether in a cellar or lab. I started out looking for lab jobs, a placement I thought I could handle. During my internship at Bear Mountain, I'd done cellar and lab work, and so most of the jobs I applied for were in quality control."

Davis, however, landed an enologist position with Beringer, which was in the midst of its growth mode. "But it didn't seem that big," says Davis. "I didn't feel like a small cog, and under Myron Nightingale I learned a lot about team playing, and in a short period of time. Beringer really lets you push yourself up."

Until she earned the big promotion at Buena Vista, Davis had little idea of what she faced once put in charge of a whole winemaking show. "I didn't realize that part of being a winemaker was being shoved out into the public," she admits. A handsome, blonde woman with an infectious, warm smile, she learned quickly, although the treatment she receives spurs some ambivalent feelings.

"I met somebody just last week who was gushing about winemakers and what I do," she notes. "Well, I'm just another person, and while winemaking is a romantic and unusual field to many people, I'm probably less creative than professionals in an awful lot of other endeavors. And yet, I can still feel that way myself, and stand there in awe around great winemakers, such as André Tchelistcheff."

Despite her rapid rise, Davis has maintained a solid perspective of herself and role at Buena Vista. Her father was a small businessman, creating a childhood atmosphere that gave her an appreciation of business. "I know that the company is not there as a palette for me to use to display my skills," she explains. "My upbringing, and knowing that fact, I think, are a couple of the reasons I've been successful here in building a relationship with the owners. We have a joint commitment to keep the business running."

Davis recognizes the risk a winery takes when it promotes a personality. "It could be a danger," she says. "I've been approached, but never tempted to move. I don't have a desire to own a winery. I want to work for a company that wants to make wine like I want to make wine. A company that has control of its own fruit; that gives direction, but allows me to have my own style. I've got no desire to be responsible for paying the payroll, but I'll do all I can to make money to cover it. Running the business would take too much attention away from winemaking."

Davis, of course, has this situation at Buena Vista, but sees the promotional end of the business as burden that must be taken on judiciously. "I can do all the winemaking and all of the travel," she laments, "but you can't do both and do them well. Obviously the quality of the wine must be a priority. I've got a good staff, but I'm a controlling type person. I make lists for myself constantly, because I find myself doing so many things at the same time."

Indeed, Davis sits in on all marketing and business planning meetings. "She's very willing to do this, is active and creative and probably gives as much input as Marcus or our controller," says Rick Raymond. "We get together on a regular basis and talk about how we'll fund the company, put together this or that program. For example, we have a twelve-month marketing calendar that we take to wholesalers and distributors, so we're always planning a year in advance. And we're thinking even further ahead, because Jill is working on a 1987 Merlot that won't be released until June of 1990. We've got to guess what market conditions will be like then, whether we should make all the Merlot we can, or sell off some of our fruit for instant cash. We control all our fruit and can sometimes do that. But it's a decision that requires a crystal ball."

Trying to focus the crystal ball is one of the reasons Davis is willing to hit the promotional trail. "It's not for the attention," she says bluntly, "because it usually makes me feel uncomfortable. In fact, it's kind of frightening to me, because when people think you're 'great,' there's a tremendous potential for you to let them down. But most important, what I get from the trips is feedback. I take all the comments I hear and bring them back to the winery, where we all talk about them. That's how our back labels came about, because so many people mentioned that they liked more information about the wine and the winery."

Davis is fortunate to be working with the fruit of some 1,700 acres of Buena Vista land in the Carneros appellation. (Despite the confusion of the common consumer when faced with further Balkanization of industry terms, Carneros

Quality Alliance members are producing consistently superior products from this superb region; it's something recognized by folks who buy wine by the case.) She acknowledges that "It would make an exceptional wine no matter what I did." But Davis has clearly done plenty in only a half-decade as a head winemaker. She will be heard from, and often, in the future.

One could argue that the Existential Enologist was also lucky, in that he hooked up with David R. Bennion in 1969, who ten years before had founded Ridge Vineyard with a couple of friends. A scientist with a Ph.D. in electrical engineering from Stanford, Bennion worked at the Stanford Research Institute when he began toying with the idea of winemaking. Along with Charlie Rosen and later Hew Crane, he revived a vineyard first planted in 1880 on Monte Bello Ridge, about 2,600 feet above San Francisco Bay. The burly Bennion, who often sported a slouch hat, was allegedly California's first second-career winemaker. He died in March of 1988, at the age of fifty-nine, a few days after an auto accident.

Bennion, however, had passed the winemaking torch to Paul Draper long before, and sold Ridge to Otsuka USA at a most perspicacious time, two days before a new United States federal tax treatment of capital gains kicked into punishing gear. Draper had earned a partnership in Ridge, but didn't have a large enough say to veto the sale, if he had wanted to. He asked only that Otsuka keep Ridge operating as it had operated for years, and he'd be glad to stay on as the masked man. The Japanese firm agreed, and Draper remains.

Changes would likely agitate the winery's clientele, who are loyal enough to make regular trips up the steep, twisting and nauseating 4.4-mile Monte Bello Road. The view of the San Francisco Bay Area from the ridge is stupendous. The winery's tasting area and retail sales outlet is the flip side. It's a decrepit old barn, more or less, but Ridge fans don't care. Indeed, for the fall harvests, Ridge takes reservations from people who want to help pick the grapes, which is limited to about 200 lucky pickers per weekend.

"Some of them come up from Southern California," says

Gary Grilli, who handles a number of duties for the lean-staffed winery. "They really seem to get into it." He admits that it's a somewhat comical business move, getting one's customers to cut labor costs. And yet Ridge thrives on the repeat business of such people, direct-mail wine-buying membership programs and word-of-mouth promotion. About the only advertising it does is an occasional spot in *The Wine Spectator*. And Draper's wines have reached a point where entering contests, says Grilli, "puts us in the 'you can only lose' category."

Producing about 35,000 cases of wine annually, Ridge will likely remain château size, unless Otsuka gets antsy for more profits down the line. But despite the enthusiasm from the core clientele, Ridge had to bootstrap over the years, still must promote, and has become increasingly cost-conscious. Draper, in fact, found himself slowly becoming as conscientious about counting the beans as he was in making wine.

Born in Illinois, on a farm that is now part of a Chicago suburb, Draper grew up helping to tend eighty acres which included about thirty head of cattle that provided meat, milk and butter for the family, chickens, ducks, hogs and sheep, bees for honey, and one of the biggest gardens around. "My father worked in Chicago until he retired," says Draper, "and also on the farm. We were basically self-sufficient throughout the Second World War." While the senior Draper worked in a stock brokerage house, "he also clearly followed his own interests," explains Paul. "He always felt that if you did something you loved and it's of service to other people in some way, then everything else will come; the money, the livelihood, will take care of itself."

While considering grad work in philosophy at Stanford, Draper fell out of love with the subject, at least as it was being taught. "I was much more interested in existential philosophy, and Stanford's has become an analytical department." He volunteered for the service during the Korean War, trained in Spanish and Italian at an army language school and was assigned to do attaché-type work in Verona, Italy. It was of course here where he developed an appreciation for vineyards and wine.

Eventually returning to California, he teamed up with an old friend from Stanford, Fritz Maytag. (Later, Maytag became responsible for San Francisco's fabled Anchor Steam Beer.) They put together a small, non-profit group to help agricultural development in South America, a soybean-growing venture in Chile. Since it wouldn't produce operating cash, Draper and his cohorts figured they could support it with a small for-profit winery. They leased a Cabernet vineyard and began making wine in 1967. Draper and his associates had to build everything, including molds for bottles. "I practically lived in a machine shop," he recalls. But while he learned his way around a winery, Chile's economic climate made both it and the soybean project downright uneconomic.

Returning to California, Draper was offered a job by Bennion. At the time, Ridge was producing about 2,800 cases a year. "We had no trouble selling 2,800 cases," says Draper, "but our job was to move up to a profitable size." And to upgrade the facilities, which weren't much to speak of, except for the hundred-year-old cellar. "We added two or three tanks at a time, at most," he says. "One year we'd get some new oak barrels, the next put a new roof on the building, a new press the year after. We didn't have the dollars for major capital investments."

Walking through the old cellar, which has been enlarged, Draper is plainly captivated by the history of Ridge, and the Monte Bello vines, which are a mix of old, 1880s plantings and others in the 1940s. "This cellar was carved out of limestone," he says, "and it, and the fields here, are not part of the Pacific Plate, like most of the other land around. It's a piece of the earth that was formed in an Equatorial Basin about 165 million years ago, by the same big plankton die-off that created the limestone that's found in French winegrowing regions. Somehow this little piece migrated, was thrust up on the Pacific Plate and is a little island in which you can grow superior grapes."

Draper appreciates such poetry, but because of the Bennion influence, hard science, too. "Dave and the others were scientists," Draper says, "and they encouraged me to do research and supplied the lab equipment to do it. We've used gas chromatography, and had access to magnetic-resonance imaging equipment at the University of California at Santa Cruz. A lot of the stuff we've learned we might never be able to apply, but we're far ahead of everyone in the state, nation and world in knowledge about tannins and color. We've even written it up in technical papers."

But the science and winemaking were only part of Draper's duties. "I think I used to write up an occasional order in the early days," he says. "We didn't have a sales director. Every couple of weeks the partners would get together for dinner, and the meetings would run until the wee hours. We were all working hard and watching the numbers, but since there were only four or five wineries in our category, catering to a small market that was very interested in wine, we really had no competition."

While Ridge probably has more discretionary money to spend today, Draper says costs are watched much more closely. "We've set up internal controls and constantly cost-out packaging and virtually every item in the winory, and try to do better. We try to reduce overtime during the harvest period. It takes discipline to check yourself all the time, but if we didn't, we'd be spending a lot more than we need to be spending. And I can see that running a tight ship has benefits besides finances; for example, employees can see that no department is lax or overspending, that we're all in it together."

This business side of Ridge is actually run by General Manager Wilma Sturrock. "It's great for me as winemaker to have a general manager of her quality," says Draper, "because she's an even greater stickler than I am." This frees him to oversee his winemakers, and to be, as he says, "the conscience" of Ridge. This is important to the operation given its new corporate ownership, and the fact that Bennion, the spiritual guide of Ridge, is now gone.

Sources estimate that Otsuka USA paid between $10 million and $12 million for Ridge. The parent company's president, Akihiko Otsuka, reportedly a wine buff, also owns a winery in the shadow of Mount Fuji. If so, the company may leave Ridge well enough alone, despite the size of the investment.

It's hard to envision Draper walking away; his home is just a two-minute drive from the winery, over the top of the Ridge, with a commanding view of the Pacific Ocean. He is closely identified with Ridge wines; the initials PD on the back of each bottle make that point pretty clear. In a sense, Draper came with the property, and he still takes fierce pride in the wines he makes. But being the superstar winemaker twenty-four hours a day is something else.

"On one hand, I'm a much more open person than I was five years ago," he explains. "On the other, I often ask myself before agreeing to do things: 'What is the sense of this?' Or, 'Will I feel good about it?' Since I got married I have a better perspective and am much happier, less tied to trivia and the emotions that come from getting upset by trivial problems."

For Paul Draper, the thrill isn't gone. "If I couldn't still get caught up in the romance," he says, "I wouldn't still be here." But to be a more rounded person, he recognizes that the thrills must come in measured doses. Draper knows well that putting on the mask of the superstar winemaker is, like many other elements in this industry, an all-consuming thing.

13

THE MANAGERS

Phil Woodward has great respect for winemakers, although he feels that acceptably talented enologists are a commodity in plentiful supply. "But a guy who can run the business and sell wine," sighs the president and CEO of Chalone Inc., the foremost publicly owned premium wine producer in America, "is tough to find."

At Domaine M. Marion, the highest-paid employee isn't Dennis Marion's winemaker. "It's my controller," he states, in a tone that suggests that he'd never have it otherwise.

When it comes to reviving a moribund winery, a company would be well advised to secure the services of Agustin Huneeus, and then leave the bright and elegant Chilean to run the place. That's what the Peter Eckes Co. of West Germany did after it paid an estimated $10 million for Napa Valley's Franciscan Vineyards in 1979, invested a couple million to upgrade it and saw the operation generally flounder until Huneeus came on board six years later. This is not the first winery he has managed into a far better financial shape.

As Brother David Brennan set out to salvage the crumbling Christian Brothers operation, his key acquisition for 1986 was Dick Maher. Broken into the business world by the masters of marketing at Procter & Gamble, Maher then served as an executive vice president of Great Western United, which owned the Shakey's Pizza Parlor chain. He worked for the Gallos, moved on to Nestlé's Beringer operation—where he was largely responsible for its sales revival—and was later president of the Seagram Wine Co. As Woodward noted, pros like Maher are certainly not a dime a dozen.

Small wineries don't need and can't afford big hitters to run the business, but they'd be wise to use a consultant like George Schofield. The former chief financial officer at Robert Mondavi, Schofield earned his stripes from his years at Price Waterhouse and at Merck, the giant pharmaceutical company. Soft-spoken and correct, he is a man who on Saturday mornings dresses in dark slacks, a blue and white pin-striped shirt, a muted red necktie, and wing tips. But his appearance is an indicator of his thoughts, which are as well organized as the business plans he prepares for about fifty small wineries. Schofield is a pure and undiluted business eminence.

Winemakers garner most of the glamour of this industry. But if it weren't for professional managers, an awful lot of winemakers wouldn't even make a dime, much less be worth one. These are individuals who understand the wine business, the few ways in which it's different from other industries, and the many ways in which it is the same. They receive little public credit, which for most is just fine; consumers don't buy a wine because the company making it has a great executive or beancounter. But in the increasingly competitive wine game, such managers may be the true superstars.

The best share certain characteristics one finds in executives in any industry. Self-assurance is one premium trait. So is the willingness to risk making a mistake, and to accept personal responsibility when something goes wrong. More importantly, they view hard experiences not so much as painful and humiliating gaffes that ought to be buried, but as pragmatic lessons that contribute immeasurably to their repertoire of skills. Thus, mistakes are put in perspective, and the experience becomes a useful tool for the future.

Moreover, all of the top wine managers seem to bring some rather simple, abiding precepts to their work. They are core or guiding principles, easily articulated and understood, from which all else flows.

In the case of Dennis Marion, success starts with the proper attitude. Not long after he started his business, Marion visited a wholesaler in Washington, D.C. When the wholesaler asked why he'd gotten into the business, Marion bluntly replied that he simply wanted to make some money. "The guy was floored," recalls Marion. "He couldn't believe that someone was treating this as a business instead of a hobby. But I've always seen wine as a business deal."

Of course, this means understanding what distributors, retailers and consumers want, and Marion has a better idea of this than most. "At our sales meetings," he says, "I stress that they're not going to be able to feed their families by discussing pH levels in soil. From my experience buying rare wines I can talk about all that, but when I first started out selling my own wines on the street, I learned real fast that you should never be smarter than the buyer."

Marion cites the example of a high-end, premium winery that was having serious difficulty with sales and finances. Its president asked Marion to come in and consult and assist on a turnaround effort. "Their product was good," he says, "but their salespeople had bad attitudes. They'd walk in and tell clients: 'You are going to like this wine.' "

Such arrogance is more likely to rile than charm a distributor or retailer. On a sales call, says Marion, "the approach has to be: 'Hey guys, what do you want and how can I help?' This makes your product a lot easier to sell. Well, that winery basically cleaned house and changed the sales force attitudes, which is mainly what turned the company around."

Cork-sniffers, as he calls them, agitate Marion. "The industry keeps talking about education, but it's misdirected," he insists. "It should have nothing to do with educating people about the technical aspects of wine, but simply be a means to make wine seem fun to drink."

Keeping it simple is yet another Marion principle, because he's found that many modern wine retailers care as little about pH and technical matters as the public. "I was down in Miami and went into a large wine shop," he explains, "and the guy there had his own tasting notes, hand-written on little cards, on nearly every wine in the house. I was impressed, and told him he'd really done a good job on rating the wines. He said, 'Nah, you got it all wrong. I've got a computer that analyzes all the tasting notes and ratings from a whole bunch of publications. I just copy the results of the consensus.' " So much for the expert.

Meanwhile, he has to appeal to consumers, to make his wine appear interesting and fun to drink. One of his most successful gambits is his "flower series" labels, eye-catching paintings of flora, an idea that is increasingly being copied. "People eat and drink with their eyes, if you will," he says. "Consumers often buy the label. And since women buy most wine, particularly in grocery stores, I wanted labels that appealed to women."

Dennis Marion is the kind of businessman who would operate pretty much the same if he were selling brooms. He loves wine, but he loves commerce even more.

Agustin Huneeus, on the other hand, once walked away from a prestigious job managing the fortunes of some three dozen wineries for Seagram International, mainly because the position put too much distance between him and the actual operations. The wineries were in such diverse locations as Germany, France, Italy, Spain, Argentina, Brazil, Venezuela, New Zealand and the U.S.

"It was a very complex thing," recalls Huneeus. "Each had a completely different set of problems, each participated in different segments of the market, and most of their products were sold locally." While the complexity didn't bother him, he slowly became "totally disenchanted with corporate life. Though I was in the wine business, my contact with it became a numbers contact," Huneeus explains. "It got so that I never had the chance to taste wines, meet with the winemakers or study their viticultural techniques. My job had nothing to do with wine, just budgets and sales figures. I could have been selling roller skates."

Born in Santiago, Chile, his family was involved in the steamship business. Educated at Fordham University's business school, Huneeus returned to Chile after graduating in 1957, and a year later began selling grapes from a small vineyard on a family-owned farm. Along with a friend, the twenty-six-year-old Huneeus spotted a possible business venture. A winery called Concha y Toro was for sale, and the two men realized that its market value was considerably less than the worth of its inventory. They planned to liquidate the inventory, and simply keep the property as farmland.

By coincidence, Concha y Toro had been founded by Huneeus's great-great grandfather in 1883. The winery, he found, had a magnetic pull on his emotions. "I fell in love with it," he says. So instead of liquidating, Huneeus began building. Indeed, between 1958 and 1970, he turned Concha y Toro into one of Chile's most prominent wineries, producing some two million cases a year. He was about to sell a 50 percent interest in the winery to Seagram, in return for a capital infusion of roughly $5 million, when the arrival of the new Marxist government of Salvador Allende Gossens soured the nation's business climate.

Leaving the business in his partner's hands, Huneeus accepted an offer to direct a Seagram operation in Argentina. "I had never considered myself a turnaround expert," he says, "but they had four companies that were losing businesses. I merged them into one, and they recovered." While in Argentina, however, Huneeus was essentially forced to let go of his holdings in his beloved Concha y Toro, which had been greatly devalued under the Allende regime.

"When I lost Concha y Toro," he says, "it was like losing my blood. My existence. I was so hurt. But I decided that from then on, you can love your kids, you can love your wife, but you can never love a company." And yet, Huneeus had learned how to make companies work, a knack that became apparent as he moved up in the Seagram operation until he left in 1977.

After being placed in charge of the many properties around the world, he explains, "I soon discovered that if I could place a good team of the right three people at a winery—any winery, anywhere—then that company would succeed. Not one good person, but three, including the president, a good marketer and a good controller. When I had this trio in place, and they each had the character traits I was looking for, I wouldn't have to worry."

Note that Huneeus didn't mention a winemaker. "That's because outside of the U.S., a winemaker is considered a good technician. He's like a baker. And since Seagram is a giant corporation, not a little American boutique that's trying to sell the winemaker's poetic insight, that position doesn't make a huge difference in the company's success. But at the top . . ."

What he looked for in an operational triumvirate was intelligence, creativity and what he calls complementary characters. "That is, if I had a very conservative general manager or president, then I'd place a real eclectic marketing guy with him," Huneeus explains. "On the other hand, if I had a real creative and undisciplined type of president, then he'd be balanced by a staid controller. At first, these personalities are going to clash. Then they begin to work together very well."

Huneeus, of course, made it clear that the inherent conflicts were not to be the stuff of mutiny, internecine warfare that hindered the business. The teams were supposed to engage in purposeful and collegial disagreements before reaching an inevitable compromise. The management brew has apparently worked, for even today, Huneeus says, "many of those teams are still in place."

But the far-flung Seagram operations enabled Huneeus to spend only one week each year on a winery. "I wanted to be back in contact with the business that I liked," he explains, "touching the earth." So he left the corporation and with a group of investors bought a bulk wine producer in California's central valley. He then bought Concannon in 1979, an old winery in the Livermore Valley southeast of San Francisco, which he says was then "a pretty disoriented company." Concannon made premium wines, but of a style that weren't in fashion, and had an image that Huneeus terms "country family farmer."

By projecting a smoother and more modern image, Concannon began to grow. In fact, it grew too fast, which Huneeus admits was a mistake. After contracts with his partners expired, Huneeus found that to keep the bigger Concannon going, he'd have to leverage it very highly, and would likely lose most control to a new investor. At that point, he simply sold out.

"It was a small jolt," he says. "But of course, I had learned to never again love a company. And I made some good money from it, which carried me over to my next job." Huneeus had earned enough of a reputation to be called in as a consultant to troubled wineries, which led him to Franciscan in 1985.

The winery had a lot going for it, including some of the best vineyards in the middle of the Napa Valley, a location right on Highway 29, and the Peter Eckes backing. The German firm had put plenty of capital into the place. Through its Franciscan and Estancia labels, the company produces about 100,000 cases of wine a year. The former is in the $8.50 to $12 per bottle range, the latter $6 to $8. Both are in the "fighting varietals" segment, the industry's toughest. "If we weren't here," says Huneeus, "if Franciscan just disappeared, nobody would notice because there are so many others in the same category."

Franciscan is now producing sufficient cash flow and is no longer viewed as a winery in distress, although Huneeus has made only minor changes in marketing and sales strategies. Perhaps this is a case of Eckes' investments finally paying off. But as president of the Napa Valley winery, Huneeus is clearly a complementary character.

Phil Woodward of Chalone is yet another professional manager, although he came to wine at a later age than either Marion or Huneeus. Born in Illinois, Woodward's family ran a small silica sand mining company. He completed his undergraduate work in Economics at the University of Colorado, earned a master's degree at Northwestern and intended to join the family enterprise. Instead, he joined the

Detroit office of Touche Ross in 1964 as a CPA on an audit staff that concentrated on small businesses.

"Half the work was terrifically interesting," remembers Woodward, a man with curly, sandy hair, ruddy skin and blue eyes. "The other half was terribly boring. But it gave me an inside look at all kinds of businesses, to see how they came together." He spent seven years with the firm, as an auditor and then on a management consulting staff. Eventually, he convinced the company to add a small-business consulting department to its San Francisco office, a location Woodward had become enamored with during his travels.

He'd also become enamored with wine, after signing up for a seminar on wine appreciation in Detroit. "I didn't grow up in a household that drank wine," he explains. "We had Virginia Dare maybe once a year. But the course opened up a whole new world to me. My wife and I even started a wine club." When Woodward arrived in California, he found himself consulting with some wineries, various partnership vineyard ventures and a few retailers.

One retailer that he patronized as a consumer needed serious accounting help; Woodward agreed to spend nights and weekends helping the business, which could only pay him in wine. In late 1970, he was rewarded with a bottle of 1969 Chalone Pinot Blanc, from a tiny and remote winery in Monterey County's Pinnacles National Monument area; a wine made by a Harvard music graduate named Richard Graff. The wine knocked Woodward for a loop.

Graff was producing only 300 to 500 cases of Chalone wine a year, hardly enough to make a living. But Woodward and Graff formally joined forces in 1972, and the businessman put together a five-year business plan to expand Chalone. As soon as he quit his job, he found himself making about 10 percent of what he'd earned at Touche Ross.

Land near the Chalone vineyard was still relatively cheap in the early 1970s, and the partnership raised enough money to plant seventy-five new acres of vineyard. They incorporated and sold shares in the company. As Graff's wine output increased, Woodward went door to door trying to sell wine and shares in the company. "To anyone who would listen," he says, "I had a story to tell and a bottle of wine to drink with it." But while Graff's reputation as a supreme winemaker grew—after Harvard, he'd gone through the Davis program—banks weren't as impressed with Chalone. "I had an almost impossible time trying to get a bank give us a car or truck loan," recalls Woodward. "Finally, Wells Fargo came through on the truck." But by 1974, Woodward's legwork had raised $750,000.

The company concentrated on the ultra-premium end of the business, a mail order list and restaurant sales. "For our kind of wine, which is all over $10 or $15 a bottle, you're not looking at stacks of it on the floor at Safeway," says Woodward, who put most of his time into convincing restaurants and clubs to carry Chalone. "Today, about 65 percent of our products are 'on premises' sales, 10 percent direct mail and about 25 percent retail."

Woodward determined early that Chalone "would grow big by staying small." That is, they would expand by buying existing wineries that also produced small quantities of ultra-premium vintages. But their progress hit a snag in 1977, when the winery experimented with a fermentation process that yielded wine way below Chalone's quality standards. "We blew it," says Woodward, "and after we released the wine and realized that it was going bad, we recalled every case, as much as we could get back. It was a terrible financial sacrifice, but I think we at least gained the respect of our customers."

In 1980, the company launched a joint venture with the Paragon Vineyard Co., Inc. to produce and market wines from the Edna Valley Vineyard in San Luis Obispo County. In 1982, Chalone acquired the fifty-one-acre Carmenet Vineyard and a 30,000-case winery in the Sonoma Valley. Two years later, with the help of Hambrecht & Quist, the high-tech venture capital firm, it went public, selling for $8 a share, making it America's only publicly traded company that is exclusively in the business of winegrowing.

The capital gave Chalone the strength to buy the financially troubled Acacia Winery in 1986, a 32,000-case, ultra-premium producer in the Carneros District of Sonoma County. "It took one phone call to get a $5 million loan to buy Acacia," says Woodward, "and all I could think of was how tough it had been to get the loan on that truck."

The affairs of Chalone's four wineries are managed from its offices on San Francisco's Howard Street. It is a quiet company, by and large, and relies on word-of-mouth to keep its sales moving. "We don't promote," says Woodward, "because in our case we would make more enemies than friends, because we couldn't produce enough wine to go around. But we also don't want to feel smug and supercilious; we try to make our products as available to as many people as possible."

Unlike many public companies, Chalone isn't under pressure from its stockholders. It has never paid a dividend, and maybe never will. Six principals in the company own about 55 percent of the stock; the other 1,000 shareholders receive discounts on wine between 15 percent and 25 percent off retail. "Many of them consider the annual meeting, which is rotated among the four wineries, as the dividend," says Woodward, who also considers them additional salespeople.

Chalone is only marginally profitable, mainly because it keeps plowing earnings back into the business. While Woodward feels the company has only about 160 competitors, including wineries in California, Oregon and Washington, he recognizes that the business could grow tighter in the future. "In the premium category that is just below ours," he concedes, "there's some real bloodletting going on."

But Woodward also says that there's more to the wine industry than "crunching numbers. Remember, I got my start in business by crunching numbers," he adds. The mentality found among beancounters in, say, the auto industry—where attempts to shave pennies here and there eventually destroy quality improvement efforts—wouldn't wash in ultra-premium segments of wine. After all, once a restaurant adds its markup, a bottle of Chalone, Carmenet or Acacia wine could add $30 to $60 to the tab.

Therefore, Chalone spends a considerable amount on labor for handling and racking its wines, on new barrels and "fancy bottles from France." For example, the extra quality in the label, bottle, corks and lead foil adds about $5 in per-case costs on the Carmenet wines. "The trick is to be able to build a brand and reputation so that when you sell the wine, people feel they're getting that reputation in the bottle." And yet, glittering perceptions aside, Phil Woodward is going to continue to crunch numbers, if only to ensure that Chalone Inc. remains above the bloodletting.

George Schofield is very much a numbers kind of guy. He publishes statistical reports on the grape crush and wine shipments, with an in-depth analysis. In article form, he contributes his interpretations to *Wines & Vines* magazine, and prepares thick *Grape Intelligence Reports*, full of bar graphs and charts, that track the acreage, production and returns on, say, Cabernet Sauvignon. Along with Jon Fredrikson, he provides the industry with some of the best data available. But to a lot of individual winegrowers who find themselves in trouble, this mild-looking, bespectacled CPA, who has a Harvard MBA, is Batman and the Lone Ranger rolled into one.

"Typically, a guy and his wife will come to me and say, 'I've been at this for seven years and I'm tired,' " Schofield explains. "He'll tell me that he feels like he's chasing his own tail around, that he 'retired' to come work with wine and instead of finding joy is putting in eighteen-hour days and is making only $10,000 for all his trouble. 'Help us understand,' they'll say."

Schofield started his financial and economic planning firm in 1983, after leaving Mondavi. He founded it on four basic axioms, which he outlines to all new clients. First, he offers "Comprehensive planning and skillful execution required to fully perceive and realize opportunities." He notes that the "Ability to compete is principally determined by ratios of quality to price and quality to cost." Schofield also feels that "Job security, freedom to act, and equitable sharing of rewards generate creativity and excellence in performance," and that "Integrity, professionalism and respect to confidentiality are crucial to effective business interaction."

In other words, he won't talk much about his clients, even in vague terms.

Schofield says that he issues economic reports for their public relations benefit, although it's material that can certainly help wineries figure strategies. His real work is providing a service to those tired winegrowers who can't afford a full-time chief financial officer, but who desperately need intervention by someone who understands the discipline. Schofield helps his clients develop financial modeling, monthly goals and three-to-five-year business plans, covering everything from the crush to the final sale of wine, "although I don't get into marketing," he adds.

He does get into tax planning, accounting systems analysis, cash management programs, computer applications and all sorts of things that aren't discussed at winemaker dinners. He also intercedes with banks, vendors and other businesses on the part of his client. "If someone is having trouble with his bank and a loan is coming due," Schofield explains, "I can go in and show them a new financial plan, or a program that puts them back on track. I've got a good relationship with the banks."

Says one Napa Valley banker who handles a large volume of winery loans: "We feel a lot more comfortable when George is involved, and when his clients follow what he outlines."

What he outlines is usually coldly realistic, given that Schofield is convinced that wine is at best a "7 percent business." He counsels clients over and over to grow slow, very slow, so that they're not stuck with unsold wine in inventory. "Ideally, at the end of the year," he says, "the winery should be one case short of the demand for its products."

While he rescues wineries with prudence, Schofield is himself in the process of what seems like a daring entrepreneurial effort. Convinced that vintners sell their wine much too early, Schofield has put together groups of investors to purchase lots of some of the best Cabernets made in California, including releases from Jordan, Beaulieu Vineyard Private Reserve, Stag's Leap Wine Cellars, Clos du Val, Robert Mondavi and several others. Although he got a wholesale license for himself to reduce the purchase price, 2,000 cases of 1982 Cabernets cost a twenty-five-member group about $275,000. For the 1981 vintage, twenty-one investors paid $187,000 for 1,800 cases.

The group actually takes possession of the wine and stores it in a temperature-controlled warehouse. Schofield's contention is that these wines are unavailable on the market when they're a decade old and at their drinkable best. He plans to package them in gift boxes and sell them through upscale stores.

Despite the initial investment and storage and insurance costs, Schofield says the wine will bring a 14 percent pre-tax annual return on investment. This, of course, is better than banks and bonds, and double the return of owning a winery. But how does he know this? Schofield has prepared a historical study of premium wine prices. He put them through the computer, and had them outlined in bars, charts and graphs. He crunched the numbers, and the beans look promising indeed.

Section Four

THE DAVIDS, A GOLIATH AND A DYNAMO NAMED BOB

14

GOOD THINGS COME IN SMALL PACKAGES

From the end of Prohibition and into the 1950s, the American wine industry was dominated by fairly large producers, including Gallo, Charles Krug, Inglenook, the Christian Brothers and a handful of others. Some made wines that were quite good, though nothing compared to the best wines of the small French châteaux. Toward the end of that decade, however, a few pioneering vintners—often plunging into winemaking as a second career or quasi-hobby—began experimenting, making small quantities of high-quality wine. It found a market in the U.S., and the wine boom of the 1960s commenced, detonated primarily by small producers.

Such businesses, which initially produced just a few thousand cases each year, have been called boutique wineries. It's a term that makes most of these vintners gnash their teeth and want to beat the breast of anyone using the word. A boutique is a fancy shop carrying expensive clothing for women, decked out in plush carpeting, baubles and bangles. Boutique wineries may make limited-edition wines that carry commensurately steep prices, but the work is too damn hard and grubby to justify the term. The preferred appellation is "small winery."

However, they do make exquisitely crafted wines, vintages unlike those made by larger producers, wines which fit a narrow niche in the market. It's a combination of quality and style that draws high per-bottle prices in the super and ultra-premium category, from $8 to $20, sometimes more. Some have been very successful, growing to become medium-sized producers. Most would be pleased to reach and stop at 35,000 cases, or "château size." This magnitude is something of a spiritual, philosophical and practical target, a French ideal where quality and a comfortable living may be conjoined.

On one hand, such winemakers face little competition from the big producers. While Beringer today makes exceptional wine that's nearly equal in quality to that of the small wineries—and probably better than a goodly percentage of them—it is perceived as a high-volume house. Consumers of super and ultra-premium wine believe that small and rare are better. On the other hand, small wineries are finding that their respective niches are growing crowded. Therefore the need for aggressive marketing and promotion, a difficult task for a thinly staffed business.

The following is a look at three small wineries. Each came into being in a different way, but all share certain characteristics. Believing the idea that small is beautiful, each has positioned his wine as a standout in origin, quality and style. Each works the hours of a Japanese factory manager; as hard as a chain-gang member under a fiendish overseer. And all had to begin by selling their wine one bottle at a time.

Patrick Campbell of Laurel Glen Vineyard founded his enterprise with a distinct niche in mind. His winery produces only 5,000 cases annually of Cabernet Sauvignon, made from grapes grown on his thirty-five-acre vineyard. Before starting it, he had looked for a property which was unique and singular, with a soil and climate that would produce a one-of-a-kind wine. This is one way to build an exclusive niche.

"My property comprises a small finger of red volcanic soil that juts out from the northern flank of Sonoma Mountain," he explains. "The vineyard there was pretty degraded, but I had tasted some of the wines made from the grapes. They were just fantastic, especially the ones that had received a vineyard designation from Chateau St. Jean. So I bought the vineyard with the idea of a small, estate-bottled winery in mind. I only wanted to make one wine; in essence, I wanted the wine to be known as 'Laurel Glen,' rather than 'Laurel Glen Vineyard Cabernet.' I wanted the name and what was in the bottle to be associated as one and the same, just as the Grand Cru Bordeaux are. You don't think of Château Mouton Rothschild as a red wine from Bordeaux that's 90 percent Cabernet Sauvignon and 10 percent Cabernet Franc and Merlot—you just think 'Mouton.' That's how I wanted it with Laurel Glen."

Campbell upgraded the existing vineyard and planted new acreage. In order to finance the expansion, he sold all the grapes from the property during the first five years of operation. "Like almost all vintners, I had to borrow," he says. "But unlike a lot of them, I had to show a profit after a specific period of time. I didn't have deep pockets. I knew I could show that profit if Laurel Glen was marketed properly, because the fruit was remarkable. But I couldn't hack it with a big debt load, considering the fact that I knew I'd never produce over 5,000 cases. Selling the fruit for five years did two things: First, it gave me a positive cash flow so I could keep my financing to a minimum while I built up the vineyard. Second, it gave me some breathing room to establish a name for Laurel Glen. My grapes went into Kenwood's Artist Series Cabernet bottling, and that got me a lot of publicity."

During the five years that Laurel Glen functioned as a grape ranch, Campbell applied himself with diligence to the study of enology. "I knew I couldn't afford a winemaker," he says. "Even now, my payroll is as lean as it can get—one full-time employee for the vineyards, and a part-time employee for the winery. But Cabernet Sauvignon is an easy wine to make, relatively speaking; much easier than Chardonnay or Pinot Noir, for instance. So I didn't have any fears that I'd blow it when it came to winemaking. Having only one kind of wine to make—and Cabernet at that—really simplifies things."

By doing most of the work himself, Campbell further reduced vineyard expansion costs. He also used ingenuity. Polio had severely affected Campbell's legs when he was a boy, but he still does his own tractor work, having welded handles on his Caterpillar's brake pedals, and operating them with his hands.

There are no lavishly appointed tasting rooms or hospitality suites at Laurel Glen. The winery building consists of one room where the primary fermentation vats sit, and another, somewhat larger room where the wine is aged in barrels. A smaller room off to the side houses Campbell's lab and wine library. The wine is bottled and stored in a temperature-controlled warehouse in Santa Rosa. "Wherever there was fat, I trimmed it mercilessly," Campbell explains. "That was the only way I could come up with a bottom line that would make my bankers happy. But I never touched the meat. I spent money freely that had anything to do with the wine itself."

Campbell didn't enter the industry at an auspicious time. In 1983, when he put his first release on the market—the 1981 vintage—he sensed that the glory days of the 1970s were already over. "That was when any small winery that had good wine and a decent label could move it out the door as fast as they made it," he notes. "Vintners got spoiled. By the time I had my first release, people were fighting for shelf space. But a lot of winemakers were still in the mindset of the 1970s. They weren't willing or able to promote their wine; either they didn't know how, or they thought it was beneath them."

Campbell didn't share this reticence. Even before he released the 1981 Laurel Glen, he was on the road whenever he wasn't actually at the winery or in the vineyards. "I poured wine for distributors, restaurateurs, wine retailers, wine writers—anyone who had influence in this industry. I flew to Los Angeles and New York more times than I'd care to recall. But it paid off. The wine showed very well, and people remembered it. They were ready for it by the time it was released."

Campbell also pushed the fact that, while his wine was equal in quality to be the best Cabs in the U.S., it came from Sonoma Mountain, which made it unique. The Rutherford Bench region of the Napa Valley has long been recognized as the prime area for California Cabernets. From here come the grapes used by Mondavi, Beaulieu and Inglenook. "The wines are rich, complex, minty and firm," says Campbell. "But I knew that my area, Sonoma Mountain, could and did produce Cabernets that were equivalent in quality. But they're different wines—more concentrated in flavor, with more cassis and chocolate overtones rather than mint—but every bit as good."

All the subtle strategies would be for naught if Campbell's wine weren't up to the hype. But his first releases met with stellar success. *The Wine Spectator* awarded it the Spectator Selection Award. Myriad independent reviewers wrote of it glowingly. Most were taken by its price as well as its quality: $12.50 a bottle.

"I knew in my guts that most small vintners were employing wrong pricing strategy," Campbell recalls. "They figured that most wine lovers would equate high price with high quality. Maybe that was true once, but wine drinkers are a lot more sophisticated and cost-conscious these days. Cash flow is very critical to my financial planning. So I price the wine as a premium wine, but I also priced it so it would move. I've had price increases since then; it now retails for around $20 a bottle. But I've always maintained my pricing structure so that it was always a bargain when compared to its image and acknowledged quality. I may not make as much per bottle of wine as some vintners, but my wine moves, and that means that my financial profile is very satisfactory."

He also emphasizes that maintaining a continuity of

quality over the years is essential to establishing brand loyalty. "I can think of several wineries that came out with fantastic releases their first few years, and then put out really inferior wines when they succumbed to overproduction," Campbell says. "Once you lose a good reputation, it's very hard to get it back. That's why I established a second label called Counterpoint, soon after my first release. All my fruit is examined before it goes into the crusher, and any that isn't of absolute top quality goes into my Counterpoint bottling."

Campbell says that it's conceivable that there could be years when he will produce no Laurel Glen, and all Counterpoint Cabernet. "And by the same token, there'll be years—quite a few years, probably, considering the good climate I usually have here—when there will be no Counterpoint. The important thing is I have the option. The Laurel Glen label will always be sacrosanct, and Counterpoint allows me to market all my wine without jeopardizing Laurel Glen's reputation."

Other vintners have capitalized on wines from specific areas to establish a distinct market presence. Dan Duckhorn of Duckhorn Vineyards in the Napa Valley, however, did not identify his wines with the Napa Valley as ardently as Campbell did Laurel Glen Cabernet with Sonoma Mountain. Rather, he has emphasized a specific varietal.

"All of our wines bear a Napa Valley viticultural designation, since we feel very strongly about the Valley's prestige in global wine circles," says Duckhorn. "We do ally ourselves very closely with the Napa Valley tradition of top quality. But we needed something more than that, since a lot of vintners push their association with the Valley. What we needed was a specific varietal that we could establish as our own. Something unique, but with a built-in constituency. We chose Merlot."

Merlot is a red grape variety from the Bordeaux region of France. In Bordeaux, Merlot is generally used as a blending grape to soften and flesh out the harder, more herbaceous Cabernet Sauvignon that forms the backbone of most of the area's great red wines. Wines made from Merlot tend to be lush, rich and heavily perfumed: a quality known as *gras* to the French, meaning literally "fat," but colloquially full, generous and velvety.

In any event, Duckhorn, a financier and wine lover who had logged a lot of time in Bordeaux, knew that Merlot had great potential in California. When he opened his winery in 1976, he had already identified several growers who produced excellent fruit. And he was heartened by the fact that the grape was still used primarily for blending. "There were some wineries who were making a varietal Merlot, but they were few and far between," Duckhorn explains. "Most winemakers were using it for blending with Cabernet. So the market was wide open in terms of the consumer identifying the varietal with a particular label. When we were able to locate growers who had mature Merlot vineyards with solid track records, I knew we were in business."

Duckhorn decided on two things right from the start: he would buy most of his fruit rather than plant his own vineyards, and he would start out small and grow as demand warranted. "Putting in vineyards is a terribly expensive proposition," he says. "And after it's in, you have to wait three years before you even get a crop. And when you're making only super-premium wine, you can't even use the fruit for the first few years; a vineyard doesn't start producing fruit of optimum quality until it's mature, which takes seven or eight years."

Duckhorn used his capital stake on production and storage facilities, and for new French oak barrels. And he started out with a minuscule production: 1,500 cases. He has since grown to 16,000 cases annually, and plans to peak out at 20,000 to 30,000. "We decided to grow piecemeal, which went completely against all the financial doctrine at the time, since it was felt that it costs a lot more to tack on additions than to build one large facility that will suit all future needs," Duckhorn notes.

"But in 1976 and 1977, interest rates were horrendous, and I was betting that they'd come down, which they did. Also, inflation has been pretty moderate in the past few years, so our additions weren't as costly as we'd anticipated. Plus, the capital we had available from not building a

20,000-case facility in the beginning allowed us to concentrate on what was really important—the wine itself. The only real drawback to the plan was the fact that we had to keep digging up our power and water lines every three or four years."

From his years in finance, though, Duckhorn had developed a healthy loathing for debt load. The idea of taking on the debt to capitalize a winery gave him "the cold sweats." He arranged for some limited partners, who provided capital, obviated the risk of rising interest rates, and enabled him to effectively plan his long-term financing. "The fact that we had ten families as partners also gave us ten more vehicles for public relations. The people who own Duckhorn are all successful, they love wine and know people who love wine, so they help to a great degree in marketing the product, however indirectly." Don and Margaret Duckhorn still hold the largest share of the company, although their power isn't absolute. He figures the trade-off in control versus freedom from debt as wholly worthwhile.

Duckhorn and his partners were aware that premium wine consumers like to associate a face with a wine. "Corporation wineries just aren't as sexy," he says. "They turn people off." It was decided that only the Duckhorns would officially represent the winery in public. "That would give the product focus and continuity," he says. "It makes sense to have people named Duckhorn talking about Duckhorn wines."

Duckhorn calls his marketing efforts "a rifle rather than a shotgun, since we don't have a lot of money to throw around." But he and Margaret are frequently on the road, talking to accounts and press people about their wine. "There's no substitute for that," he says. "The people who sell your wine want to meet the people who make it—not some sales rep. And we always spend a lot of time on our package."

Duckhorn knew he'd never make it as a high-volume business. "We had to make as much money as we could on every bottle. It didn't take us long to figure out that the best way was to handle our own distribution, to eliminate the middleman. We distribute directly to our accounts in California, and sell directly to our distributors in out-of-state markets. We don't use brokers like the great majority of small wineries do. We also have a big direct mail program in the state. Finally, we chose to build the winery on the Silverado Trail, which gets a lot of tourist traffic. That means we sell a lot of wine right at the winery, at full retail price. All in all, that adds up to an average F.O.B. [i.e., per case profit] of $110, which is really very good."

Duckhorn Merlots have received almost fulsomely positive reviews, which Duckhorn attributes to the fruit. But now that more vintners are playing the Merlot game, he's having to become more aggressive in securing grapes. This, of course, puts the best growers in the driver's seat. Consequently, Duckhorn is considering a vineyard acquisition. "It will be expensive," he admits, "since we'll only want mature vineyards in prime locations, but it will give us the security we need, as well as provide a means of increasing long-term equity."

In 1975, Daniel Gehrs had not a dime of equity, formal training or any appreciable experience in winemaking, although after two years of directing tours at Paul Masson it was something the twenty-five-year-old was pretty sure he wanted to do. Businessman Vic Erickson had a decrepit piece of property in the Santa Cruz mountains above Saratoga, called Congress Springs. It included an old vineyard first planted by French immigrant Pierre Pourroy in the late 1800s, and an extremely funky building called Ville de Montmartre, built in 1923 with concrete walls thick enough to withstand a direct nuclear strike.

Gehrs thought he could revive the old vines in what had once been a prized viticultural area called the Chaine d'Or—the Golden Chain—but which had been eclipsed by the Napa and Sonoma regions. He offered Erickson diligence and sweat. The elder man, who'd made his fortune in steel fabrication and other development ventures, was quick to sense the innocence of a pigeon.

Erickson agreed to fund the enterprise to the tune of $25,000, let Gehrs and his wife, Robin, move into the Minuteman silo, and signed a fifty-fifty partnership dated

January 1, 1976. Even if the winery didn't pan out, Erickson knew, the land and property would be upgraded. "Vic was looking for a bargain," says Gehrs, with a sardonic grin. "In fact, both of us were kind of looking for something for nothing."

What they got a dozen years later—though not without some love-hate beefs and costs that far exceeded the seed money—was a small winery that's making some of the finest wine in the country. Congress Springs' 1985 Santa Clara Chardonnay hit a grand slam the following year, winning five golds, three silver and two bronze medals in top competitions. It received rave reviews and an award in every fair where entered; no other Chardonnay came close to being so honored.

When Gehrs was a tour guide at Paul Masson, he talked them into paying for U.C. Davis Extension courses in viticulture and enology. He needed vines and grapes to practice with, and found them in an old vineyard near the house he and Robin rented. Tended haphazardly by an Iowa hog farmer who ran a tractor service and had little interest in viticulture, the caretaker allowed Gehrs to keep the fruit if he could keep the vines alive.

Gehrs spent all his spare time on the vineyard throughout 1975, and when he sold the fruit and calculated his time, figured he earned about fifty-six cents an hour. "It was," he says, "just another in a long series of rude awakenings." And it also hooked him.

A rangy, craggy-faced man with a wry, sophisticated and self-deprecating sense of humor, Gehrs one day tried to throw an interloper off the vineyard property, as the care-taker had told him to do. "But I own the place," protested Vic Erickson. And the two were soon in business together.

"Neither one of us had any idea it would cost as much as it did," says Gehrs today. "The $25,000 was complete pie-in-the-sky. We had to clear land, plant vineyards and buy equipment, starting with a hand-operated basket press."

At first, he didn't have the slightest idea of what to charge for his wines. "Pricing," says Gehrs, "was pin the tail on the donkey. I did no analysis of the cost of goods to pricing. Since this was a backwater business to Vic, it probably helped me that he didn't help. Without a business background, I was learning by the seat of my pants."

Gehrs, however, figured he could charge near the top of a given category because of the hand-made quality of his wine and the limited availability. "If Zinfandels were selling from $2.50 to $8 a bottle, I offered it for $7.50," he explains. Going door-to-door at liquor stores and restaurants, Gehrs portrayed Congress Springs as having a European château image and as a product that was reviving the lost esteem of the Santa Cruz Mountains viticultural area. He also tried to capitalize on the fact that he used natural, organic farming methods on his vines, shunning chemical pesticides. A sizable contingent of California's populace eats that kind of stuff up. "But it never panned out as a sales tool," laments Gehrs, who is still reluctant to wage serious chemical warfare on pests.

The battles with Erickson also began, inevitable conflicts, says Gehrs, "because the investment thing was screwy from the beginning. Both Vic and I started with a wrongheaded understanding of the industry. We just didn't think it would cost so much. Consequently, the thing about contributing equal money unraveled within two years. He started investing cash and I couldn't."

Eventually, Erickson put nearly $200,000 into the business, compared to Gehrs' $10,000. "I felt we were equal partners," says Gehrs, "while he came to regard me as an employee, which made the partnership difficult. The difference in our ages also made it difficult. Vic is in his seventies, and to him, I was, am and always will be a kid."

While Congress Springs wines were gaining a following through Gehrs' legwork, profiles in local newspapers, and festivals held on the winery's scenic grounds, the early 1980s crunch started to hit even small operations. "We'd established a small beachhead on the East Coast and suddenly that market dried up," he explains. "And it looked like the whole market was starting to suffer from boutique burnout, which was unsettling and scary."

He found difficulty moving wine through liquor stores and the larger chains like Liquor Barn. Erickson didn't like the idea of offering discounts, which limited Gehrs' flexibility with high-volume outlets. "What carried us through were the local markets, loyal clientele, our events and staying open six and then seven days a week for visitors to buy directly from the winery," he explains.

With a nominal supply of equipment, purchased used or just rented, Congress Springs boosted its production to 5,000 cases in 1981. Its wines had been winning a few ribbons here and there, but 1982 was a benchmark. "I really wanted to try and grow," recalls Gehrs, "and to make more money. I like what I'm doing, but I had two kids and I never took a vow of poverty. So I started being more aggressive, active and independent. We needed more grapes, and I went shopping, almost over my partner's objections. But Vic let it go."

Gehrs found the Chardonnay he was looking for at the San Ysidro Vineyard in the southeastern portion of the Santa Clara Valley. He paid $1,000 a ton for the grapes, sold the wine for $12 a bottle and knew he was on to something good. It was the San Ysidro fruit that has subsequently yielded gold medals at the Orange County Fair, the Los Angeles County Fair and, among others, the American Wine Competition in New York.

However, as Congress Springs' production exceeded 7,500 cases—including several different varietals—Gehrs realized he couldn't sell it all personally. He initially farmed out sales to brokers who received a 10 percent commission on the invoice. "The problem is that brokers never own the wine themselves," Gehrs explains. "If they don't sell the wine, they don't get a commission, but they also don't have a big financial stake in the thing."

He then considered going with wholesale houses, which buy the wine and therefore are more compelled to move it along. But wholesalers take a bigger piece of the cake. When Gehrs did the work himself, he could hold on to revenues equal to about two-thirds of the retail price of total wine sales. But with either the delivery and warehousing charges he'd pay to support brokers, or the take requested by wholesalers, Gehrs would see his revenues fall to less than 50 percent of the retail price.

He concluded that wholesalers, even if he had to accept

between 46 and 48 percent of retail, were the best, if only "because it's a lot less trouble." But Congress Springs still sells 20 percent of its products at the winery or through mail order, getting the full take. And the reduced margins were worth it, says Gehrs, "because the wine moved and it helped establish a greater reputation for Congress Springs."

In buying grapes from vineyard owners, Gehrs often "took what I could get. I couldn't afford someone who already had a big reputation, nor did I have the clout to get it from them." When he contracted to have the grapes he couldn't handle at his own winery crushed at a commercial crusher, he had to wait his turn behind bigger customers. "Sometimes the fruit didn't go in at the best time," he says, "but it doesn't do much good to jump up and down and make a scene. I've always found that I could make some technical changes down the line to compensate."

This relaxed and almost laconic demeanor no doubt helped his partnership with Vic Erickson endure until it became successful. Gehrs was forced to trade away some of his sweat equity for more capital, but production is now about 20,000 cases a year and climbing toward a target of between 30,000 and 35,000. Moreover, in 1986, Congress Springs turned a profit for the first time, a cool $100,000, while holding no debt.

"But that was only a temporary situation. We'll be going into debt and into the red again because the winery is going to expand and grow," explains Gehrs, as if this irony were some kind of cosmic joke endemic to the business of small wineries. However, he's optimistic, because in 1987 a British firm, Anglo-American Agriculture, bought out Erickson, who indeed saw his property greatly upgraded, and was rewarded for his patience and impatience with his young partner.

Gehrs still holds a meaningful ownership stake in Congress Springs, though far less than 50 percent. But like Paul Draper at Ridge, he is somewhat inseparable from the winery. He also thinks that he's ready to run a well-capitalized outfit. "I think if we'd been well funded at the start it might have been a hindrance," he notes. "If I needed a nickel, I sure wouldn't get a dime. But because I started out that way, I was on a pretty steep learning curve."

Gehrs now has ten employees at Congress Springs, including his brother, Jim, who has been at the winery since 1978. He also has several bright-eyed, eager and enthusiastic youths who work in the tasting room, who are willing to do just about anything to get a chance at making wine. Gehrs sees particular promise in one of them, a young college student who looks like he just picked up his Eagle Scout badge. One Saturday afternoon at Congress Springs, after this employee reported on a minor matter and hurried back to the tasting room, the wizened winemaker cringed in mock pain, and then gave a slight grin at the eager and earnest manner.

"He's just a kid," mused Gehrs. "And to me, he's always going to be a kid."

15

THE GALLOS THANK YOU FOR YOUR SUPPORT

Virtually every player in the wine industry faces certain competitive constraints and limits to business performance. And then there are the brothers Ernest and Julio Gallo. Any similarities between this pair of septuagenarians and the rest of the industry are, by and large, coincidental.

For decades, the Gallos have stood alone atop the business, crushing challengers with an ease akin to pressing overripe berries. They have been the Exxon, IBM and General Motors of winemaking wrapped into one. Their domination continues even today, for E. & J. Gallo Winery—an empire that actually includes four wineries—produces more than a quarter of all wine sold in the United States. The nearest competitor, Seagram & Sons, sells less than 10 percent.

More important than the seven Gallo labels that are found among the top twenty brands in America—which include Gallo generics, Carlo Rossi, Bartles & Jaymes, André, Thunderbird, Gallo dessert and Gallo premium varietals—is the fact that the brothers maintain a vertically integrated operation to a degree other winemakers cannot even approach. Not unlike a major oil company, Gallo controls its fortunes in nearly all facets of the wine business.

For example, to haul raw materials into its 400-acre winery in Modesto and product out, the company fields the Fairbanks Trucking Co., one of the largest intrastate truckers in California. Some 200 semis and 500 trailers not only bring in grapes and move out with wine, but carry sand and lime, much of which comes from the Gallo quarry near Sacramento. Sand and lime? Well, these materials are used by the firm's plant that can reportedly spit out two million glass bottles in a day. Moreover, Gallo's Midcal Aluminum Co. punches forth the metal screw caps to seal many of the vintages.

While most wineries must hopefully cajole wholesalers and retailers to move their product, Gallo guards its downstream business by owning distributorships in a dozen major markets. Although laws in many states prohibit the company from owning the more than 300 independent distributors Gallo uses, the brothers keep a close watch on these businesses. Gallo products, advertising and marketing techniques can make a distributor rich. But like Sinatra, these gentlemen do things their way; cross them, or fail to follow their exacting procedures, and they'll likely just roll the business over to a competitor. He'll get rich, and you will struggle.

The Gallos hold an unsurpassed measure of power in the industry, and know when, where and how to apply it. While they own about 5,000 acres of vineyards, the brothers buy almost a third of all wine grapes grown in the state. About 95 percent of Gallo's crush comes from roughly 1,500 growers, loyal farmers who are, for the most part, at the mercy of this winemaking leviathan.

Gallo, and Gallo alone, sets the price it will pay at its three crushing plants, in Livingston, Fresno and at the Frei

Brothers winery in Sonoma County. Many growers have no idea of what they'll earn in a given year. They may be richly rewarded, pulling in, say, $300 a ton for grapes that meet the Gallos' specifications in color, acid and sugar balance. But since judging grapes can be somewhat subjective, others come away disappointed, seeing a harvest downgraded to less than $150 a ton, sometimes below production costs.

"Gallo has been generally fair with the growers," says the manager of one Lodi winery, an area where the brothers buy about 90 percent of the Tokay grapes that are used for brandy and fortified wine. But as he adds, "There is a tremendous amount of Lodi's future in one guy's hands." Indeed, if the Gallos concluded that the market for Tokay-based products is kaput, they could shift production with relatively few problems; the growers, however, would be stuck.

The Gallos are picky about the grapes, says a grower who sells to them. "I wish they'd pay a little more," he notes. "Still, they treat us decently, and most importantly, they pay in cash within two or three months of delivery."

Those who bitch about Gallo, bitch quietly. With its economic sway and litigious attorneys to protect the company's interests, Gallo is perceived as an ominous presence. When *The Wine Spectator*'s Jim Laube interviewed about fifty people for a couple of articles on the Gallos, only a few agreed to attribution. Likewise, when *The Stockton Record* prepared a piece about the brothers, reporter Gary Strauss noted that: "Farmers' horror stories are often followed by 'but don't quote me on that.' " There is fear that Gallo wrath could ruin a business or career. And yet, the brothers are in turn quite generous, donating money to numerous civic organizations and projects, including $3 million for a San Francisco clinic and center to research alcoholism. These men clearly have many sides.

Power, though, is not the primary reason for Gallo success. It is an outgrowth of success, forged by personality traits that include drive, skills and wisdom not found in any other vintner in America, if not the world. These things flow from what elder brother Ernest calls, "a constant striving for perfection in every aspect of our business."

While this company comes up with some of the most downright friendly advertising campaigns in the nation, it is one of the least amiable firms in terms of public relations. While it seems that many winemakers get into the business mainly for the psychic strokes of schmoozing with visitors and holding tastings, the Gallos have no public tours. "We don't socialize much," explained Julio to *Fortune* magazine's Jaclyn Fierman, who described him as the more affable of the brothers. "There's not much to talk about." Or see, if you wanted to. Gallo's buildings are not marked; Lawrence Livermore Lab could wish for such security.

The 1986 *Fortune* interview marked a temporary coming-out for the Gallos, after a refusal to speak to the media for many years. The magazine ran a laudatory cover piece that called the men "Marketing Marvels." It also mentioned in brief some slightly eccentric behavior among the Gallo children, and what Ernest and Julio contend was a sensationalized version of their parents' deaths in 1933.

It was Napoleon who said that he feared the power of only three newspapers more than 100,000 bayonets, and Ernest—born in 1909, a year before Julio—shares this dread. Such feelings, perhaps, set the foundations to the brothers' angry response to an article that taken as a whole portrays them as business and winemaking deities. Boiling over what they termed as "vicious and damaging inaccuracies," they pulled $650,000 worth of advertisements from Time Inc., *Fortune*'s publisher.

And they've gone back into the closet. In an otherwise remarkably open business, the taciturn brothers keep their own counsel, sharing their deliberations with the world about as often as did the old Politburo. They are the wine industry's Supreme Anomaly.

The word *gallo* is Italian for rooster; Ernest and Julio's father Joseph, a tough and determined bird, came from the Piedmont region in the northwest part of that country. After arriving in California, the senior Gallo started a vineyard in Modesto, putting his boys to work during their non-school hours. A rather small-time grape grower and shipper, the immigrant struggled during Prohibition. While his grapes went into wine for religious and medicinal purposes, so did the fruit of others who weren't put totally out of business. Low demand meant low prices for harvest. Meanwhile, Ernest graduated from Modesto Junior College; Julio stopped his academic education after high school. Their best lessons came from Joseph Gallo. Says Julio: "He believed in hard work and no play. None at all."

During the Great Depression, the family business nearly folded. Then, in late June of 1933, in Fresno, for reasons never fully determined, Joseph allegedly shot his wife and turned the gun on himself. The apparent murder-suicide left behind twenty-four-year-old Ernest, twenty-three-year-old Julio and a younger brother, Joseph Jr., then thirteen.

That same year, as Prohibition was headed for repeal, the brothers decided to switch from growing grapes to making wine. The young men asked the state of California for permission to continue the business of growing their grapes, but with the proviso that they could "hold the juice"—a Prohibition cipher for wine—until selling alcohol for purposes other than medicine and religion was again fully legal. With the great sham about to end, vintners could obtain interim permits to get business underway.

According to official Gallo doctrine, the elder brothers had no idea of where to begin, but received guidance from a pair of pamphlets found in the Modesto Public Library. More important, the brothers maintain that they started their operation with precisely $5,900.23 of their own money. This contention is a cornerstone of the Gallo legend, for the men were competing against some 600 other new wineries, all looking to capitalize on the public's long-denied alcohol thirst. But while it seems admirable that Ernest and Julio Gallo built an empire off this relatively small stake, the legend, after a half century, finally accumulated a touch of tarnish, the result of an imbroglio with Joseph Jr., who is claiming a third of his brothers' business.

All three had gotten along well throughout most of their lives, attending family gatherings, giving the outward appearance of harmony; or at least as much as any outside observer could tell with this secretive clan. Ernest, named Joseph's guardian in 1933, often gave his brother business advice. Joseph eventually became a wealthy landowner, farmer and cattle rancher in Merced, California.

Problems erupted when Joseph began marketing a brand of cheese under the Gallo name. Ernest and Julio had dealt with trademark questions before, preventing an Ohio woman, one Mary Gallo, from using her name in the wine business. She tried in 1949, but E. & J. had it first. It's been suggested that the older brothers were willing to let Joseph sell his cheese if he'd only signed off on a no-fee licensing agreement. (The brothers, for example, don't seem bothered by the Gallo Salami Co., since it's not selling wine.) But Joseph wouldn't agree, and Ernest and Julio sued for trademark infringement. Joseph countersued, and the cooperage holding the origins of the Gallo legend began to burst at the seams. (Joseph lost his cheese case; the other suit goes on.)

Through Merced Attorney John Whiting, Joseph contends that his brothers denied him his rightful inheritance and the legal right to use the family name. Moreover, he has brought to the fore new evidence that Joseph Sr. and Susie Gallo were in the wine business before 1933. In fact, Ernest allegedly claimed—during their action against Mary Gallo— that his father and grandfather had been in the wine business since before Prohibition. As early, in fact, as 1909.

More critical to Joseph's inheritance claim is whether Ernest and Julio used resources and knowledge from Joseph Sr. and Susie to found E. & J. Gallo Winery. The brothers now say they didn't. But wine historian Leon Adams believes that the boys knew the old man made bootleg wine, and actually watched him do it. Although the pair borrowed to finance the business, some of their debts, claims Joseph, were paid out of estate funds.

According to court records, Joseph Sr. owned more than 500 acres of land in the state, and stock worth $16,000. His wife was worth nearly $9,000 at the time of her death, a sum that apparently included stock in the Transamerica Corp. Joe Junior's lawyer claims the older brothers eventually sold this for more than $33,000.

John Whiting, no minor-league strategist, has taken the case to the media, the glare of which makes the elder Gallos cringe. He has in fact used the press, pointing out juicy dichotomies that make for hot print. For example, while the brothers have made much of the $5,900.23 they had saved to start the winery, Whiting has a Treasury Department document filed in 1935 that shows they invested $160,000 in their winery over a two-year period. Production leaped from 200,000 gallons in 1933 to more than double the next year and in excess of a million gallons in 1936. Positive cash flow aside, one likely needed considerably more capital than $5,900.23, even then, for such rapid growth.

The 1949 trademark testimony could come back to haunt. "Millions of cases of grapes were shipped with the brand name on it," Ernest had testified. "Our company, the E. & J. Gallo Winery, then continued with the brand in 1933 when we started business. We always sold wine under the brand name Gallo." Moreover, Susie Gallo's will, hand-written in 1928, divides her personal property and stocks equally among her sons, "as soon as each one becomes 21 years of age." Joseph's suit alleges that his brothers never fully informed him of the inheritance and commingled the estate's assets with their new winery. This, he claims, gives him a stake in E. & J. Gallo.

Although Joseph Gallo may or may not have a rightful claim, it was indeed Ernest and Julio who built an enterprise with estimated sales in the neighborhood of $1 billion per year. After interviewing dozens of current and former Gallo employees, industry experts and competitors, *Fortune* guessed that the privately held company earns at least $50 million a year on such sales. To put this in perspective, consider that in 1985, Seagram had about $350 million in wine sales, but actually went in the red on its best-selling table wines.

The Gallos' company is divided into two segments. Julio is president and presides over the upstream, tending to the grapes, winemaking and product research and development. Chairman Ernest controls marketing, sales and distribution. Curiously, the two have relatively little day-to-day contact. In their neoclassic headquarters on the grounds of the Modesto winery—which local wags call Parthenon West— Julio presides over the first floor. Ernest, in an office decorated with statues of roosters, commands the second story.

The two actually compete between themselves; Julio, it's said, wants to make more wine than his older brother can sell. Ernest wants sales to strain Julio's production capacity. Their two staffs are allegedly prohibited from discussing business. Basically, Julio wants the world to recognize Gallo as a quality winemaker; his brother sees the wine as a means to harvest cold cash. This is synergistic sibling competition at its best, all the best, if you will.

With an agrarian soul, the younger brother enjoys walking the vineyards "with the old-timers." In a jaunty straw hat, linen trousers and wing tip shoes, he looks like a benevolent Central American plantation owner. And yet, while associates say Julio is more easy-going than Ernest, it's only a comparative measure; he is no soft touch, monitoring the amount of fertilizer used on the vineyards, research on grapes and the blending of wine. He enforces high standards and participates in the winery's morning tastings.

No stranger to enological science, Julio pioneered the use of stainless steel tanks for bulk white wines, since redwood and concrete casks can breed bad-tasting bacteria. In the 1960s, he made a then-unheard-of offer to a number of grape growers. In return for a fifteen-year contract, the growers agreed to rip out their vines and replant with better grapes. He's probably hired more Davis graduates than anyone, and set them to experimenting with grape varieties, and it could be argued that in some respects, the Gallo researchers are ahead of the university's faculty. It's because of Julio, for whom the wine is everything.

Ernest thrives on marketing and sales, and he seems to care little about much else. According to former employees, he interrogates more than he talks and is impatient when employees don't come up with answers or information. Says George Frank, who directed Gallo's East Coast sales effort for thirty years before retiring in 1985: "If you try to cover up, he'll expose you." And when Ernest came to visit the distributorships, as is his common practice, "I never knew if he was checking on the marketplace or on me," adds Frank.

Ernest was a magnificent prowler, legendary among Gallo old-timers for the way he'd visit a market area, walk around observing stores and for the way the Gallo displays were positioned. He'd check out bars and even garbage cans, which provided a kind of instant end-use survey of consumption patterns and Gallo's market share, something he encouraged his sales force to do as well. Ernest would stroll into black communities on Saturday nights, to ask folks who were hanging out what kind of wine they liked to drink and what radio stations were playing the gospel and blues, after which he'd know exactly what to advertise, where and when.

Distributors who got rich with Gallo were the types not afraid to venture into mean pool halls and brothels, and stand around on street corners asking people what they drank. Gallo's advance men also gave away Thunderbird on the street, imbibing along with a cluster of future customers, and pretty soon these people would be asking for the 'Bird at bars and liquor stores. Salesmen didn't come much tougher.

From the beginning, Ernest Gallo knew how to find and impress customers. When a Chicago distributor wrote to California's newly licensed wineries following Prohibition, inviting samples, Ernest immediately headed east, and sold the man 6,000 gallons at fifty cents each. He kept going, and didn't stop until he'd completed transactions for E. & J. Gallo Winery's total first-year production, pulling in a profit of $34,000.

Although the Gallos sold their wine in bulk during their first five years of business, they began doing their own bottling in 1938. The company encouraged its distributors to hire separate sales forces to handle only Gallo products. Gallo would sometimes drop distributors who wouldn't go along, saying they couldn't do justice to Gallo by also moving competing brands.

In the mid 1970s, the Federal Trade Commission charged Gallo with unfair competition practices. The brothers signed a consent order that prohibited the company from making distributors reveal their sales figures for all brands, and prevented Gallo from dumping on distributors that wanted to sell wines of other companies. The FTC set the order aside in 1983, after the Gallos made a convincing argument that the wine business had become more competitive, and that the order gave others an edge over Gallo. This allowed the brothers to once again make exclusive arrangements with distribution firms.

The Gallos always seem to have an edge, if only because of Ernest's sixteen-chapter, 300-page sales training manual that details his precepts on the business of selling wine. There are sections and diagrams on how to display Gallo products in stores. For example, the most highly advertised products are placed at eye level, while those that might be impulse purchases are spread across the shelf waist high. According to Ernest, Gallo products should take up exactly seven feet horizontally on each of five shelves, ostensibly the largest expanse that human eyes can scan and focus upon in a retail store.

Salesmen are ordered to place larger size bottles to the right of smaller ones if there is a decided price advantage in buying the bigger volume. (Since Ernest is a master of merchandise display, employees simply don't fool with the formula; it just works.) The book contains tips on retailer behavior and attitudes, noting that "An off-color joke may be great if you're selling pornography, but it's a little difficult to use this opener . . . to sell the retailer on cold-box placement for wine."

And the Gallo sales force is constantly pushing for the best placement. Talk to just about any wine retailer and they'll claim that if you turn your back on a Gallo salesman for a minute, he'll turn your store into an exclusive Gallo outlet. Mick Unti, a beverage merchandising manager for the Safeway supermarket chain, buys a considerable amount of Gallo products, but he is troubled by the company's ethics in the field.

"Up in Washington state we found that by cutting down on Gallo's space and boosting it for other brands, we had a wine sales increase," explains Unti. "We knew this from internal sales figures. But a Gallo team came in and gave us a forty-five-minute presentation with charts and figures and tried to tell us we were wrong. They'll show you reports that say you will lose money on other winery brands. It's a bogus marketing report and they're masters at that."

Unti does appreciate the fact that Gallo offers the same prices to everyone. "That's the most ethical thing they do, and not many others follow it. They don't manufacture different prices for various accounts." It's clear that Gallo, like any large and successful entity, has traits that people love and loathe.

Gallo makes wines for everyone, from jugs to premium varietals. But it has long struggled with an image that it inadvertently forged in the late 1950s, with the introduction of Thunderbird. A radio jingle pushed the stuff: "What's the word? Thunderbird. How's it sold? Good and cold. What's the jive? Bird's alive. What's the price? Thirty twice."

Thunderbird proved incredibly popular. Unfortunately— at least in terms of cachet, but not for cash in the till—it went over best with winos. So did brands like Ripple, "With that ring-a-ding flavor." Following were other market hits, such as Night Train, Boone's Farm, Spanada and Tyrolia, none a tremendous threat to the houses of Bordeaux. The Gallos also stuck with screw caps, correctly believing it better sealed the bottles. Consumers of premium wine, however, perceive this as low-quality cheapness.

Despite the image, Julio began to improve the quality of Gallo's wines. He bought better grapes from the North Coast, and mixed the wine with that from the Central Valley. Gallo's Hearty Burgundy, which has a backbone of Petite Sirah, is a good example of a wine that is consistently solid and has more flavor than similarly priced offerings of competitors. Both Julio and Ernest realized that the average jug wine consumer doesn't detect a great difference between plonk and superior plonk, but the businessman accepted the higher costs incurred by his brother. Keeping Julio's quest aflame was more than worth a slightly reduced profit margin.

According to Unti, the Gallos have fallen, though, with their premium varietals: Chardonnay, Cabernet Sauvignon, Sauvignon Blanc, Gewürztraminer, Johannisberg Riesling and Zinfandel. "I've talked with Gallo people quite a bit, and they could have bought wineries like Beringer, Beaulieu Vineyards and some others, and used the Gallo field force to really build a market for fine wines. They could have assisted tremendously in the growth of varietal consumption. But Ernest is Ernest, and he wanted to do it his way.

"If it weren't for the field force," confides Unti, "I believe their varietal program would be dead. Gallo is the Phi Slamma Jamma of the wine field, and their merchandising makes up for a lot of mistakes. The thing is, Gallo has the potential to be real progressive. But a lot of people think that they're dinosaurs, and their presence is prohibitive to expanding the fine wine business."

Ernest and Julio Gallo inspire fear. Few competitors, current or former employees are willing to talk on the record about them. Some growers, marketers and competitors have good cause to dislike the pair. But nearly everyone in the industry acknowledges that the Gallos have been good for the wine business. They have expanded the wine market in the United States—for everyone.

Neither Ernest nor Julio seem wont to retire. Although between them they have four children, twenty grandchildren and six great-grandchildren, a succession is not yet totally in place. Ernest's sons, David, forty-nine, and Joseph, forty-seven, work with him. They're well educated, with undergrad degrees from Notre Dame, and the younger is a Stanford MBA.

Julio's son Bob, fifty-four, and a son-in-law, Jim Coleman, fifty-two, are conversant with the first-floor business of Parthenon West. While these two have been given some authority, neither of Ernest's children seems ready—or perhaps fully capable, say some observers—to take over.

Most of the top senior Gallo executives are near retirement age themselves. For most of their years, say insiders, they've generally said yes to Ernest's policies, and capably executed them. But there's a leadership vacuum, evident in the fact that Gallo is missing perhaps two generations of its former middle-management. Former Gallo execs litter the upper ranks of other wineries throughout California and the United States. It has been a place to learn well, learn the hard way and move on.

For whatever can be said about Ernest and Julio, they have indeed done the most to popularize wine in America, providing better quality in volume than is found in France or Italy, and at an affordable price. They have served as a U.C. Davis finishing school, training hundreds of crack winemakers. The brothers have trained growers to raise better grapes, and set standards of consistent quality.

They have also, in their eighth decade of life, begun to shed the stigma of screw tops and a wino clientele. *Fortune's* Jaclyn Fierman spotted a cartoon from *The New Yorker*, proudly framed in Ernest's office. It shows a couple drinking wine in a restaurant. "Surprisingly good, isn't it," says the caption. "It's Gallo. Mort and I simply got tired of being snobs."

16

THE BOY FROM LODI

At the Robert Mondavi Winery, they call it The Speech. They've heard it many times, and expect to hear it again. And soon. With only minor variations, Robert Mondavi has been giving The Speech for the past four decades. He gives it to writers, distributors, retailers, restaurateurs and strangers he meets during the course of his daily life. Indeed, he gives it to his own family members. And today, during the 1987 annual family report to winery employees, he gave it again.

Son Michael had already spoken on the financial status of the winery, revealing details on bonuses, raises and an updated retirement plan. Son Tim had talked of the wines themselves, advancements in the cellars and vineyards. Then Bob got up to talk, and at the podium radiated his characteristic energy, an aura which is almost palpable. Short, bandy-legged and muscular, he looked considerably younger than his seventy-three years, a little gimpy in one leg, but otherwise in flagrant good health. The craggy face was tan, and split in an aw-shucks grin that provided a pleasing frame to the looming prow of a nose. His voice was gravelly, the words stentorian, even messianic.

"Let me just say this," he began. "What we need here is complete dedication, complete devotion. That's how we got where we are. If you can't give 110 percent, then you should go somewhere else. We've accomplished tremendous things—but I'll tell you, the future is ten times more exciting than the past." The words took no one by surprise; some employees, in fact, moved their lips as the chairman gave his spiel, like understudies to the lead actor in *King Lear*.

"Our wines now stand with the finest wines in the world," Mondavi continued. "We are on the verge of a golden age of wine and food in this country. We have it all—the soil, climate, the skills, the beef, seafood, the vegetables and of course, the wine . . ." His voice droned on, like moderate surf rolling up on a cobbled beach.

The man is a one-message prophet. But he has pushed his prophecy so long and so hard that it's become self-fulfilling. He had a dream, and dreamed it with such vigor that it became reality. It was essentially self-centered, but the wine industry is better off because of it.

Bob Mondavi is an anomaly in this business, no less than the Gallos. The Robert Mondavi Winery is a large winery which produces wines equivalent to the finest boutiques. A vinous oxymoron, this house produces more than two million cases of premium varietals annually, some of which retails for $40 a bottle. Visitors to Mondavi's Napa Valley facility are often surprised to see the legions of stainless steel fermenters in the building behind the stucco archway and Spanish-style tower. They'd be even more bemused by the gigantic sister facility in the Sacramento Delta town of Lodi, a winery that looks more like a mid-size petroleum refinery.

Thus, Mondavi effectively negates the industry adage that you can make good wine or a lot of wine, but you can't do both. Mondavi's premium red and white jug table wines compete with Gallo's, siphoning consumers up to a higher level of quality. His ultra-premium varietals go head-to-head on restaurant wine lists with the Chalones and Laurel Glens. He does both.

Mondavi has often been described as a genius. If force of will, intuition and an almost preternatural marketing sense are definitions of the term, then he is certainly a genius of the first water. He is the eldest son of Cesare and Rosa Mondavi, two Italian immigrants from the impoverished, mountainous Marche region northeast of Rome. The Mondavis settled in the Iron Range of Minnesota, where Bob was born.

Cesare operated a saloon and a modest hotel in the mining town of Virginia; the quintessential shrewd Italian peasant, it didn't take him long to figure there was more money in purveying goods and services than in grubbing for ore. To supplement his income, he imported grapes by freight car from the Lodi region of California, which he sold to fellow émigrés for their home winemaking ventures. Even in the New World and in the midst of Prohibition, no Italian could conceive of life without vats and carboys of wine in the cellar. Moreover, it also became apparent to Cesare that there was even more money in shipping fruit than in running a hostelry, so he moved the family to Lodi in 1923.

By 1936, Cesare had become the president of a winery in the town of Acampo near Lodi, and secured a partnership in the Sunny St. Helena Winery in the Napa Valley. In the same year, Robert graduated from Stanford University with a degree in economics. He originally planned to pursue a graduate degree, perhaps a doctorate, but Cesare wanted Robert back at his side and convinced the young man to return to the family wine business.

Robert went to work at Sunny St. Helena as a cellarman and wine chemist. His father did not believe in overstaffing; all the work there was done by Cesare, Robert, brother Pete and two hired hands. Among them, they made 500,000 gallons of wine annually. Bob turned every task, no matter how small or mundane, into a competition. He couldn't help it; he'd always been that way.

Bob threw himself into the family business with gusto. It

was his early—and unorthodox—contention that the Napa Valley was as capable of producing super-premium wines as Bordeaux and Burgundy. Most people didn't share his opinion, and those who did still weren't inclined to care one way or another. People made decent money selling bulk product. The upgrading of skills, knowledge, equipment and vineyards necessary for the production of supreme varietal wines was a concept that most of the valley's vintners found unappealing.

Mondavi, however, knew of the monomania that had marked the efforts of the early settlers; the wines of Captain Niebaum, Charles Krug and Count Haraszthy, which were celebrated on both coasts. Post-Prohibition vintners weren't interested in taking up the old standard, but Bob Mondavi agitated for bucking the trend, sometimes to his father's great irritation. Cesare was conservative in all things, especially money. "Leverage" was as foreign to him as Amazons from the moon. Still, Bob proved influential enough to convince his dad to purchase the old Charles Krug winery when it was put on the block in 1943. The winery was large, and it was surrounded by a hundred acres of degradated vineyard which Bob planned to replant.

And replant it he did, with superior clones of Chardonnay, Cabernet Sauvignon, Pinot Noir, Johannisberg Riesling and Sauvignon Blanc. He refined Krug's viticultural techniques and upgraded equipment. Through the 1940s and 1950s, Mondavi traveled Europe, learning as much as he could about winemaking. He began marketing an exclusive line of premium Charles Krug wines, bottled and distributed separately from the winery's generic line. He hosted public tastings, and initiated innovative vinification techniques such as cold fermentation and oak aging. He took a slow-selling wine called White Pinot, cold-fermented the grape and sold it as Chenin Blanc, the sobriquet it goes by in France. The product took off like gangbusters.

Despite the success at Krug, things weren't going swimmingly in the family arena. Bob's younger brother, Peter—known in the family as Babe—had gone off to war in the 1940s, while Bob stayed home to tend the business. When Peter returned, he wanted a major say in the way things were run. Tensions between the two brothers increased throughout the 1950s, beyond Cesare's death, and finally culminated in a 1965 fistfight. Rosa, who held the majority of stock in the business, relieved Bob of his duties. He eventually sued his family for breach of contract, won a ruling that left him with more than $500,000, and opened his own winery fifteen miles down the Valley in Oakville. Winning the suit enabled him to buy out his creditors and aggressively attack the field that had always best suited him—marketing and public relations.

Robert Mondavi does not advertise. But he does spend millions for his public relations program, which works on a variety of levels, all exceedingly well funded. Robert Mondavi is also good copy, candid to the point of ingenuousness, and as charismatic as Billy Sunday. And he loves publicity. Mondavi is comfortable with writers and the camera. Unlike many CEOs, he doesn't need to be prodded by his PR people; he merely needs to be aimed.

Even Mondavi's sales force contributes to the public relations program. The winery maintains over forty sales and distributor reps across the nation, as well as a staff quartered in London for the European market. A sales staff for the Pacific Rim is planned. In all, Mondavi wines are sold in more than twenty nations besides the U.S., and wherever they go, the sales force moves wine and rainbows with a Mondaviesque twist. They spend more time, for instance, hosting comparative tastings of Mondavi wines against European top growths than twisting arms of recalcitrant distributors. They are instructed to "present" the wines, not push them.

The World According to Mondavi is a perfect place in which there is no sin save the Sin of Not Living Graciously. It's a world peopled entirely by willowy women and courtly men, a world that's pruned, cultivated and spotless, a kind of adult Disneyland; a world, in short, where all come to pay obeisance to wine, a substance which Bob characterizes as "that most moderate and civilized of beverages."

Where the Gallos' personal style is low-key and no-frills, the Mondavi style could be best described as Lucullan, with Bob as the Roman general and his family the most privileged

Centurions. Michael and Tim also live on the family's Oak Knoll ranch, a 600-acre tract of vineyard and riparian woodland in the southeast Napa Valley near the Stag's Leap area (daughter Marcia lives in Manhattan), but Bob's house sits on the highest promontory. The boys' homes are on knolls with arresting views of the Valley, but still well below their father's aerie.

Designed by Cliff May—who also did the Oakville winery—and completed in 1985, the house is an architectural marvel, stylistically based on California's Spanish missions. At the apex of Oak Knoll, it commands a 360-degree view of the entire Napa Valley, from Napa in the south to St. Helena in the north. It is huge, sprawling over 10,000 square feet of hilltop. Yet it has only one bedroom and a small dining room. (Nearby, however, is a guest cottage.) Mondavi likes to dine with small, intimate gatherings here; larger soirées are accommodated at the winery. As might be expected, the house has a large kitchen and spacious wine cellar. There's also a tower accessible by a spiral stone staircase.

Most of the home is taken up by a vast central room that occupies two levels. The upper story is a large lounging area, while the lower features a Romanesque pool with a rolling skylight above it. The pool is right outside the bedroom Mondavi and his second wife, Margrit Biever, share. He's in a habit of climbing directly out of bed and into the pool for a few laps before breakfast.

Mondavi has always believed that he is selling a lifestyle, or even a philosophy of life, rather than a product. In this he holds an unwavering enthusiasm and sincerity, and when seeking employees, he endeavors to find people similarly inclined. Mere competence—or even genuine talent—is not enough. He ain't kidding when he says he expects "total dedication." Like himself, he expects his people to exist for wine.

Mondavi employees use the same vocabulary as he, and what they're selling is Robert Mondavi, not Cabernet Sauvignon and Fumé Blanc. It's not surprising then that entrepreneurial or creative sorts don't usually fare well at Mondavi. They need too much latitude, too much autonomy. Mondavi is always somewhat susceptible to sycophants, since he genuinely likes to be liked. Thus, a certain amount of deadwood has cropped up at the winery, mere courtiers. But he has also attracted a superb corps of worker ants, gifted employees who are dedicated and make the winery—and Bob Mondavi—the focal point of their lives.

The winery has a rigidly vertical management style. Mondavi's children are in the business on the executive level, and termed "general partners." Michael oversees sales and marketing strategy, Tim handles production, and Marcia sales implementation on the East Coast. But it is Chairman Bob who has the last word on any decision.

He's a details man, as apt to tend floral arrangements in the Vineyard Room hospitality suite and settle personality conflicts between administrative assistants as study the winery's operating budget. He eats the food prepared in the Vineyard Room, smells the roses in the garden and is always prowling around the winery, watching, prodding, exhorting, sniffing and tasting. He's like a racehorse owner who insists on currying and training his own animals. Mondavi is not comfortable with delegating authority.

This has led some industry pundits to wonder about the winery's direction when Bob is no longer alive. Though in his mid-seventies, he still evinces the energy of a man twenty years younger, thrives on four hours of sleep a night and still spends half his time hobnobbing at wine functions around the world. But the day must come, and Mondavi does not want to see a Krug redux; he wants the winery to carry on intact with all his children in accord.

Either Michael or Tim is sure to succeed Bob after his death. Though they share common bonds of family affection and fealty, each is strong-willed. Each would like the job of running the winery. Like his father, Michael is extroverted, fond of public speaking, gala events and the marketing and public relations end of the business. Tim, on the other hand, is spare and diffident. Where Michael favors a trim moustache, $60 haircuts and tailored clothing, Tim wears a beard and modest apparel, which makes him look vaguely like a Mennonite. Tim detests public events, and is wont to spend all his time in the cellars and vineyards.

These are two men with very different areas of expertise, not unlike Ernest and Julio Gallo. Their skills would prove complementary should they maintain their partnership after their father sloughs off the mortal coil. Of course, each would probably prosper if they chose to separate as did their father and uncle. But the pie would be split by more than half, given that a lot would go to lawyers and sister Marcia. In any event, each would have to hire someone with the same talents as the other brother. For the time being, though, the brothers continue to work in their own spheres, under the aegis and, at times, pointed directions of their father.

Mondavi has shown a remarkable propensity for taking great risks over the years, and dragging along others in joint ventures. The most famous is a wine called Opus One. A Napa Valley Cabernet Sauvignon produced in conjunction with Château Mouton Rothschild, the first releases—of the 1979 and 1980 vintages—came out with as much hoopla as the unraveling of the Dead Sea scrolls. The wine met with almost as many accolades, the $50-per-bottle price tag notwithstanding.

Currently made at Mondavi's Oakville Winery, a separate facility for the project is on the drawing boards. Demand for the product has slowed, perhaps in resistance to the price, increased production and the fact that the novelty has worn off. But the venture is still an extremely profitable item for Mondavi and his Gallic partners.

The same cannot be said for Vichon, a winery Mondavi acquired in 1985. Purchased from a partnership, it had a reputation for complex, concentrated—if somewhat ponderous—wines. They were distinctive, but not marketed effectively and consequently languished on the shelves. The Mondavis figured that their army of sales reps and PR men could turn the tide in short order. The flood of increased sales, however, didn't materialize.

Even Robert Mondavi couldn't change public perception of the heavy and tannic wines—when they were perceived at all. He appointed Tim Mondavi as president of Vichon, and the son hired a talented winemaker named Mike Weiss to give the line an enological face-lift. Draconian price cuts were needed to reduce the Vichon inventory, and some of the efforts are paying off, although it is taking several years longer than Mondavi anticipated.

The size of the entire Mondavi operation—it employs more than 450 people full-time, and many more during harvests—is creating some difficulties. Although Mondavi exhorts his employees to "communicate," and insists "I don't want any walls between departments," walls are inevitable in an institution of this magnitude. Decision-making, moreover, becomes a more laborious and circuitous process. The winery doesn't move as fast as it once did, can or should.

One project which Mondavi has failed to turn into a coup is The Mission. The idea has existed, inchoate, in his mind for a long time. Basically, he feels that wine—along with art, architecture, medicine and basic agriculture—forms one of the cornerstones of civilization. "When Noah stepped out of the Ark after the flood, the first thing he did was plant vines," he is fond of noting in The Speech. "Wine has been praised by poets, artists and philosophers through the millennia."

Angered at the meddling ways of "neoprohibitionists," Mondavi decided to launch a campaign of his own—The Mission. His idea was to infuse the concept of wine as a "civilizing beverage of health and moderation" into the American psyche. Echoing this Jeffersonian viewpoint, Mondavi has wanted to sponsor panel presentations by experts around the country, panels composed of learned physicians, celebrated artists, and revered men and women of letters. To date the response has been underwhelming, falling somewhere between "Huh?" and "So, who cares?" Undaunted by the program's foundering, Bob Mondavi presses on with it, although many of his subordinate executives no doubt wish he would abandon his battle with this windmill as quickly and quietly as possible.

Still, Mondavi retains much of his old Midas touch. A recent program that displayed this gift was the winery's futures program. True, Bob Mondavi was not the first vintner to offer futures on his Cabernet Sauvignon. Caymus, Diamond Creek and several other top boutiques have been at it for a while. But no one of any size has taken the plunge. Mondavi smelled a buck in the idea, and followed his proboscis.

He offered his 1985 and 1986 Reserve Cabernets on a futures basis in 1987. The price worked out to between $17 and $25 retail—for wines that would likely sell for $35 to $40 on release. The response was immediate and enthusiastic, despite the fact that the 1982 Mondavi Reserve was on sale at discount retail outlets in California for around $17 on the day the futures program went into effect, a point that a few wine and business writers acidly noted.

"In my heart, I know we belong with the great wines of the world," Mondavi exclaimed at a San Francisco luncheon that kicked off the program. Plenty of wine lovers agreed with those tender sentiments. The wines were sold on allocation, and the offered lot of 7,000 cases was snapped up. The program is providing welcomed cash for the winery, a fact that no doubt keeps smiles on the faces of Mondavi's anonymous, hard-working beancounters.

Money from the futures program is needed because parsimony has never been Bob Mondavi's style. He's no good at tightening his belt. Moreover, he enjoys the fact that his enology staff spends several thousand dollars a month on first-growth European wines to taste against their own blends. He likes the floral arrangements in the winery, as well as spending money in the course of business.

Although the wine market is generally sluggish, the high premium end on which Mondavi mostly concentrates is more than holding its own. Still, Mondavi, more than any other American winegrower, is trying to make the world his dominion. He has spent hundreds of thousands of dollars on promotional programs and tours abroad. He publishes glossy promotional brochures in Japanese, French, German, Italian, Chinese and, detail kind of guy he is, "British" English.

There are many in the wine industry who have found his ceaseless promotion of himself and his winery tedious. But even critics will admit that no one has contributed so much to the upgrading of Napa Valley wine and the promotion of the area as a world-class viticultural region. He has never doubted that his wines belong to the world.

Moreover, rain forests may be disappearing, AIDS may be wreaking social havoc, a depleted ozone layer may allow ultraviolet rays to fry humanity, and the global economy may be jouncing around like an autistic kangaroo—but according to Bob Mondavi, the Philosophy of Gracious Living, marked by the consumption of fine wine, will inexorably continue to gain converts. That's his gospel and the sum and substance of The Speech. And he'll keep giving it to anyone and everyone who will listen.

Section Five

CONFLICTING OPINIONS

17
FAMILY FEUDS

Bug-eyed with rage, Bob Mondavi had his brother down and in the dirt, his hands locked around Peter's throat. "I warned you not to call me a thief," he roared at the younger sibling. "I warned you . . ." The two men, both in their fifties, rolled in the dust like a pair of kids, punching and cursing one another.

Finally back on their feet, Robert stepped away, quivering from adrenaline overload, while Peter rubbed the welts on his neck. They stared balefully at one another, knowing that something between them had been irrevocably shattered. It was 1965, and the long-simmering animosity between the brothers finally burst into open hostility. The brawl served as the Pearl Harbor of the Great Mondavi Family Feud. The real war, however, was yet to come.

Blood and money can make for a volatile brew in any industry, and the wine business is no different. Trouble in a family enterprise usually begins when the founder is incapacitated or dies, and rival siblings vie for control, cash or both. Divorce has also threatened to split wineries asunder.

The long-running CBS television program *Falcon Crest* has come to epitomize family feuding in the wine business; at least in the perceptions of the TV-viewing public. But as with most soap operas, reality is stretched as thin as a molecular chain of tannins.

There have been some whopper feuds, though. Considering his personality, it figures that Bob Mondavi's would be an epic.

The punch-out with Peter started when the younger brother asserted that Robert's extravagant marketing programs constituted a theft of the family's financial resources. Bob took it personally, and proceeded to take it out on Peter's throat. But the boys had been at each other's larynxes for years, especially since Peter returned from the service after World War II.

The conflict manifested its first flashpoint shortly after Pete's 1946 return, when Bob cornered a huge inventory of wine grapes. Peter was chary of the move. But Father Cesare agreed with Robert's assertion that the deal represented enormous profit potential. It was one of the few times in his life that the old man made a truly bad business decision.

Wine was in short supply at the time Bob cut the deal with a number of Eastern wine distributors. The price for bulk wine was high, nearly $1.50 a gallon. However, a number of other winemakers had been working overtime to produce the plonk to meet anticipated demand. By the time the delivery came due, the market was flooded, and the price of bulk wine plummeted. Those distributors that Bob had so assiduously cultivated blithely broke their contracts, and Krug was stuck with a loss, an astounding $370,000. Cesare was forced to borrow heavily to keep the winery afloat. An operation which had functioned in the black almost from its start suddenly found itself awash in red ink.

When Cesare died in 1959, the leadership of Krug fell to his wife, Rosa, who held 60 percent of the company's stock. Robert and Peter each held 12 percent, while Mondavi sisters Helen and Mary owned 8 percent apiece. The strong-willed Cesare had always been able to keep the boys in line, but Rosa was not so adept. Her expertise lay in the kitchen.

The physical altercation between Bob and Pete deeply

disturbed Rosa. Though she loved both her sons, she usually sided with Peter in his disputes with Robert. The sight of bruises around her younger son's throat compelled her to take action. She called together Peter, Helen and Mary; decisions were made, and Bob was informed of them through a family friend. He was, Rosa had concluded, to take a six-month "leave of absence." The action stupefied the hard-charging executive and he felt betrayed, doubly so when he learned that Rosa had told Bob's son Michael that there would be no place for him at Krug when he graduated from college the following year.

That did it for Robert. If the family didn't want him, he didn't want the family. He would open his own winery with Michael in Oakville. Fred Holmes and Ivan Schoch put up $100,000 in seed money, and Bob crushed his first grapes in 1966, at a crusher that wasn't even covered by a roof. He was fifty-four.

But Mondavi still had financial interests in Krug. He still retained his stock, and remained a director of C. Mondavi and Sons, the partnership established by his father in 1943. Sales were brisk there; more than $7 million in 1970. And Bob needed more money to expand his new winery—lots more.

Meanwhile, back at Krug, the family had discovered that the partnership could be manipulated to avoid double taxation on share dividends. That is, all profits on wine sales could go directly to the members of the partnership without being subject to corporate taxation. This arrangement suited Robert just fine, since he needed the large infusions of cash. But he was then outmaneuvered by Peter, who set up a partnership that reduced Bob's status in the organization. Under the new corporate structure, Robert was limited to the position of limited partner, which left him with a much smaller percentage of the company's shares—and profits.

Once again, that did it for Bob. He sued all of his family in 1965, save for sister Helen, who joined him in the legal action. Bob aimed at the sale and dissolution of Charles Krug. His mother, Peter and Mary countersued. The trial changed the acrimony between the brothers from a private affair into a public spectacle; it lasted for 103 days.

When the dust of this one settled, presiding judge Robert Carter saw things Robert's way. Carter ruled that Rosa had conspired to undermine Krug's profits with Peter's collusion; the object was the transference of shares to Peter's children without the incurrence of heavy gift taxes, since the rate of tax depended greatly on the winery's profits. Rosa and Peter had devalued company stock by buying and then selling wine to Krug at exorbitant prices, and paying equally inflated prices for grapes the company purchased. Thus, the family was acting as the corporation's own middlemen. Though the value of Krug went down, the new partnership's profits went up. Rosa was able to pass on shares to her grandchildren without paying onerous gift taxes.

Judge Carter said that this was a fraudulent fiscal device, and that it deprived Robert of his rightful share of the company and its profits. He also dismissed two of Peter's contentions; namely, that Robert was only interested in acquiring Krug stock to sell for his own pocket, and that he was trying to finagle a slippery deal that would enable the company that had become his chief partner—Rainier Brewing—to take over Krug. Instead, Carter maintained that Rosa, Peter and Mary had concealed an offer from the Schlitz brewing interests, tendered at $32 million for Krug. The upshot of this messy business is that Carter finally ruled that Robert was entitled to $538,885.

Rosa Mondavi died in 1976, before the final disposition of the case; a blessing, many in the Napa Valley thought. She was eighty-six, and the court proceedings had devastated her. Rosa was never cut out for such corporate hardball. She was an uneducated peasant woman whose universe revolved around the kitchen and the family members who ate there. She was used to feeding people, not fighting them. The lawsuits made her last years miserable. Both sons felt considerable remorse and guilt over the pain they'd caused their mother, but both viewed it as a necessary, though tragic ancillary. The animus they had for each other preordained it.

Although the two couldn't stand the sight of each other,

their children remained friendly. Michael and Tim continued to hunt and fish with Peter's sons, Pete Jr. and Marc. The bonds that had been so bitterly severed by one generation held together with the next. And then, in the spring of 1985, a seemingly impossible thing happened. Peter and Robert sat together at the same table, broke bread and drank wine. The occasion was a retrospective tasting of Krug and Mondavi wines. Proceeds from the affair went to a scholarship fund for the U.C. Davis enology program.

People at the event were incredulous and the tension in the air palpable. Bob and Peter sat stiffly through the first part of the tasting, exchanging nothing more than polite observations. As the affair progressed, their conversation became more animated. And when the last wine had been evaluated by Michael Broadbent, they were talking and laughing together like most brothers are wont to do. Finally, Bob and Peter stood up, took each other's measure and shook hands. Then they hugged spontaneously. The room burst into cheers and applause.

Not surprisingly, however, the men are still not exemplars of familial warmth. They don't spend Sundays chowing down on their mother's old recipes, reminiscing about old times and old wines. The relationship is marked more by politeness and restrained good will; they act more Norwegian toward each other than the Italians that they are. But they visit each other's wineries now and then, and talk. They have only good things—though vague—to say about each other in the press. Fifteen years ago, nobody would have thought such a limited rapprochement possible—least of all Peter and Robert Mondavi.

Maybe Don and Sam Sebastiani will attend a tasting together sometime in the year 2005. Then again, maybe not. But in many ways, their feud seems like a reprise of the Mondavi imbroglio. Indeed, here we have two brothers who intensely dislike each other—perhaps even more so than Peter and Robert disliked each other. In fact, Sam and Don Sebastiani are as different as two brothers can be. And here, as with the Mondavis, we have a mother who holds most of the corporation stock and favors the younger brother above the elder. There is a difference in the two stories, but it isn't in the way the piece is set; it's in the outcome.

Sam Sebastiani vividly remembers when the boom fell. It was in a meeting with Don, Sam, and Sam's wife, Vicki, on the second day of January, 1986. As president of the winery, Sam had agreed to the meeting because he thought that his brother was a proxy representative of his mother, there to handle negotiations on a long-term employment contract for Sam. But Sam didn't get the contract. Instead, Don blandly informed him that he had been relieved of the presidency, and no longer worked at the Sebastiani winery. Vicki, who'd handled winery promotions, also got the sack. Furthermore, Sam was told that if he contested the action or attempted to hinder it in any way, he'd lose everything.

Initially stunned into silence, Sam finally realized he was getting whacked, and in his own home to boot. "Get the hell out of here!" he screamed at his dapper, slick-haired, younger brother. He then threatened to smack Don in the chops.

Don did as he was told, gathering up his papers and scurrying out of the meeting. He didn't want to engage Sam in anything that amounted to a physical confrontation. That wasn't Don's style. Besides, the tall, muscular elder Sebastiani would have made mincemeat of Don, who wears wire-rimmed glasses, smokes a pipe and is the antithesis of a tough guy.

The breach had been a long time coming. Sam's relationship with Don could be characterized, at its most charitable, as rocky. Sam was twelve years older, and their lifestyles and life philosophies were as different as fried catfish and nigiri sushi. Sam was cast in the old Sonoma mold; agrarian by inclination, disposed to rural pleasures and homespun ways, in spite of an M.B.A. from Santa Clara University. He liked to wear blue jeans, scuffed cowboy boots and rodeo belt buckles as big as Frisbees. Even when the demands of the winegrower profession forced him to dress up, he favored Western-cut suits and bolo ties.

Young Don, on the other hand, had a taste for three-piece suits, polo shirts, Guccis and power neckties. The only cowhide one was liable to find near Don was the makings of his briefcase. He'd made a name for himself by his late twenties as one of the most conservative and provocative members of the California State Assembly. He discovered early in his political career that he could get a great deal of print and air time if he said things that were so outrageous that they bordered on the lunatic.

It was Don Sebastiani who made the AP and UPI wires hum when he suggested that women astronauts should be given one-way tickets to space. Predictably, this got feminists in a lather, and they immediately called for a boycott of Sebastiani wine and threw up a picket line at the winery. This was particularly ironic because Don had nothing to do with the winery at the time, save for his name, and Sam's politics were so distinctly mainstream that they seemed positively quaint.

Another stunt of Don's was his 1983 reapportionment campaign, which aimed to push the state's Democratic legislators out of the Assembly and Senate and into the Pacific Ocean. California's Demos began sharpening their long knives and howling for Don's head. So much pressure rained down upon Sebastiani Vineyards that Sam telegrammed his brother, informing the young renegade that he would do everything possible to see him whipped like a dog in the 1984 elections, if not like Walter Mondale.

Sebastiani Vineyards got an inauspicious start in 1904. In that year, Samuele Sebastiani, an immigrant from Farneta, Italy, made some wine from money he'd scraped together, loaded it into a tank on a wagon, and sold it door-to-door around San Francisco. He earned enough to make even more wine the following year, and before long was really prospering. He invested in real estate, including a large cannery and other property near Sonoma. By the time of his death in 1944, Samuele's family was established as preeminent in Sonoma's business and social circles.

Son August took over after the founder died, and he demonstrated even more fiscal and marketing acumen than Samuele. Sam Sebastiani has observed dryly that "my father had pretty good business sense. He knew how to sell wine." That, in fact, is putting it mildly. August adopted a plot common among savvy country folks. Though he had a mind like a No. 2 Victor steel-jawed animal trap, he enjoyed playing the rube. He favored bib overalls for his daily wear. What a lot of people didn't realize was they were custom-tailored. He launched advertising and public relations campaigns that portrayed him as a gentle, avuncular man of the soil; and indeed, he did have his gentle side, especially when it came to the care and propagation of his collection of rare waterfowl. But he was also a hard-as-nails businessman.

Sebastiani was the first vintner to put varietal wines in jugs, and he knew how to bully everybody from growers to distributors. The consumer may have thought of August Sebastiani as a Little Old Winemaker in Bib Overalls, but people in the business knew him as one tough cookie. Under his direction, Sebastiani Vineyards became one of the ten largest wineries in California, with sales topping three million cases.

August married a local girl, Sylvia Scarafoni, in 1935. They had three children over a period of twelve years: Sam, Mary Ann, and the youngest, Don. August never really groomed Sam as his protégé; rather, he badgered him to the point where it was impossible to think of anyone else taking the job. Sam, in short, paid his dues under an imperious father.

By the late 1970s, August had a case of cancer that was to prove terminal, and he knew it. Impending death had mellowed the old man somewhat, and he handed the reins to Sam gracefully and faced his demise with dignity and courage. Sam ran the show during August's long and painful decline, and ran it well. The end came on February 16, 1980. One of August's last pieces of advice to his eldest son was to make wines "that will make Sonoma proud."

If there were any uncertainties that Sam would take his father's words to heart, they were quickly dispelled as soon as he knew the helm was unequivocally his. Sam was determined to change the direction of the winery by 180 degrees. Under August, the company had become known as a large producer of serviceable, if essentially mediocre, wines. Good-selling wine, but not great wine. Sam felt the future belonged to premium dry varietals.

He not only believed that virtually all of the low end of

the market was headed down the hungry maw of the Gallos and a few foreign producers; Sam also wanted to make fine wines. But the commitment took money, and lots of it. Sam invested heavily in new oak barrels and fermentation equipment. A new waste disposal system was installed, as was an upgraded executive tasting room and wine library.

Millions were spent on advertising and public relations. In this latter regard, Sam seemed to display particular flair, with Vicki making all the arrangements. They specialized in lavish barbecues at their Eagle Ridge Ranch. All the industry's movers and shakers and press bigwigs were invited to these events, which proved very effective in getting Sam print. They also cost a mint. One such blowout set the winery back around $60,000.

Naturally such heavy investments in equipment and promotion shaved company profits. The company lost $250,000 in 1982, a fact that horrified Sylvia. It was the first time the winery had ever posted a loss; she had even more room for despair in 1983 and 1984, when Sebastiani Vineyards ran up $1.2 million and $1.7 million, respectively, in red ink. Things got a little better in 1985, if one could call it that, when it lost only half a million. Still, the Bank of America had heaved Sebastiani into the bad loan department, which convinced Sylvia that the winery was on a downward slide to perdition. Sam steadfastly maintained that the bottom line had to suffer if Sebastiani Vineyards was to tool up sufficiently to become a major player in the premium wine game.

Sylvia, however, was also unhappy with Vicki, Sam's second wife, a former real estate agent he met the same year August was diagnosed with cancer. Sylvia had formerly headed up the company's food and wine promotion program, and compiled a cookbook that had become a modest best-seller. Sam married Vicki in an impromptu ceremony in January of 1980 and told his mother about it only afterwards. And after August died, Vicki's star at the winery ascended while Sylvia's waned. Although she owned 95 percent of the company, the older woman felt left out, that Sam and his bride were pushing her to the sidelines.

She was also distressed by Sam's attitude toward Don. All

these things—the company's lackluster performance, the hemorrhaging of capital, Vicki's growing role, and the conflict between the brothers—convinced Sylvia that she had to reassert herself. It had become a matter of honor, not only a mere business decision.

And yet, Sam didn't have the slightest inkling of what was in his mother's mind. In fact, he was ebullient in November of 1985. The aortic pumping of red ink had slowed to a trickle; the years of massive capital outlay for production and promotion were beginning to pay off. Best of all, the company's beancounters figured that 1986 would bring nearly $2.5 million in profits. To Sam, things were looking awfully damn good.

Sylvia, however, called for a meeting with her elder son. Sam figured she'd come to praise him. Mom was already thinking of ways to bury him, organizationally speaking. Right in front of Sam's staff she lashed out at her son and his treatment of Don, who had temporarily bowed out of politics in 1984 and was planning a new wine venture that included the Sebastiani name. Sam had sent Don another message, warning that such use could jeopardize the old operation.

The Sebastiani president was stunned that his mother would humiliate him in such a forum. He aborted the meeting and stormed out fuming, with Sylvia hounding at his heels, continuing her attack, claiming that she'd do something "drastic" if he didn't start treating his little brother with kid gloves. Still upset, Sam arranged a meeting with Don at a Sonoma restaurant to thrash out their differences man-to-man. He laid out his views, once more, on Don's politics and new business plan. He threatened to quit Sebastiani Vineyards if Don continued in the wine business.

Finally, they got around to discussing the possible sale of the winery. Sam, under the circumstances, was for it, and left the meeting thinking that Don was in agreement on the benefits of such a step. But in an interview with Jim Wood for a *California* magazine article, Don claimed that he was nodding his head as an acknowledgment of Sam's statement, not as an acquiescence to his proposals.

Sam should have known that an agreement concluded by

a nodded head, to paraphrase the Sam Goldwyn rule, isn't worth the paper it's written on. But he felt that his younger brother had indeed agreed that he would remain as president until the company was sold; he also assumed that Don had agreed to discuss the situation with Sylvia. Since nothing came about, Sam went to his mother himself, and once more said he thought it best that he quit. Sylvia assured him that such a move wasn't necessary.

Still, Sam continued feeling insecure, and so requested an employment contract from his mother. She must have nodded, because Sam thought she was favorably disposed. Only later, after getting axed by Don, did he learn otherwise. He didn't even get a chance to quit for real, and the firing seemed calculated to humiliate him publicly. Indeed, within weeks of the dismissal, Don was telling *The Wine Spectator* that Sam's management of the winery was "weak, very poor, horrendous." Don said the firing was a business decision, claimed he wanted to demur on specifics, and then talked of excessive personal and corporate expenditures by Sam and Vicki. Don also added, "I don't want to see his [Sam's] talents wasted. He's a very intelligent guy." The younger brother's political skills were showing; Sam was damned, and then given faint praise. The words seemed designed more to make Don look like a generous and gracious spirit than to bind Sam's wounds.

Devastated by his dismissal, Sam Sebastiani didn't languish about. He immediately plowed everything he had into a new winemaking venture, which he initially called Sam J. Sebastiani Vineyards. And he concentrated on what he'd learned to do best: the painstaking production of a limited number of excellent wines.

In early 1988, he decided to change the name of his venture, since he found there was considerable confusion about the brand. Consumers and tradespeople alike were mentally mixing it up with the wines of Sebastiani Vineyards, despite all the publicity over the Cain and Abel parting. Sam didn't want this to happen—and Don probably wasn't happy about it either—and so he renamed his venture Viansa and completely redesigned his packaging. Sebastiani also bought property outside of Sonoma that will ultimately be used for his new winery and vineyards. Viansa is meeting with enthusiasm in the marketplace, the sweetest revenge.

Both brothers have made their own way, but nothing seems able to assuage the acrimony and bitterness that's come between them. As with the Mondavis, the Sebastianis constitute a house divided. There doesn't even seem to be the faintest glimmer of reconciliation. Sam is a cowboy, and Don is a supply-side yuppie. Even if they didn't dislike each other so completely, the only thing they have in common is their surname.

Personalities, conflicting visions, different philosophies of winemaking and wine marketing all contributed to the Mondavi and Sebastiani feuds. With the Heck family and the Korbel winery, cash was always the thing. Money was the one and only issue from the first round, along with the question of who was going to get it.

Korbel is a venerable industry institution, founded in the nineteenth century by a group of Bohemians. With its stone edifice on the banks of the Russian River, this winery soon became known as a producer of excellent wines. Fortunes for Korbel was up-and-down throughout the century, however, and the management sold out to Adolf Heck and his family in 1953. Prices quoted for the purchase ranged from a low of $400,000, according to Gary Heck, Adolf's son, to the $700,000 that was quoted by local newspapers of the day.

Adolf Heck was a master vintner who was the third in a generation of family winemakers. He served a lengthy apprenticeship at Europe's most prestigious wine academy, the Geisenheim Wine Institute, and his specialty was champagne. At Korbel, Heck established himself as one of America's most technically proficient winemakers, and his champagnes were the standard by which other domestics were measured throughout the 1960s and 1970s. He also made excellent brandy.

Heck was responsible for one of the most significant innovations in the modern wine industry: the automatic riddling rack. Riddling is a process necessary for the production of fine champagne, and involves turning the bottles daily in a special rack over a period of several months during the secondary fermentation. This gradually forces the dead yeast to the neck of the bottle, where it may be disgorged prior to corking. It is an extremely boring, laborious and time-consuming process, long the scourge of sparkling-winemakers around the globe.

"I had hand-riddled bottles for three hours a day for seven years in dark, wet cellars," Heck was quoted as saying. "I only had candles for light. I knew there had to be a better way." There was, and it took Heck to envision it. The automatic riddling rack uses a special rack and a forklift to accomplish in a few minutes what once took hours or days. For that alone, Adolf Heck will long be remembered in the wine industry.

Unfortunately, he'll also be remembered for the spirited legal fights which his death precipitated. And even before his death, Heck faced legal action from his brother Paul. In 1978, Paul filed suit against Adolf, claimed he'd been cheated of his rightful share of Korbel's assets. Paul died before the final disposition of the case, but he would have taken little comfort in it had he lived.

Adolf had made substantial and numerous loans to his brother, and the collateral offered was Paul's stock in Korbel. Paul frittered the money away in ill-begotten business deals, the judge ruled, and the final increment of money he'd received from Adolf was in fact a sale of stock, not another loan. The court found that Paul had no one but himself to blame for his financial state. Adolf was absolved of all responsibility.

Paul's widow, Anne Marie, was not happy with the ruling. In 1984, she filed suit for $6.5 million against Adolf. Ben, Adolf's older brother, was a co-plaintiff. They claimed that Adolf had "squandered" the assets of the family partnership. The case remains tied up in court, with no resolution seen in the near future.

Adolf died in 1984, however, at the age of sixty-eight. And it was his departure that really started the imbroglio royale. Adolf had a wife, Richie, the mother of his son, Gary, who currently runs the winery. But he hadn't lived with her for more than twenty years. They were separated but never divorced; and for those two decades, Adolf had cohabited with a woman named Veronica Ann Miramontez. Adolf's will left Richie his share of Korbel. To Veronica, he left a $50,000 life insurance policy, seventy acres of vineyard, and his interest in Santa Nella Winery, a property adjacent to the Korbel holdings.

That wasn't enough for Ms. Miramontez. She hired famed "palimony" attorney Marvin Mitchelson and filed a $40 million suit against the Heck estate, claiming that it was worth between $80 million and $100 million, and that she was rightfully entitled to half. She also filed to have her surname changed to Heck. "Everybody in Maui (where she lived much of the year with Adolf) thought I was Mrs. Heck," she mused to *The Santa Rosa Democrat*.

The local newspapers had a field day as the events unfolded, and Sonoma County residents followed the proceedings with a relish that is only evinced when wealthy people air their dirty laundry in public. In the end, the Hecks settled out of court with Miramontez. They agreed to pay her $3.5 million, and acknowledged her right to a condominium and a bank account in Maui, which contained somewhat more than $100,000. According to the Hecks' lawyer, however, the monies awarded to Miramontez are in an escrow account that is being held against her impending federal estate taxes. At least $2 million of the award will go toward those taxes, and the final tally may well wipe out the total amount. In the end, the Heck family—and the Korbel winery—came out as the uncompromised victors.

Korbel continues to turn out well-made champagnes that are an artful blend of premium North Coast grapes and bulk Central Valley grapes. The wines are good and moderately priced, representing both the technical legacy and spirit of Adolf Heck. And that's as it should be, and what he deserves to be remembered for—not the squabblings of his survivors.

Well-funded, successful family wineries are a rarity in the industry. They may become even more rare. Not only are they facing exterior pressures, including rising production costs, intense competition and a tough marketplace; they also face divisive pressures within. Business partnerships are usually just that—strictly business. But family ties, and occasionally weird knots, complicate the equation.

The lines between respect and envy, hate and love are fine indeed. When the tensions that are inherent in any family are combined with the rigorous demands of running a business, especially a business as angst-ridden as a winery, then the end results can be pyrotechnic, driving spouses, mothers and brothers to rage.

18

THE GOLD STANDARD

Everybody loves recognition, including vintners. They like good reviews for their products, they like to be feted at honorary dinners—and most especially, they like to win medals. Or at least, most vintners and winery executives do. Gold medals and blue ribbons look good in the trophy case or on the fireplace mantel. More important, medals are a major tool for selling wine.

Indeed, a winery's merchandising materials—little table tents in restaurants, signs and shelf-talkers, those increasingly ubiquitous hand-written cards one finds in liquor and grocery store wine sections—will crow about them. Winemakers will put little faux foil medal stickers on each bottle. Paid advertising will feature the golden kudos of a particular release, although less likely the silver and bronze.

American consumers also like and gravitate toward

medal-winning wines, unlike their European counterparts, who are more apt to trust their own palates than those of a panel of wine judges. But this is probably a direct manifestation of American culture. Since medals are won at contests, it's a qualitative verification that simplifies decision-making. The wine has undergone a trial and the judges have found it worthy, a verdict plenty convincing to Edith and Elmer Rosencrantz, insurance that they won't be embarrassed by serving it at their suburban dinner party.

Never mind that wine-tasting is a terribly subjective phenomenon, or that wines that do well in big contests don't necessarily show well at the table, since they often tend to be excessively fruity, extractive and high in alcohol. Never mind that the subject of medals creates great contention among winegrowers.

Of course, there's no disagreement among those engaged in the race for gold that winning at fairs and expositions is good business. For some winemakers, the risk of losing is bad business, which is the main reason they avoid entering. But even they acknowledge the marketing boost from winning medals. The controversy boils down to emerging points of consensus:

1. A number of contests are poorly run because they use judges who are inexpert, men and women who are often tarred and labeled with that heinous and pejorative word—celebrity.

2. A number of contests are poorly run because they use judges who are experts; winemakers to be specific, ones who will certainly pick winning wines that are just like the wines they make at home.

3. An even greater number of contests, it's agreed, overwhelm judges—expert and inexpert alike—with too many wines to sniff and sip. With hairs burned out of their noses and tongues righteously crisped, Jack Daniel's could get slipped into the sequence and they wouldn't know the difference.

4. Contests award far too many medals, some in excess of 50 percent of the wines entered, which is only slightly less

generous than youth soccer programs. The effect is to devalue the gold standard.

5. There are too many contests. The effect: ditto.

There are also suggestions that contests aren't always on the up-and-up. Given the profit incentive of winning, this would seem to put winegrowers in the position of construction contractors, and judges in the role of New York building inspectors. Of course, the contests are blind tastings, so unless a steward were in on the action, nodding at a particular wine, this type of malfeasance would be tough to pull off. Vintners, however, mutter darkly about their suspicions, prefacing comments with: "Well, I don't know personally if this is true or happens, but . . ." and then they spin out a scenario.

No concrete evidence of cheating on wine contests has emerged, although the subject generates an awful lot of smoke that doesn't quite flash into fire. In any event, honest wine contests by themselves produce more than enough conflicting opinions. Respected wine experts may not be able to agree in precise terms what constitutes a great wine, but they are virtually unanimous about the characteristics of a bad wine.

Naturally, some vintners are in a better position to profit from the medal circuit than others, and their enthusiasm for the competitions usually runs in direct proportion to their potential for turning the ore into increased sale. "We don't enter any of our wines in medal competitions," says Harvey Posert of Robert Mondavi. "Our wines are occasionally entered in those that buy the wine off the shelves, and they usually do quite well. But we really can't derive any major benefits from the circuit. We already have name recognition, and we get very good press. A bronze medal might do us more harm than good."

To serve Mondavi's interests, Posert admits, "it has to be gold or nothing." But he also claims that Mondavi wines aren't designed to win contests. "Medal winners are often very 'big' wines. They have to have a lot of fruity flavors, aromas and oak if they're going to stand out from the scores or hundreds of other wines being tasted. Our wines are designed to be complex and subtle—it's easy for them to be blown away by overpowering monster wines."

Other winery principals are less circumspect than Posert in their disapproval of the medal chase. "We simply feel that they're meaningless," says Sandra MacIver, a co-owner and president of Matanzas Creek winery in Sonoma County's Bennett Valley. "They aren't an accurate reflection of the actual quality of wines that are judged. We've entered wines in competitions in the past, and we've done very well with some of them. But we don't believe that the basic process can be trusted. It's essentially a rip-off. We just don't enter competitions anymore."

MacIver thinks that many of the citations presented at competitions are undeserved; others are simply dog and pony shows, outright travesties that have nothing to do with determining wine quality. "The Los Angeles County Fair is a good example," she fumes. "Supposedly, this is one of the most prestigious wine competitions in the country. But they didn't award a single gold medal to a California Chardonnay—not one. Now, it goes without saying that the best California Chardonnays stand with the best white wines of the world; some are invariably included in any wine expert's list of the greatest wines. So it's strange that none of the California Chardonnays entered won a gold. But what did win a gold medal? André Cold Duck! That's a sparkling wine made by Gallo that sells for about $2 a bottle. It's like sparkling Welch's grape juice. I mean, give me a break. I haven't tasted André Cold Duck lately, but I think I can say without fear of contradiction that it's not a great wine."

The Matanzas Creek executive also feels that judges are by no means resolute in their individual opinions while judging. "They don't arrive at clear-cut decisions, stick to them, and tabulate the results of their preferences," she claims. "They dicker. They bargain. They horse-trade. They'll swap votes for silvers and bronzes in order to reach unanimity on golds. They'll also submit to predetermined criteria for a tasting. At one competition we went to some time ago, the sponsors actually gave the judges printed instructions for the tasting. It directed the judges to rate the wines according to certain characteristics that were nothing more than the personal biases of the sponsors.

"That just shows me that the whole medals circuit is a travesty," MacIver continues. "It doesn't do what it claims to do—determine the best wines that are out there in the marketplace. Also, the more wines you enter in competitions, the more medals you'll win—it's as simple as that. If you keep submitting wines, you can be assured of garnering an impressive array of medals."

Naturally, not everyone shares MacIver's splenetic views on medals; in fact, her position of disdaining the contest process and the medals appears to be a minority one. A lot of winegrowers quibble with the process, but see medals as a valuable and effective marketing device. Vintners suggest that a gold from the Orange County Fair, for example, may be worth a $2 per bottle retail price boost, or as much as a 10 percent increase in what the winery gets per case. Moreover, a release moves and depletes faster, a boon to cash flow.

Some winegrowers, such as Patrick Campbell of Laurel Glen Vineyard, feel that contests do a fair job of establishing wine quality. "Or at the least, they do a fair job of identifying wines that are of good or excellent quality," he says. "Granted, they don't necessarily identify the very best wines consistently. But you'll probably have a wine that runs anywhere between sound to truly superior if you buy a medal winner—particularly one that has won medals in more than one competition. That's helpful to the consumer, and valuable to the vintner. With all those wines out there on the shelves, a shelf-talker with a medal sticker on it next to your bottles really helps make it stand out. Medals may actually stimulate increased wine sales, and I think that's good for the entire industry."

Some competitions definitely carry more weight than others. Among the most prestigious is the Orange County Fair, acknowledged as one of the most effective merchandising mechanisms in the industry by even the most cynical vintners. "The Orange County Fair has integrity and it's well known," says Jerry Mead, the competition's chairman and co-founder. "It's not surprising that winemakers like to get medals from it."

Mead is one of the nation's best-known syndicated wine writers. He's been at the game a long time and is known as a tireless booster of both domestic wine and his own profile. "I'm not shy," he admits freely, "but then, I never pretended to be." And Mead isn't particularly enthusiastic about the general ruck of wine contests. "A lot of the competitions are medal mills, it's true," he observes. "Particularly some European competitions. There, if you enter anything you'll get a medal, as long as it isn't industrial toxic waste. Those outfits don't even award bronze medals. They award double golds, triple platinums. If you get a gold, I mean a single gold, it's equivalent to a bronze in other contests. Of course, that's total bullshit. It puts the entire competition concept into jeopardy."

The Orange County fair, Mead notes, is the only major wine competition that uses only winemakers and enologists for its judging panel. "That's one of the reasons we have so much credibility," he says. "You don't have self-appointed experts judging these wines. You don't have people who may know quite a bit about wine from an objective viewpoint—say, restaurateurs and writers—but whose palates aren't very sophisticated. Instead, you have only the people who actually make and judge wine on a daily basis on the panel."

Such a panel, Mead insists, is "much more likely to come up with a roster of truly superior wines than a panel of 'experts' or celebrities. Tasting and evaluating wines is the business of our judges. They do it for their livelihoods. If more competitions followed our lead in this, competitions as a whole would have a lot more credibility."

In order to keep his judges' palates up to snuff, Mead limits the number of wines they taste in one day. "I once went to a competition where we had to taste 175 Chardonnays in one day," he recalls. "It was ridiculous. It was also painful. I think that's why a lot of fruity, relatively simple, slightly sweet wines win so many competitions. The sugar soothes your mouth after an entire day of tasting dry, high acid of tannic wines."

Orange County also maintains its reputation by insisting that all wines used in the tastings can also be found in retail stores. "That guarantees a couple of things," says Mead. "I'm not saying that there are vintners who would enter a ringer, but that possibility exists when you ask for free samples. Next, we're guaranteeing a fair representation of the marketplace. We don't taste wines that are only available at the winery, or wines with severely limited distribution."

Orange County also includes wines that might otherwise not be voluntarily placed in such a hunt. Some small wineries can't afford to give out the samples, even if it might win gold. Others are dragged in, despite kicking and screaming back at the winery. "When we first started out, I had vintners calling me up and telling me they were going to sue if we tasted their wines," he reminisces. "I said, 'So sue.' You can't sue anybody for reviewing wines, just as you can't sue anybody for reviewing movies. I knew that—and their lawyers knew that too, since nobody ever sued. But you really can't have an objective competition if the only wines you taste are those submitted by the winemakers."

One other device used by Orange County to maintain credibility is the separation of the wines by price category. As Mead explains, "People don't expect the same things from a $5 Cabernet that they could from a $35 Cabernet. It's ridiculous to taste wines from widely disparate price categories. A wine that's a bargain at $7 may be a rip-off at $15. We want to give vintners the opportunity to price their wines fairly. If they make a good wine and it's priced right, then they should do well at the Orange County Fair."

Just as wines compete, so do competitions, so to speak, for credibility. And the promoters of various contests can get reasonably nasty with each other as they attempt to bolster their own projects at the expense of their col- leagues. The Orange County may be the biggest competition, but not everyone shares Mead's high opinions of his own gig.

One who isn't shy about expressing his disdain is Anthony Dias Blue, a *Wine Spectator* columnist and the wine editor for *Bon Appétit*. Blue lambasted wine competitions in general in one of his *Spectator* columns, singling out the Orange County Fair for particular ridicule. He claimed it handed out too many medals, and that winemaker judges are really only qualified to judge their own wines. Instead, Blue championed the San Francisco Fair, maintaining that the judges represented a broader spectrum of qualified palates, and that it handed out far fewer awards—to about 20 percent of the entries, as opposed to 33 percent at Orange County. Blue, it may come as no surprise, judges at the San Francisco Fair.

Mead fired back in his syndicated column, calling Blue's statements on the inadequacy of winemaker judges "asinine." He added: "Come on, Andy. Do you really think that the men and women who make the great wines of California don't know the difference between excellence and mediocrity? Greatness can't be achieved by someone incapable of recognizing it. . . ."

Many winemakers like judging at fairs because they get a chance to check out the competition and taste a lot of wine for free, a double-gold opportunity. Of course, it's work when the contest organizers load on too many wines. And apparently, it's kosher when a vintner's own wine is entered, mainly because there are so many others. After tasting dozens and dozens of Chardonnays at one big contest, Congress Springs' Dan Gehrs was asked if he recognized his own wine. "Yeah," he groaned, "at least five times."

Counties and cities throughout the nation have added wine tastings to their fair agendas, right along with the hog judging, baked goods and preserve contests. That means more ribbons and medals. So, as Jill Davis of Buena Vista explains, "If you buy a wine because it won medals, you have to look at the pedigree of the competitions." Among the more credible and significant ones, Davis lists Orange County, San Francisco, the Sonoma County Harvest Fair and the Atlanta Wine Fair.

Beringer vice president Tor Kenward seconds that motion. "We enter established fairs, fairs that have good reputations, and the ones that we can effectively use in our marketing campaigns. It's not in our interests to enter every one. And I think we're reaching a saturation point. If we have too many of them, people aren't going to care about them. I think it'd be in the interests of the industry if the second-rate competitions would fall by the wayside."

Kenward's emphasis on the marketing potential of medals is a succinct distillation of the one and only reason vintners care about medals. True, some winemakers bemoan the inequity of something that should mean so little meaning so much; but not much in life is fair, least of all marketing and sales. Perhaps competitions are too flawed to be used as definitive guides to wine quality. But consumers like those medals, no matter how much wine mavens and winemakers rant and rave. Gold speaks a language they understand.

"Our medal winners outsell all other wines by three to one," says an employee at the Napa Liquor Barn store. Liquor Barn is a chain of large stores that carry beer, spirits and literally hundreds and hundreds of wines from all over the world. The Napa store—located as it is in the heart of California's wine country—boasts both a particularly knowledgeable staff and a wine-wise clientele. Here, if anywhere, one might expect the medals hoopla to have little effect. But this isn't the case. Customers buy medal-winners by the case in Napa, just as they do in New York, Dallas or Chicago.

"Even people who know a lot about wine tend to buy medals winners," says the Liquor Barn employee. "You can't possibly taste all the wines that are on the shelves, even if you're really into wine. So, maybe you'll buy some that are old favorites, maybe you'll buy some that were reviewed well in *The Connoisseur's Guide* or *The Wine Spectator*, and then maybe you'll try a few wines that took gold or silver medals at Orange County or the Sonoma Harvest Fair. We like medal winners, because they move off the shelf quickly. They make money."

Wineries seek glory from competitions, and use the

judges' positive verdicts as a confirmation, questionable or not, that someone with some knowledge liked the wine. For the consumer who can't trust his or her own palate, can't afford to try every wine in the house, and has the Dingle-mans coming over for dinner in an hour, reaching for the gold is about as safe a move as a wine-buyer can make.

19

GRIDLOCK IN GRAPELAND

It is 0900 hours on Monday, and the traffic is heavy and slow. Clench-jawed commuters in Hondas jockey with smoke-spewing eighteen-wheelers loaded with perishables, while Harley riders occasionally ease onto the right-hand shoulder and pass the creeping traffic millipede. It is just another manic Monday, the kind expected in any urban area, where people grind and honk and crawl and crash their way to work.

Only this jam also contains dazed septuagenarians in Winnebagos, and even more folks in BMWs, Volvos and Fords who aren't in the least bit of a hurry to get to work. They don't work here. This is Highway 29 in the Napa Valley, a two-lane road that skirts 25,000 acres of the world's most celebrated vineyards as it wends its way from San Pablo Bay north to the town of Calistoga. Most of these

266

people are going wine-tasting. They're there for fun. And they've created a transportation gridlock as bad as Manhattan's.

Fun has never been so trying. The Napa Valley is in danger of being loved to death. As a California getaway destination, it runs second only to Disneyland—and Disneyland is a lot better able to handle the crush, surrounded as it is by a serpentine tangle of freeways and enough motels and restaurants to service the entire population of Taiwan. More than 2.5 million tourists descend, locust-like, on the narrow, twenty-five-mile long valley each year, most of them in the summer.

But the horde doesn't come empty-handed. In 1987, visitors dropped over $135 million in the Napa Valley. No matter how you cut it, that's a lot of wine, and a lot of dinners, hotel rooms, T-shirts, corkscrews and souvenir tote bags.

These tourists therefore translate as either a blight or a blessing, depending on whom you talk to in the Valley. One thing's for sure, though; if the throngs of visitors and the services that must be maintained to support them continue to proliferate unchecked, the very basis for the Valley's prosperity—viticulture—is threatened. Like Southern California's Orange County, where they now grow housing developments and malls instead of oranges, Napa Valley will be associated with winegrowing in perception only.

Twenty years ago, this place was a sleepy little agrarian backwater north of San Francisco. It had some modest renown for its wines, of course. But the business of the Valley was making wine, not hyping it. Visitors to Napa in the 1950s and 1960s were as apt to be there to take mud baths and thermal soaks at Calistoga's health resorts as to taste wine; more so, in fact. Any tourist industry that existed at the time owed its genesis and prosperity to the mantle of red-hot magma that existed under the north Valley near dormant Mount St. Helena. (Not to be confused with Mount St. Helens in Washington, which isn't, obviously, dormant.) The mineral baths were good for what ailed you, and thousands of Bay Area health aficionados made use of them.

People still take the waters up in Calistoga, but it's wine, not steaming mud, which has made the Napa Valley the teeming hotbed of tourism that it is today. Starting in the early 1970s, the fame of the area's wine made the transition from the regional to the national scale. After that, vociferous local boosters and the growing legions of wine pilgrims who were anxious to make the trek to their vinous Mecca did the rest. Tourism took off, and it's been growing at a headlong— even metastatic—pace ever since.

Moreover, many Valley bigwigs seem intent on increasing the tourist load rather than containing it. Such attitudes are the cause of fractious debate here, pitting advocates of growth against those who fear for their quality of life and the viability of the Valley's spiritual core, winegrowing. But the pro-tourism forces are pushing forward. And the most striking example of this compulsion to stuff the golden goose until its liver explodes is the Napa Valley Wine Train.

The Wine Train first reared its ugly head in 1986, when Vincent DeDominico, a multimillionaire who had recently divested himself of some very lucrative holdings— including Golden Grain Pasta Co. and Ghirardelli Square in San Francisco—started looking for a venture suitable for major funding. He decided to buy up the rights to the railroad spur that ran the length of the Valley. DeDominico's plan was for a pleasure train that would haul tourists through the Valley at a leisurely pace, stopping at various wineries along the way. The train would feature luxuriously appointed cars, three-star meals and wine service on board. DeDominico estimated that the train would be hauling 450,000 passengers annually by 1990.

That was the problem, the last thing the Napa Valley needed was an additional half-million tourists, critics argued. "We don't need Disneyland in the Napa Valley," growled Louis Martini Winery president Michael Martini, who worried that the extra crush of bodies might ultimately interfere with the real purpose of the business: making wine.

Since the train would cross Highway 29 at several points, further slowdowns on the already egregiously congested road seemed inevitable, in spite of DeDominico's assertion that it would relieve traffic, not contribute to it. Almost forty wineries have formed a coalition to fight the Wine Train, headed by St. Helena insurance agent Norm Manzer. He contends that the train will severely disrupt the lives of Napa Valley residents.

"First, you have them spending $1 million in promotion to attract people to the Valley," Manzer argues. "In spite of their denials, that's going to bring thousands of new tourists to Napa who won't even ride the train. Then you have the interference with Highway 29. And since the train is required by state law to blow its whistle at intersections, we're going to have major auditory pollution. There are 110 crossings between downtown Napa and downtown St. Helena—with the scheduling they're proposing, that's 4,000 to 5,000 blasts daily. Also, there are safety gates at only twenty-seven of the 110 crossings, so you have major traffic risks as well."

Other residents point out that many of the train's stops are for wineries on the other side of Highway 29. "They're serving wine on the train, so a lot of people will be lushed," says one St. Helena resident. "They'll stagger across Highway 29 and splat! They'll be flatter than a possum under a Peterbilt. Talk about a public relations catastrophe . . ."

Clearly, then, most Napa Valley residents view the Wine Train as anathema; they see it as one more straw, and they see themselves as the camel's back that has to support the touristic load. Most Napa Valley natives will tell you they don't want to discourage tourism; they simply want to discourage excessive tourism, so they can preserve the things that make them want to live in the Valley in the first place: clean air, elbow room and reasonably uncrowded highways.

The fact is that virtually all the winemaking enterprises in the Valley want a certain level of tourism. The retail trade that the tourists represent is essentially found money for many vintners. They sell their wines at full retail price. And sometimes even more, so as not to undercut and anger their friends in the retail business, upon whom the vintners must really count. They're getting the full take from direct sales, instead of only half by running it through the wholesale middleman and the retailer. Tourist sales are a gold-plated, cash Holstein.

Some wineries, though, have so many visitors clogging the facilities that they occasionally interfere with production and shipping. A few have instituted a series of subtle measures to reduce traffic, such as requiring reservations to get tours, charging a small fee for tastings and so forth. But it hasn't worked. The tourists still come like waves of Chinese infantry throwing themselves at Pork Chop Hill. Most vintners graciously host the throng, and grumble about it after hours.

There is one Napa Valley winery, however, which does not view such trade as bothersome in the least. In fact, tourists are the raison d'être for the V. Sattui winery. The St. Helena facility, located hard by Highway 29, sells nearly all of its wine, more than 20,000 cases annually, right out of the winery and at retail prices. About 10 percent of its sales are mail order, but you can't find V. Sattui in any store. To get it, you gotta write or come see Darryl in person.

Darryl Sattui is an anomaly in Napa wine circles, a good ol' boy who cheerfully admits that he grew up on Ripple and Red Mountain. Even though his palate is somewhat more developed now, he still doesn't seem struck from the Napa mold. In fact, the mold was broken before they made Darryl Sattui.

His attire is casual to the point of outright disregard, his hair obviously cut by the local barber rather than a stylist, and he sports a large, sterling silver vampire bat on a chain around his neck, jewelry that would befit the gizzard of any head-banging metalhead headed for a Mötley Crüe concert. Still, on a summer afternoon at the winery, ambling across the parking lot, the angular, raw-boned Sattui has a tuxedo slung across his shoulder. That evening, he's going to a winemaker dinner. But for the most part, Sattui listens to a drummer no one else in the industry can hear.

The V. Sattui winery is not merely a winery; it's also a delicatessen and rest stop. It supports a large picnic area where visitors drink the wine and eat the bread, cheese and salami they purchase from the retail shop. A disproportionate number of the folks sprawled out on the grass bear little resemblance to the thin, well-coiffed, impeccably-though-casually-dressed young professionals who predominate in crowds at other Napa wineries. No, these folks are in baseball caps and jeans, K-Mart dresses and monogrammed windbreakers. They are visitors from Gary and Fargo, not Tiburon and Newport Beach. Many would normally have a can of Bud in their hands, except for the fact that they started out wine-tasting for the day and ended up at the most hospitable place they could find, with picnic tables and food to boot. These are people who look just like Darryl Sattui, except for the fact that they don't have bats around their necks, of course. Sattui understands them. In fact, they were just the folks he had in mind when he built his winery.

In 1972, Sattui returned from a two-year tour of Europe with $5,000 and a Finnish wife. He took a series of odd jobs at various wineries, doing everything from guiding tours to shoveling pomace. He also picked every brain he could sink his teeth into, so to speak. What he found wasn't encouraging. Most pundits advised that he'd need a minimum of $1 million in start-up capital for a wine-making venture. Sattui did some calculations. "I found that I'd be over 125 years old before I'd have that kind of money," he recalls.

Sattui scraped, scrimped, cajoled and begged investors, and finally put together about $50,000 in 1974, enough for a down payment on a parcel. He raised most of his funds through limited partnerships. Other investors contributed time and building materials to construct a modest winery. Sattui's office desk was an old door on sawhorses. His total equipment purchases for his first crush in 1975 consisted of forty-five barrels, a small general purpose pump and one hundred feet of hose. He rented everything else he needed.

V. Sattui Winery opened on March 4, 1976. On his first day, Sattui grossed $141. But by the end of the year, he'd developed a modest following among the tourist trade. Sattui disposed of 1,800 cases of wine, a goodly amount of cheese and mortadella, and turned a profit of $2,600. Given that new wineries usually don't get into the black until seven or more years from their inception, Sattui was on to something.

His wines aren't cheap, ranging on the average from $10 to $15 a bottle. And they win an exceptional share of gold medals. Sattui's staff makes a visit seem wondrous to the throng; each bottle of Cabernet is numbered, like limited edition Warhol prints, and clerks pour deliberately small tastes, explaining that the wines are "scarce" or "special." Sattui has developed quite a fan club among people who feel like insiders and part of the winery, since average folks can't buy Sattui wine at the liquor store. This marketing tactic does make his operation unique, and thus his wines special.

Sattui's success has made him a prototype for others to follow. Napa is increasingly becoming a valley of tourist wineries, and this fact is the basis for an issue as divisive as the Wine Train.

These wineries are different from V. Sattui, which makes wines only from Napa Valley grapes. The great blocks of trailer parks, sprawling condominium tracts and retail business developments going up in St. Helena, Yountville and Calistoga are bad enough, drawing the eye away from the vineyards. But the new tourist wineries aren't quaint, artfully built little structures; they're big, sterile, concrete tilt-ups or bizarre architectural jabberwockies that say more about the twisted egos of their proprietors than they do about living in harmony with the land. They are mock palaces of wine. And though they're located in the prestigious Napa Valley, some of them don't make a drop of Napa Valley wine.

Growers see some of the most profitable wineries in the

Valley making their fortune off the good name of the region—and cheaper grapes from other areas. At the same time, the growers are squeezed by high land prices, high production costs and zoning restrictions. They want all Napa Valley wineries to use Napa Valley fruit exclusively, thus ensuring good prices and long-term contracts; essential guarantees if the Valley's economic base is to remain viticultural. Yet they also want the option of selling their land if farming becomes unprofitable—that is, if the land is worth more as a site for a carpetbagging winery, a golf course or a condo complex than as a vineyard.

Local politicos have locked horns with residents over what seems a very basic question: what is, exactly, a Napa Valley winery? Is it a wine-producing facility that makes wine only from Napa grapes? Can a winery be an entertainment facility, with a year-round agenda of concerts, conventions and special events?

Yet another question is whether a winery can be an art showcase, or a piece of art itself. That seems to be the primary intent of Jan Shrem, the proprietor of Clos Pegase, whose architecturally controversial facility is dedicated to Pegasus, the winged horse whose hoofs struck Mount Hellicon and allowed the spring of the muses to first flow. Shrem appears considerably more interested in fine art than fine wine, and his vast, sprawling facility may be better described as a museum than a winery.

Such matters would never be raised in France, where great winegrowing regions are considered national legacies and treasures. Construction is strictly regulated there, and the rules which specify which grapes from certain vineyards may be used in certain wineries are pointed indeed. But Napa isn't France, and the thought of that type of regulation in the American wine business might make any vintner a bit uneasy. In terms of land use, Napa is 200 years behind Burgundy. The trouble is, the Valley's vineyards may all be gone by the time the rules catch up with reality.

Land use in Napa County is determined by its Board of Supervisors, which is comprised of elective seats. At this point, most of the upper valley is an agricultural preserve—a designation that effectively protects viticulture. The trouble is that land use is much like the practice of law; each change in the status quo sets a precedent. Thus, a variance which allows the construction of a small bed and breakfast inn in an area that was formerly an unsullied tract of vineyard doesn't only affect the quarter acre required for the construction site; it affects the entire area, for hundreds of acres around. The inn serves as a cell, from which grows the cancer of further development. That danger already exists in Napa, since land use policy can change as easily as an elected board can change.

Johnny is not his real name, since he doesn't want his real name used. He works in an up-valley winery as a warehouse foreman, a good job, considering that he is nineteen years old. He is a born and bred resident of Napa; the town, not the Valley.

Residents here live either up-valley or down-valley, and the Mason-Dixon line for this demarcation is just below Yountville. It is a social and economic division more than a geographical one. Napa is a gray, somewhat gritty working-class town. There is a deep and almost palpable resentment in down-valley Napans, an underlying class-based animosity directed against up-valley swells.

Like many working-class youths, Johnny seems both older and younger than his years. Street smarts coexist with a kind of recalcitrant naiveté that would be considered ignorance, were it not so assiduously cultivated. "I don't give a shit about wines" he says. "I like Jack Daniel's with a beer shooter."

Johnny works hard, but he harbors a private disdain for the wine business, which he considers much ado about nothing. But he takes pride in the fact that he puts in more than a day's work for a day's pay. On weekends, he likes to fish or water ski at Lake Berryessa, ride dirt bikes or get high.

He wants to buy a small house. Not up-valley, of course. Johnny doesn't have that kind of scratch. And that's precisely what pisses him off.

"My grandfather has some acreage north of town, in the ag

preserve area," he says. "He's getting on in years. And when he dies, the only way our family will be able to pay the estate taxes and make any money on the piece is to split it for houses. But the plan won't let us do that. I mean, it really burns my ass. Here we are, natives of this goddamn valley, and we can't even build in it. It's gotta be saved so all the assholes coming up from San Francisco can have some place to go on weekends to look at grapevines. This ecology crap is getting out of hand. This place has to grow if regular people like me can make a go of it."

The effects of the development heretofore allowed is most evident from the top of Mount St. Helena, if not the cause. But Dave Steiner understands the root of the problem, as he stands at the summit and looks south to San Pablo Bay. Steiner likes to climb this mountain in the early spring, looking for the savory boletus mushrooms that sprout abundantly in the duff at that time of year. His sack is full of the delectable fungi, and he pauses to take in the view before heading down the slope. To the Sonoma grape grower, the patchwork of development and vineyard speaks all too eloquently.

"It's scary," he says. "I stand up here and I see Sonoma County in twenty years. We're going to have to be making the kind of decisions these guys are making now—or better, the decisions they aren't making. The fact is, you have to choose at a certain point. Is the greatest possible good, the highest use for the land, tourism or viticulture? If you decide it's tourism, then what the hell; pave the place with bed and breakfasts, hotels, restaurants and wineries, and use out-of-area grapes, leaving a few token vineyards for show. But if it's viticulture, then you have to do everything possible to make sure that grape-growing is given every priority, from land use to tax structure. The thing is, once it's gone it's gone for good. I've seen a lot of vineyards go under to housing developments and shopping centers. But I've never seen anybody tear up a development and put in a vineyard. It only goes one way."

Which way the Napa Valley will head is uncertain. The standard of living for many of its people depends on a

275

thriving tourism industry. At risk is one of the world's greatest viticultural regions. But while the Napa Valley's future is uncertain, it's clear that economic, political and social conflict, along with 2.5 million visitors each year, has created a binding gridlock that is both physical and spiritual.

20

BIG PLAYERS, NEW PLAYERS: THE CORPORATE AND FOREIGN INFLUENCE

It is a business that sent Beatrice, Pillsbury and Coca-Cola packing. While renowned names in marketing, these corporations tried the wine game and came away greatly disillusioned by profit margins much thinner than expected. The industry's difficult distribution channels, many of which reflect the Frankenstein monsters of tortuous state laws, made wine much harder to move than soda pop, cake mixes and other consumer goods. And in the considered opinion of Agustin Huneeus, such enterprises and wine simply do not mix.

"I'm convinced that big corporations have no place in the

wine business," he says. "Big corporations can make money
in all areas, or at least make it look like they're making
money. Where a big corporation thrives is in areas where its
very bigness, its vast resources, can play a role. But in the
wine business, there's nothing that a big company can do
better than an entrepreneur can do. In wine, the big company's liabilities come into play."

There have been notable examples of corporations that
have done well with wineries. Nestlé with its flagship
Beringer brand and other subsidiaries of Wine World Inc.—
the Nestlé division that runs all the U.S. properties—is one.
Another is United States Tobacco with its Stimson Lane
stable, led by Château Ste. Michelle.

Corporate money is also seductive. A financially strug-
gling winery may see capital salvation in selling a sizable
interest to a large company. Or, the owner could sell the
whole thing, walk away with the accrued equity and feel
that his or her baby is in good hands. And to a bone-weary
vintner, the marketing muscle of a big corporation can make
a joint venture look awfully attractive. With that very
bigness, as Huneeus says, major companies appear as if they
can do wondrous things with and for a winery.

Since the start of the wine boom in the 1970s, an increasing number of corporations, many of them foreign, have
bought into the American wine industry. Wineries have
drained a number of corporate profit lines; these can be
written off as bad breaks and forgotten. But what a few
corporations have done to wineries and vintners cannot be
so cavalierly dismissed. To a small winegrower, a bad
corporate break can wipe out his entire stake.

Huneeus once worked for Joseph E. Seagram & Sons, and
still has many dealings with the giant Canadian distiller.
But while largely successful during his tenure there, he
personally observed a downside in the way in which
corporate liabilities can rear up, big and ugly. "I now
believe that a wine business should be a family or entrepreneurial business," he says. "I was very sad at Seagram
because we were taking over family businesses; we bought a
lot of personal companies, and on those we didn't do well."

As Huneeus suggests, the total personal involvement of

an owner or CEO who has the autonomy to make fast and concrete decisions is critical to a winery's success. Corporate bureaucracies work against such action. For example, when wine executive Paul Schlem visited a Paul Masson vineyard several years ago—which was then owned by Seagram—he found grapes still on the vine two weeks past when they should have been picked. When Schlem asked the Paul Masson enologist about what stopped the harvest, he was told: "We couldn't get clearance from New York."

Among the other liabilities corporations frequently carry is impatience, particularly on the part of companies that are publicly traded. Stockholders—including institutional investors and those who may be poised to launch a takeover attempt or force a greenmail buyout—compel corporations to seek substantial and early returns on an investment. It's a common complaint among American executives that such pressure forces them to manage a company toward short-term profits, at the expense of long-term strategies.

But wine produces earnings almost exclusively in the long-term, if then. Generating winery profits—given the required upgrading of vineyards, purchase and maintenance of equipment, and the time red wines must age in inventory—is a low and slow proposition.

U.S. Tobacco and Nestlé are noteworthy in that they have taken the long view in winery earnings. Moreover, they generally let their wine enterprises run themselves. And corporate executives aren't all necessarily boneheads when it comes to vineyards and wine. Many of the large companies that invested in the industry, such as Beatrice, Coca-Cola and Pillsbury, did so when the wine boom promised (and for a brief time delivered), sufficient—and sufficiently fast—returns. But as the boom diminished, so did the ability of corporations to apply their muscle.

In 1983, Coca-Cola sold its group of wine properties to Seagram for $200 million. But less than four years later, Seagram, along with a pair of other giants—National Distillers & Chemical and Heublein—were engaged in a virtual orgy of corporate winery sales. In an attempt to handle a flat market, these other corporations began playing hot potato with wineries, restructuring, wheeling and dealing, trying to find a magic blend of business structuring.

In January of 1987, Heublein agreed to buy Almadén Vineyards from National Distillers for an estimated $150 million. Just ten days later, Grand Metropolitan announced that it was buying Heublein from its owner, RJR Nabisco, for $1.2 billion. Seagram, in turn, was said to be losing $8 million to $10 million a year on its Paul Masson and Taylor California Cellars brands. So by April of 1987, it sold these, and a number of other wineries and properties, to a newly formed company called Vintners International, headed by Schlem and Michael Cliff, both of whom had ties to Seagram.

Schlem figured he could do better. A veteran who had built New York's Gold Seal brand before selling it to Seagram nearly a decade ago, Schlem took the troubled properties off Seagram's hands with a highly leveraged deal estimated at $220 million to $250 million. It reportedly included a $205 million loan from Citibank, and $20 million worth of debt that Seagram can convert into 20 percent equity in Vintners International. In return, Vintners got companies that produced about $250 million in annual revenues. Schlem quickly sold off about $40 million in excess inventory to reduce his bank debt, and planned to sell about $20 million worth of assets.

He may do just fine. When the sixty-three-year-old Schlem visited his newly acquired bottling facilities in Gonzales, California, he claimed that he felt as he did as a young soldier entering liberated Paris. The employees were ecstatic to have a real wine person back in charge. Paul Gillette, editor and publisher of The Wine Investor, an influential insider newsletter on the business, calls Schlem "one of the brightest guys in this industry."

Shifts of ownership, asset sales and the like are more than multi-million-dollar bank transfers and new faces in corner offices. Careers, jobs and lives twist in an uncertain wind— or hang on meathooks—before, during and after the corporate maneuvers. The situation can be psychologically and financially bruising to employees, suppliers, customers and the company itself. There's a human element here, to which corporate animals aren't always sufficiently sensitive.

Which brings us back to the story of Carneros Creek, Francis Mahoney and Joseph E. Seagram & Sons. Seagram has since made several vintners happy with the way the company has marketed their wines. Perhaps it learned something from Carneros Creek. Mahoney will never forget his lesson.

To put the piece into perspective, one must first consider the workings of Seagram, the nature of its leadership and the company's general experiences in the American wine industry during the 1980s. Founded in 1928, the distiller is best known for its brown hard liquors, including VO, Seagram's, Chivas Regal, Crown Royal and Seven Crown. It also sells about 150 brands of wine worldwide, and after E. & J. Gallo, has been the second largest marketer of wine in the U.S.

The company earns a thin return from its spirits and wine businesses, though; in 1986, it had profits of $103 million on revenues of $3.3 billion. In that same year, it earned more than triple that amount from its 22.6 percent holding in the DuPont Co.

About 38 percent of Seagram's stock is owned by the family of Edgar Bronfman Sr., who serves as chairman and CEO of the company. Edgar Bronfman Jr. is, at the age of thirty-four, the head of the House of Seagram and has been named the heir apparent to his father. Headquartered in New York, the House controls most of the company's American wine properties and its wine cooler business. His older brother Sam Bronfman II, thirty-six, runs most of the company's California wine interests and is based in San Francisco.

In the wine industry, Sam is probably the more respected of the two. He once sold advertisements for *Sports Illustrated*, and has worked his way up in the wine business managing products for Paul Masson and other Seagram properties. (He was also the Bronfman who in 1975, at the age of 22, was allegedly kidnapped, ransomed for $2.3 million and released. The two men charged in the case were convicted of extortion—the money was recovered—but acquitted of kidnapping. They claimed Sam arranged his own abduction to get the money. The family dearly wants to forget the episode, whatever really happened, and consistently refuses to discuss it.) While being a Bronfman has surely helped Sam's career, to a degree he's gone through the ranks.

Edgar Jr., on the other hand, has been described by Seagram's President David G. Sacks as a youth who was "rebellious, overweight and very show-bizzy, with a gold medallion hanging around his neck." He hung out in Hollywood, dumped a lot of family money into theatrical productions, most of which failed, and showed little interest in the family business. But his father talked him into giving it a try. Noted *The Wall Street Journal*: "He is young. He is inexperienced. He didn't go to college. If he weren't Edgar Bronfman Jr. there isn't a chance in the world that he would be, at the age of thirty-two, the head of the House of Seagram and his father's designated successor."

But he is Edgar Jr., and immediately launched an ambitious, $100 million campaign to push Seagram's Golden Wine Cooler, the most money ever put behind a new Seagram product. He signed actor Bruce Willis to a three-year contract to pitch the product, a package that reportedly could earn the star of television's *Moonlighting* series $6.4 million. And Edgar did it even before Willis was recognized as a Hot Property. In just eighteen months, Seagram's Golden Wine Coolers climbed from fourth place in the cooler wars to a tie with Gallo's Bartles & Jaymes brand, and then began edging ahead.

By 1988, however, *Moonlighting* was beginning to lose some of its steam, Willis hadn't quite made it as a feature film star, and the cooler sales growth was slowing. As Paul Gillette noted, Edgar chose coolers "as his moment of truth." Nearly everyone at Seagram agrees the kid has tremendous instincts. As the *Journal* reported, "Some see young Edgar as a bit of a bully," alternately "a genius and a brat." Even Michael Mondavi has been stirred enough to note for the record—unusual in the wine business—that "he believes that because he's Edgar Bronfman Jr., and has the power of Seagram, he can do exactly as he pleases."

Seagram has often done as it pleased, the punishing limits of the jug wine market aside. After several beefs with the Wine Institute, it withdrew from the organization in 1986, which cost the Institute about $100,000 in dues from the wineries Seagram held before their 1987 sale. When Seagram purchased Winery Lake Vineyard from Rene di Rosa, and dedicated those grapes to its Sterling Vineyards winery, an esteemed source of fruit simply disappeared for a large number of premium vintners.

For $8.5 million, this was a brilliant move that other vintners only wish they could have made. Sterling is guaranteed ultra-premium grapes from a vineyard with a highly marketable track record, one that enabled wineries to tack on roughly $2 a bottle because of the Winery Lake designation. Some critics think that the Seagram connection will devalue the Winery Lake mystique. Of course, that comes from vintners who will no longer get its grapes.

Seagram treated Rene di Rosa well, which clearly pleased his friends and associates in the industry. Recently, Sam Bronfman approached Peter Mondavi with a proposal to have Seagram Classics Wine Co. market Charles Krug worldwide. Mondavi agreed, and the companies signed a long-term contract.

In recent years, Krug has shifted from generic wines to a greater emphasis on premium varietals, substituting volume for quality and selling the wine for higher prices. But its marketing is frequently at odds with industry norms. Krug often releases vintages two or three years after other wineries. Consumers are actually getting a good deal for the extra aging if they buy the wine, but may perceive the older vintages as unsuccessful remainders. Under Bronfman, Seagram Classics Wine means to spruce up the Krug and C.K. Mondavi brand images through ads and public relations, while marketing them much more aggressively than the Peter Mondavi family.

For example, Seagram promised Francis Mahoney the moon, and then left him on the dark side.

By 1983, Carneros Creek produced about 13,000 cases of ultra-premium wine, and its profits had climbed from $45,000 to $50,000 and then to $80,000. But despite the reputation and good press, Mahoney found it took longer to sell his wine. He could see the wholesale and distribution system starting to unravel, as a number of smaller, reliable distributors who had worked hard moving Carneros Creek wines dropped out of the business. He saw Seagram, Heublein and National Distillers getting into wine, and knew he didn't have the clout to match that kind of marketing strength. And then along came Seagram, with its new Classics Wine Division, designed specifically to market and distribute wines from producers just like Carneros Creek. Mahoney and four other wineries—Robert Keenan, Château Chevalier, Lambert Bridge and Bandiera Winery—signed on with what was originally called the American Classics program.

"Seagram had a great image," says Mahoney today. "We were very respectful of the fact that they were one of the largest beverage companies in the world, and if they couldn't sell our volume of wine, who could? The idea is that I was to develop a château or estate plan, a model for what we'd do for the next fifteen years. They said, 'We're going to develop you to the point where, except for a few promotional appearances, you can stay home and devote yourself to making great wine.' And I was seduced by the incredible power and economic force of Seagram. Maybe it was a warped view, but I thought to myself, 'Seagram doesn't make mistakes. Lee Iacocca doesn't goof.' "

Emboldened by his new partnership, Mahoney started putting in new tanks and cooperage with his own capital. By the end of the third year of the contract, he planned to be producing 25,000 cases of wine. The people he signed the contract with, says Mahoney, "were very honorable. They had experience in this segment of the business, had sold the program to their superiors, and had good intentions. But six months after we signed, Seagram purchased the Coca-Cola properties. And I then heard nothing from them but silence."

Those properties not only included the jug wine producers, but the premium Sterling and Monterey Vineyard wineries. Mahoney asked what would now happen, and was told that Sterling might join the American Classics line.

In 1984, the name of the program was changed, and a number of other brands, including Mumm Champagne, joined the group. "They came out and assured us that we had nothing to worry about," Mahoney says.

But it slowly dawned on Mahoney that he had plenty of worries. For one thing, Seagram salespeople clearly had more incentive to put efforts into the Sterling and Monterey Vineyard brands, since they were Seagram house brands. "Sales is a tough business," notes Mahoney, "and their staff was overwhelmed with work for Sterling. In general terms, Seagram ended up not putting any incentives there for the sales force to sell our wine, since their quotas and bonuses depended on Sterling and Monterey."

Mahoney expected that 15,000 cases of his wine would be sold, possibly more considering the other members of the original group. He found that about 9,000 moved in each of the two years. "The rest was kind of shoved in a warehouse, with the idea that they'd get back to it." By the end of 1985, Mahoney learned that about 6,000 cases of his wine were warehoused. "But I still didn't pick up on the fact that trouble was in the offing, because I was still on a cloud. I'm backed up 6,000 cases? It's nothing, the No. 2 beverage company in the world will take care of it."

But when he closed the year for 1985 and found that he'd taken a $250,000 beating, well, that was when Mahoney felt like a fool. "I wanted to be a team player. I had blinders on." He was told that the market was soft. And then the guillotine really fell.

"I was invited to breakfast at San Francisco's Stanford Court hotel," he recalls. "It was in an elegant suite. Sam Bronfman and some of his people were there. And he said, in essence, that it was all over, that they wanted out of the contract as of January 1986."

Mahoney had thought Sam could work Bronfman magic. Now, he realized that: "Sam was only thirty-two years old at the time, had always had it easy, and had never experienced a really tough moment in his life. He'd been given a toy, a $200 million toy. And for me, it was over."

Mahoney quietly left the suite, too shocked to know what to say. In a daze, he got to his car and doesn't even remember how he got the key in the ignition. He felt like he'd been tossed in San Francisco Bay with an anvil around his neck. "Shit," he muttered to himself before driving home, "what do I do now?"

Mahoney agreed to the terms Seagram offered on the broken contract. But with no excess cash or room to move, he felt helpless. He did find that he could buy some of his own wine back, at $2.99 a bottle. It was both an opportunity, and an insult. "I went to Los Angeles to sell some of my wine," he explains. "Tough city. Guys said, 'Why should I buy your wine when the last time I did it got discounted down to nothing.' "

Mahoney, however, didn't cave in, but grew more determined. In fact, the more he began to think, the more creative he became. He did some custom crushing for other vintners, which earned much-needed cash. He went back on the road and sold 26,000 cases of his wine himself. He had to re-earn the respect that had once simply gravitated to the "genius" winemaker.

In 1987, Mahoney filed a $60 million breach-of-contract suit, a figure that includes punitive damages. In preliminary legal maneuvers, Carneros Creek won the right to have the trial held in a federal court in San Francisco, rather than in Seagram's ballpark back East. It took considerable soul-searching, says Mahoney, to bring the action.

Mahoney is no hypocrite. He's forthright and honest enough to admit that $60 million would do wonders for the winery and his peace of mind; money is the object. But it's not the only object. Seagram, he feels, has never acknowledged that they did him wrong, and in this they have besmirched the spirit of the fraternity of winegrowers, a sin that demands retribution.

The real point, of course, is that the agreement meant everything to a business as small as Carneros Creek, including stable growth and a reasonably normal family life for Mahoney. To Seagram, it was just another deal, the kind big companies make all the time. In terms of cold numbers, it was no doubt in Seagram's interests to get out of the deal. The result was a sharply contested lawsuit against Seagram by Carneros Creek, which is still pending and being actively litigated by both sides. A federal court will decide on the legality of Seagram's move, while vintners can spend the next few years sitting around a cracker barrel arguing the ethics of the entire affair.

The most successful and stable corporate investments in the American wine industry—and which seldom cause big trouble—have been made by foreign companies. More than thirty-five California wineries are wholly or partially owned by non-U.S. firms, including several major and prominent operations. Together, they produce approximately 15 percent of California's wine. Although silent partners and hidden ownerships make it impossible to get a precise fix on the foreign dollars invested here, some estimate it in excess of $500 million.

A couple of reasons for this interest are security and political stability. According to George Vare, a wine industry consultant: "Putting your money in California is a good investment. The economic and political climate is more settled here, less uncertain than in Europe." Californians accustomed to goofy state ballot measures and politicians who frequently stray off the wing tips, both left and right, may find this statement odd. But the Warsaw Pact doesn't have divisions stationed in British Columbia.

In addition, nations like France and Italy have long supported schizophrenic political personalities, with a profoundly socialist side that can pop out—like one of the more malicious faces of Eve—during any given election. Placing money in the American wine industry gives European investors a hedge should governments turn punitive or confiscatory toward business. While serving as a liquid Swiss bank account, such an investment is also leverage should the U.S. grow more protectionist and attempt to restrict wine imports. Therefore, some European winegrowers can play both sides of the Atlantic. As for the Japanese, they've simply got so much excess cash that they'll buy anything that isn't nailed down.

Although wine country land has appreciated so that it seems phenomenally expensive to Americans, it's still dirt cheap compared to prime winegrowing parcels in France and Germany. Indeed, $20,000 for an acre in Napa Valley is nothing when one considers that an acre in Champagne costs more than $80,000, and in Bordeaux $100,000 to $140,000. And because of the jigsaw nature of the many small, independent vineyards in France, putting together a spread of fifty contiguous acres could take fifty years.

This, in fact, is what brought the prestigious champagne house of Moët-Hennessy to the Napa Valley in 1973. The company had doubled its champagne acreage between 1955 and 1970, and squeezed its production rate from two tons per acre to five tons. But the 1971 harvest was abnormally low, as was inventory the following year, just as demand for champagne was increasing in Europe and elsewhere. In essence, Moët-Hennessy could go no further on the Continent. So, in California, it constructed an ambitious sparkling-wine facility, and a restaurant and called the operation Domaine Chandon. Today it produces more than 400,000 cases of sparkling wine.

Moët was followed by the Ferrer family of Spain, which recently spent $11 million to build a winery and hospitality facility outside Sonoma. The family owns wineries in Spain, France and Mexico, and is accustomed to foreign investment. But according to Begonia Ferrer, a principal of the new Gloria Ferrer vineyard complex, the move into the U.S. produced a few second thoughts. "Wines and spirits are regulated to a far greater degree here than they are in Europe," observes Ferrer, "and licensing and production is a very complicated procedure."

Europeans are patient, and invest for the long term. And nowhere is that more true than with Nestlé, the 130-year-old Swiss food concern. When Nestlé purchased the crumbling Beringer Vineyards in 1972 for $6 million—in conjunction with the Labruyere family, which owns a gasoline company and a chain of convenience and grocery stores in its native France—it was clear that at least a decade and an awful lot more money would be needed to bring the winery to prominence. The Swiss sent the money. Beringer upgraded its facilities, put some polish into Frederick and Jacob Beringer's tourist trap Rhine House, bought more prime vineyard and gained the prominence they sought. And then, between 1985 and 1987, the Swiss sent even more money, $21 million to buy even more vineyards and get better equipment.

As Dick Maher, currently of Christian Brothers, once said of his former employers: "It's the kind of company where if you ask for $500,000 to improve sales by 10 percent, they'll ask you what you can do with $1 million."

Nestlé's Wine World subsidiary now handles six labels. The flagship is Beringer, which produces more than a million cases of premium wines annually. It is also producing Napa Ridge vintage dated varietals, which compete in the fighting varietal category, a cut below Beringer prices. Nestlé spent $9.5 million to buy Souverain, a promising Sonoma County winery that was started by Pillsbury in 1973, but had always lacked stable ownership and direction. It spent more than $4 million to upgrade the production facilities, the exterior of the winery, then renamed it Château Souverain. The company also produces the Los Hermanos brand of jug wines—although it is curtailing production—and bought a one-third interest in Maison Deutz, which produces sparkling wines in Santa Barbara county. Wine World also runs C & B Vintage Cellars, which imports a number of European wines.

What Nestlé gets for all this is a group of companies with sales rapidly approaching $100 million a year, and assets in excess of that figure. But while it puts its name on chocolate bars, the Swiss are as low profile as a secret numbered bank account when it comes to wine, preferring consumers to perceive Beringer and the other properties strictly as American wineries. It probably shouldn't fear. No other well-capitalized winery of Beringer's size generates so little ill-will. During the tenure of Maher and through the current Wine World president, forty-eight-year-old Michael Moon, executives at this company are admired throughout the industry and are genuinely liked.

This may be due to the fact that Wine World executives are given the investment funds to do things right. The company makes long-term commitments to its acquisitions, partners and the vineyard owners with whom it has signed contracts. Wine World doesn't make disruptive, panicked moves that rattle lives, careers and other businesses. It is often cited as the best-managed company in the industry, and to this degree could be called the Hewlett-Packard of wine.

Nestlé and Wine World have been expansion-minded, but in 1984 it lost out on one big winery to another foreign bidder. Moon started out with $24 million to bid on Chateau St. Jean, an esteemed white wine producer that had been founded in 1973. When the bidding went past $38 million, Moon and Nestlé dropped out. For a cool $40 million, Suntory International of Japan had purchased one of the top Chardonnay makers in the States.

Suntory wasn't new to the wine business; it has owned Japan's largest winery for nearly a century, and in the 1970s, Suntory chairman George Harada bought a one-third interest in Santa Barbara County's Firestone Vineyards, after talking wine during a golf game with Brooks Firestone. Industry analysts figured Suntory had paid way too much for St. Jean, and that profitability would be a long time coming given the price. But Suntory invested another $5 million in new equipment, and Harada said he wasn't particularly worried about a quick return. In fact, he said, "Even if it takes thirty or fifty years, that's okay. We're not short-term people."

Such thinking is almost un-American, of course. It's also a bit un-corporate. And yet, patience is a key to successful corporate involvement in the wine industry, and this may be why foreign companies are behind some of the more prosperous—and potentially prosperous—ventures in the game.

Section Six

PUSHING
THE
PRODUCT

21

STREETWALKING

With substantial advertising budgets and large economies of scale, wine marketers like Seagram and Gallo can create awareness of their products through national television, radio and print ad campaigns. Other companies can afford to advertise on selected radio stations and place ads in *The Wine Spectator* or other publications catering to food and wine buffs. And for those on the tightest budgets, the winemaker can always take to the hustings to promote the product at wine club tastings. All these things are important to moving bottles. But the real battles in the wine industry are waged at the point-of-sale.

Marketers of consumer goods are aware of the importance of attractive packaging, signs, positioning on shelves and the like. It's a factor in the sale of crackers, soda pop, potato chips, spaghetti sauce and just about any item where competing brands offer a choice. And yet, most of these products are supported by advertising. Since few wineries can afford to forge consumer perceptions in this way,

293

point-of-sale, then, is where most of the wine business goes to war.

Few products are as dependent on point-of-sale marketing as premium wine, although women's magazines and the weird weekly tabloid business are similar, in the way they fight at grocery store checkout counters. But point-of-sale is important to wine mainly because the bulk of American consumers know relatively little about the beverage, face dozens of choices and are frequently reticent to ask questions.

Even if the shopper understands the difference between table, appetizer, dessert and sparkling wines, each category can present a daunting array of price ranges and labels. Therefore, supporting information can go a long way toward helping make a sale. This can take the form of a small sign, noting that a certain group of wines are red, dry and go well with meat and cheese. It can be a shelf-talker, proclaiming that a particular wine has won more gold medals than Mark Spitz. Or it may include a friendly and unintimidating offer of advice from a sales clerk.

In any event, the skirmishes are waged in grocery stores, liquor stores and restaurants. Vintners need the hearts, minds and premium shelf space at these retail accounts. They want the sales staffs and waiters to tout their wine to consumers, whether for its high quality, or because it's a bargain, or both. They want their wine featured on restaurant "table-tents," at eye level on grocery store shelves, or on special display stands.

Winegrowers want the retailer and restaurateur to care as much about moving the wine as they do. Retailers and their sales staffs will care, of course, if the incentives are high enough. But there are a lot of vintners going after those hearts and minds. And before a winery can help merchandise the heck out of their products at the point-of-sale, the wines have to get on the shelves in the first place. One gets them there only by walking some mean streets.

A goodly number of winery owners and winemakers take the point, knowing that they are their product's most effective soldier. But they can see only so many accounts each year and still run the business back home. Besides, vintners still need brokers and wholesalers to move the product into stores, and count on them to see that retailers are paying enough attention to their wine. However, because the number of American wholesale houses is shrinking, and the remaining ones are each carrying more brands, it has become awfully easy to get lost in the shuffle.

In addition, says an executive wine buyer for a major liquor store chain, "The big distributors carry a full line of products, and usually put their most talented people into liquor sales. They don't train wine salesmen very well. The talent level ranges from used car salesman to shoe salesman to the very knowledgeable, although the latter are few and far between."

Therefore, winegrowers must hire and dispatch sales representatives to educate, encourage and support the wholesalers, and also help the retailers and restaurant owners with merchandising. But other winegrowers do the same thing. So discounts and other sales incentives are offered, and the competitive climate just gets rougher, and profit margins thinner. If a vintner really sat down and thought about it beforehand, the prospects for success generally look about as promising as another Asian land war.

One person who has expended a great deal of shoe leather working the pavement is Alex Morgan, now the sales and marketing director for Sutter Home Winery. A 1980 *summa cum laude* graduate of the University of California at Berkeley, Morgan helped put himself through school by working in a JV Liquor store as a clerk. He gradually developed an interest in fine wine that ultimately blossomed into an all-consuming avocation. By the time he was nineteen, Morgan was the wine buyer for the entire eight-store JV chain. Though he had planned on a career in law, Morgan's budding involvement with wine superseded his original ambition.

"Besides, I noticed that most of the lawyers I knew were raving assholes," he says. "I was enough of an asshole already, so I figured I didn't need to compound the offense."

After graduation, Morgan went to work for the Grape Empire Wine Company, a wholesaler of modest size based in San Francisco's East Bay region. He was given a territory that was turning $18,000 a month when he took over. Six months later, the territory was turning over $85,000 worth of wine monthly. The principals of the company were impressed. They made Morgan sales manager. A few years later, the gargantuan distributor Southern Wine and Spirits bought out Grape Empire. At the age of twenty-three, Morgan found himself supervising 164 people.

Morgan left Southern for Sutter Home in 1985. It's different for him now; he sells as a primary producer rather than as a wholesaler. His goals and techniques are somewhat different. But he remembers what it was like on the street.

"It's never been exactly genteel," says the husky, bearded executive. "The difference between wholesaling now and ten years ago is the consolidation. There are fewer distribution houses now, but the same game is being played out there. In fact, things are probably meaner than ever." A decade ago, when there were far more distributors, he notes, "little guys could make it. Now, they've all been bought out or beaten out."

Like agriculture, the operative phrase in wine wholesaling is to get big or get out. And the big houses, such as Southern Wines and Spirits, Peerless and Jalco, now have a full nelson on the industry. There's little room for the small specialty house, run by the feisty entrepreneur with grit and intelligence. And the trend has stripped vintners of many of their options in marketing their wines.

"It used to be that a small or medium-sized vintner would go with a good, small distribution house, because he knew that the small house would fight for him," says Morgan. "At one time, all the brands were in competition with each other, since they were all represented by different houses. Now you have mega-wholesalers selling multiple brands that are competing in the same market niche, for the same shelf space. So even if the brand grows, the chances are your competitor's brand is growing as well."

The concentration of wholesaling power troubles Jason Lewis, a buyer for the Liquor Barn chain's Southern California stores. "I don't understand the situation," he says. "On one hand, the wineries are permitting this to happen. They're not pulling together and helping and supporting the smaller distributors. And on the other hand, they then complain that they don't have options anymore. Bull. I don't know if this is some kind of lack of will or backbone, or whether these guys really feel that one distributor can do as good a job for all of them as several working with fewer wineries."

Most small California wineries can't afford to hire trucks to deliver their wine throughout the state. Likewise, when selling wine elsewhere, they must go through a state-approved wholesaler, which Safeway's Mick Unti calls "a link built into blue laws, a niche protected by government in most states." So, vintners are often stuck with whatever distributor they can get.

For wine, says Unti, there are two major kinds. "One is the big, high-volume house that also handles spirits. They tend to be less concerned about small wineries, and more concerned about those doing large volumes. The small ones don't get a lot of follow-through from the big distributors." The fast-growing, high-volume wineries such as Glen Ellen or Sutter Home—even with wines that are low priced for a premium—grab a distributor's attention.

"The other kind of distributor," continues Unti, "specializes in wine. They exist around the country, although in Northern California this kind of business is more often handled by a broker, who is more of a liaison between the winery and the retail account. But even they like to focus on wineries with huge production, as well as those few wines that bring them the most dollars." A 25 percent to 30 percent slice from a bottle of $20 Cabernet or Chardonnay—for filling out some paper work and delivering the wine to a store—isn't chump change.

Alex Morgan feels that the trend toward the concentration of distribution power is bad for both wineries and consumers. "Face it," he says, "the only people it's really good for are the few distributors who are calling the shots. And they're calling the shots for the whole industry. The consumer suffers because he doesn't necessarily find the wine he wants. What he finds are the wines that are profitable for the distributor."

The system is hard on vintners, Morgan adds, unless they're high-production wineries that make wine that's in demand. "But it's the mid-size producers who make mid-range wines that are really taking it in the shorts. Their wine doesn't have the snob appeal to warrant work on the part of a good broker, and the big distributors aren't interested in them because they're too small."

The number of distributors is shrinking even as the number of wineries continues to grow. "Ten years ago a large distributor represented maybe fifteen wineries," Morgan explains. "Today, that same distributor may represent seventy wineries. But the thing is, their volume hasn't changed all that much. They're doing the same amount of business, but it's divided among a lot more wineries. Well, it's obvious that a lot of wineries are going to get short shrift."

Winegrowers who aren't hot property have to provide support, including constructing displays and putting merchandising materials in retail stores. "But you also have to entice them with 'incentive programs,' which means that you essentially kick back money to them for every case of wine they move," says Morgan. Liquor Barn's Lewis has seen an increase in these kinds of offers. "Some wineries have come up with a rebate coupon, $5 off on a case. Or they'll offer truckload discounts."

While there are few industries that don't offer volume discounts, Lewis views some of the wine rebate action as signaling trouble at the vineyard. "I liken it to the automobile industry, where you know an auto company is having problems moving cars when it offers 1.9 percent financing. When has Rolls-Royce offered rebates? You see ads for Hyundais, but they don't need to talk about rebates."

But even solid wineries such as Buena Vista occasionally offer rebates on specific wines. "You simply have to offer sales incentives," says Mary Brown, who makes forays to the East Coast and Midwest, trying to whip up enthusiasm for Buena Vista wines among distributors, retail store accounts and restaurants.

"In some places, it seems like distributors are Buena Vista all the way, which is a good feeling," she explains. "In others, we're just one wine in a huge portfolio. And distributors and retailers are always looking for a deal." The personal attention by a winery representative does help, adds Brown. "In one place, a distributor said they couldn't get us in restaurants. Well, in a week we visited about twenty, and got a dozen to order cases."

However, even if a winery somehow strikes a chord with a retailer, the vintner is still at the mercy of the distributor. "Say you managed to get your wine in a chain store for a special program," explains Morgan, "a wine-of-the month promotion. Then you still have to have a distributor who has the people and clout to support you. Because if a chain store manager agrees to that kind of program, he wants the wine now, he wants the merchandising now, he wants it all now. Your distributor better like you, so your wine and material moves out of the warehouse when the retail people want it. Otherwise, you're screwed."

The realm of wine distribution is occasionally besmirched with tales of dirty tricks; Morgan doesn't discount this, but emphasizes it is a problem not restricted to this one particular industry. "Hey, it's the real world out there," he says. "Big money is involved. The biggest distributors aren't just moving wine. Wine, in fact, is incidental. The real money is in spirits. I know one distributor who moves 1.4 million cases of Scotch each year and makes $40 off each case. You think he does business with kid gloves? These are guys from New York and Chicago, who have been playing hardball for a long time. At the top, who knows what arms get twisted—or broken. At the bottom, you have guys pulling competitors' wines out of cross-merchandising racks in stores and putting their own wines in. Or they'll drill holes in their competitors' corks so the wines spoil. These guys can take their business pretty seriously."

Big distributors who handle many different wines also

have some leverage on retail outlets. "I know that smaller stores, if they want a particularly good wine for which there's high demand and a low supply, are sometimes forced to take ten cases of ordinary wine or slop to get that one good case," says a buyer for a large chain. "We're big enough so that no one can really pull that around here. But there are certain requests that are made, if you will. But with us, that's about all that are made—requests."

Curiously, one of the most powerful "distributors" in North America is a government agency; the Liquor Control Board of Ontario (LCBO), which buys nearly all of the foreign wine—whether it's from the U.S., France, Germany or Australia—consumed in Canada. It also buys a tremendous amount of the wine produced in the Great White North, although Ontario wineries can sell their own wine, and that's all, through winery-owned retail stores.

According to Dave Hulley of Ontario's Hillebrand Wine Estates: "The LCBO has a certain percentage they take, but you can set your price. It's a good deal, because we don't have to worry about a lot of distributors." American vintners must work hard to make deals with the powerful LCBO, but generally hold it in high regard, saying it's run by straight-shooters.

However, the recent free trade agreement between the U.S. and Canada promises to remove all of the barriers to American wine's northward movement. This undoubtedly will hurt companies such as Hillebrand, although rebelling nationalistic Canadians—who are distressed by American economic hegemony—will continue to drink Canuk wine, good and plonk alike, out of spite.

One of the most intriguing street battles is shaping up in the western U.S., between several large wine purveyors. Store Wars, as it could be called, is downright fascinating, in that the Safeway chain appears bent on killing its own child, the Liquor Barn chain, a subsidiary that it sold in 1987. Other giant wine discounters are entering the fray. If these giant stores war long enough without mortally wounding each other, accepting razor-thin margins—and perhaps even losses—to move wine, then this could attract consumers to buy more wine. It could thus prove the one bright spot for beleaguered wineries, a chance for vintners to see their products profitably used as weapons.

In the big scheme of things, this is but a small bit of fallout from the corporate raider mania of the mid-1980s. As a subsidiary business, Safeway had built up its Liquor Barn chain to 104 stores in California and Arizona, averaging 20,000 to 25,000 square feet in size. These whoppers carried beer, spirits, beer nuts, chips, smokes and a few other drinking products, and the most formidable selection of wine in America, if not the world. Ask just about any vintner, and he or she will tell you they "love selling to Liquor Barn." With literally thousands of wines from around the world, the chain generated annual sales of more than $330 million a year.

Faced with a hostile-takeover attempt in 1986, Safeway took itself private. In the extremely leveraged deal, the grocery chain ostensibly racked up $4.2 billion in debt. To raise capital to pay it down, Safeway sold Liquor Barn in 1987 to Majestic Wine Warehouses Ltd., of London, for a sum variously reported as $100 million and $105 million.

Majestic is owned by a pair of young Brits, Esme Johnstone—thirty-six at the time of the Liquor Barn acquisition—and Giles Clark, then thirty-four. It was a pretty audacious move on their part, given that Majestic owns twenty-one discount stores in the U.K., with annual sales estimated at around $25 million. But the two have been credited with revolutionizing the British wine merchant tradition, selling only by case and at a discount, remaining open for long hours, seven days a week. Johnstone and Clark planned to merge the American firm with Majestic, and within five years issue stock publicly in the U.S. and U.K.

Shortly after the purchase, Johnstone outlined what he had in mind for Liquor Barn. He planned to install computerized sales systems to free managers to spend more time on the floor helping customers; previously, Liquor Barn managers spent about half their time on paperwork. He wanted to do more newspaper advertising. The new Liquor Barn would push wines much harder than spirits, and actually cut back on the liquor lines. It would sell a couple of stores in what Johnstone thought were poor locations, and open a few new ones.

However, he also said he would use the same buying strategy used at Majestic, whereby the retailer would determine the price it wants to sell a wine for, and then figure backwards to what it would offer the winery and its broker or distributor. Johnstone planned to centralize wine buying, and cut down on the store manager's ability to cut deals. He added that Safeway Stores' and Liquor Barn's previous executives "were basically grocery buyers dabbling in liquor. They weren't wine buyers."

Johnstone may know how to buy and sell wine in the U.K., but he wasn't winning friends and influencing people in the States. "The new guys at Liquor Barn are arrogant and awfully rude," said one winery owner, who sold a considerable volume through the chain. "And I think that within a year or two, they're gonna be out of business." His words proved prophetic.

In late 1988, Liquor Barn went into Chapter 11 of the U.S. bankruptcy code. It is now undergoing a lengthy—and one may assume somewhat humiliating—financial restructuring. British and American financial institutions now own 66 percent of the company, and a crack turnaround specialist, John Thompson, was brought in to resuscitate the ailing firm.

A former president of Elson Cos., an Atlanta-based newsstand and gift retailing chain, Thompson blamed Majestic's British owners for much of the Barn's troubles. He tightened spending and worked to boost the morale of employees who felt "discounted" by the Brits. He also fired more than a few management types to save money.

Majestic's management have no one but themselves to blame. For example, Johnstone's verbal digs at Liquor Barn's previous management didn't sit well with Steve Boone, who founded the chain, served as its president under Safeway, and lost out in a bidding war for it with Majestic. After failing to get the Barns, the thirty-nine-year-old Boone pulled together his group of investors and paid $46 million for the Cost Plus Imports chain of stores. With outlets in five Western states, Cost Plus sells $82 million a year worth of plates, rugs, wicker furniture, exotic food and knicknacks from Southeast Asia and the Indian subcontinent. Boone now means to convert some of the stores and expand to build Cost Plus Wines.

With help from other former Liquor Barn staffers, Boone started in the San Francisco area and planned to eventually open operations in Oregon, Washington, Florida and, perhaps, New York. "There are a lot of consumers who don't want to shop in a store with 9,000 items," he told *The San Francisco Chronicle*. "They want fine wines at competitive prices sold by a knowledgeable staff. We think we can offer better prices than Liquor Barn by focusing only on those wines that are hot—say sixty or seventy of California's 600 or more Cabernets."

Moreover, Safeway concentrated on its own wine business, free from the worry of hurting its subsidiary. The cash sale to Majestic put no restraints on the grocer, and during the 1987 Thanksgiving and Christmas season, Safeway came out smoking, advertising champagnes and top-quality wines at astonishingly low prices. As one independent wine and liquor marketer said: "Some felt this was a declaration of war on Liquor Barn."

And Safeway had the heavy ordnance. "Safeway can take a loss on its liquor and wine till water freezes over and drive them out of business," said Pat Andress, manager of a Trader Joe's outlet in Pasadena, part of a twenty-seven-store chain that has been No. 2 in wine sales behind Liquor Barn. Trader Joe's has worked a slightly different strategy than Liquor Barn, selling only a limited selection of heavily discounted wines. But it too plans to expand, opening more stores in Northern California, and will try to take away some of Liquor Barn's action.

Moreover, discount "membership" warehouse operations, such as the Price Club chain and its clones, are also stocking increasingly large volumes of wine. While Price Club limits its memberships to small-business owners, government employees and credit union members, the stores are packed with folks buying pizzas, paper towels and tomato sauce by the case. There's no sales help, and nearly all the items in a Price Club are cheaper, ounce-for-ounce, than one can find them anywhere else. Its wine is no different.

But few kinds of retail enterprises can merchandise and move wine as well as a grocery store, if it so chooses. By featuring wines in its regular newspaper advertising—which isn't an additional expense, since grocery store chains do it every week anyway—it can make consumers aware of good wine values. In terms of merchandising, it has unlimited opportunities to pair wine with food, creating situations that can compel consumers to make impulse purchases. However, both the wine and supermarket industries have been slow to tumble to this fact.

"In the late 1960s, it was a pretty radical thought in the supermarket industry for a major chain to pay any attention to wine," says Mick Unti, Safeway's beverage merchandising manager who buys liquor for the chain's Southern California stores. "For one thing, wine requires more knowledge than other products, and supermarkets lacked the expertise to have a marketing program for fine wines. Plus, the fine wine industry was very reluctant, to the point of adamantly opposing, the idea of fine wine in grocery stores."

The wineries, Unti explains, felt that they would lose presence in a high-volume, low-service environment. But of course, that was when premium wineries could sell all the wine they made. Today, vintners need every outlet they can get. But in some supermarkets, even their fears of low service are being eased. More supermarkets are emphasizing specialty sections, including bakeries, delis, fresh seafood counters and wine sections. For the latter, some even assign wine-wise attendants to help shoppers with selections.

In an industry accustomed to making a penny or two on a dollar of sales, premium wine provides heady returns with its 30 percent markups. Only fresh seafood carries as high a price and as big a return as premium wine, while even jug wines bring an 18 percent to 23 percent profit, says Unti. "And you don't have to worry about losing any of the wine to spoilage, as you do with seafood. You don't have to put wine in a cooler, so you don't have refrigeration costs. It's one of the few nonperishable goods in a grocery store that sells for more than $5."

But merchandising is still critical, says Unti. "You cannot underestimate or place enough emphasis on shelf-talkers. If I'm in a store and ask a shopper in the wine section if they need help, they may or may not accept it. But if I put up a shelf-talker, they immediately walk up and look at it. I tell store managers that they can't have enough information up in the wine section."

Liquor Barn's Lewis is also a believer in shelf-talkers. In fact, there aren't many wines in Liquor Barn that aren't accompanied by some kind of little sign explaining a bit about the wine, its aromas, flavors, what food it might best go with, its track record in contests and so forth. "But the ones that work best are handwritten, or at least look as if they're handwritten," Lewis adds. "It doesn't work if the shelf-talker is typeset, printed and carries the Mondavi logo on it. It's got to look like someone at the store took the time to quote reviews by Robert Parker or Jerry Mead."

This is where the winery's support personnel often come in, going around to liquor and grocery stores hanging shelf-talkers on their bottles of wine. The tags might be color photocopied, but the ones that work best will appear to have the personal touch.

Not every grocery store manager buys the approach, says Unti. "I was hired to increase wine sales," he explains, "and I've had to go against management in many places to do this, to train them, to get them to fund advertising. It's still a new idea for some of them, and they resist. But the stores that have done this have had phenomenal success selling wine. I've seen it in Phoenix, Dallas, Seattle, Los Angeles, any place where you can sell wine in supermarkets and the grocery stores make the effort."

Unti is, however, disappointed that not all wineries make the effort to assist the stores. "It's one of my biggest gripes.

If a winery like Château St. Jean would send someone out to spend a couple of weeks going through stores, assisting with marketing, putting up merchandising displays and talking to customers, their sales would take off. But the only ones who are really working the streets hard, especially outside of California, are the Gallos. What premium wineries need are more working missionaries."

This is a marketing point where wineries have great opportunity, and where they need to do a better job. Few distributors will do it for them. But it could be the one major arena where flat wine sales can be increased. Moreover, discount wars between Safeway, Liquor Barn, Trader Joe's and Price Club-type outlets may also prove a boon for wineries. The survivors won't be identified until the smoke clears. But if consumers can get most of the wines they want while also buying groceries, the boys from Britain may find the words about Liquor Barn's previous owners coming back to haunt.

Food and wine also conjoin in restaurants, and it's a symbiotic relationship important to both vintners and restaurant owners. For the former, restaurants are another outlet for products. But it's also a particularly prestigious and effective one; when the wine is matched with good food, the consumer thinks of it kindly, may seek out bottles to drink at home and recommend the brand to friends and associates.

Some winegrowers, such as Chalone, concentrate on the restaurant game. About 65 percent of its wine moves through on-premises sales, which befits its image more than the Safeway shuffle. At more than $15 a bottle, says president Phil Woodward, Chalone wouldn't sell many bottles there anyway. But while there are relatively few wineries in Chalone's ultra-premium category, he adds, "this is not to say that there aren't some wine lists that we don't fight over to get on."

Except for restaurants that specialize in wine and retain large and diverse inventory, most carry a limited selection in several price categories. Just as on the retail shelves, winegrowers do compete for places on the lists—if they can get the restaurant owner's attention, that is.

"People think that wine lists at restaurants are arrived at only after extensive and critical competitive tastings," sneers Alex Morgan. "That's bullshit. There aren't many restaurateurs who have time for that kind of thing. And a lot of them don't know much about wine. What happens is that a restaurant owner will sit down with one or two wholesalers. He'll tell them what he needs—so many whites of a certain price range, so many reds, so many domestics and imports—and the distributors essentially make the decision for him. There may be incentives, but they're financial incentives more than they are ones related to the relative quality of wine and how it fits with the food in the place."

Morgan is correct to a large degree, but it depends on the establishment. Rene Verdon, who served as White House chef for President Kennedy, and until recently owned the Le Trianon restaurant in San Francisco, tasted an awful lot of wine over the years, looking for what might please his customers. When he opened Le Trianon in 1972, explains Verdon, about 90 percent of the wine he served came from France. By the time he sold it in 1987, the list was split about evenly between French and California wines. Besides the vintners who came to him, Verdon also visited a lot of wineries. "For one thing it was fun," says the outgoing Frenchman. "But also you have to keep moving on, adjusting your cuisine and wine list for what your customers want."

Moreover, he adds, wine is an important adjunct to the restaurant trade, a business that's even more perilous than running a winery. Unlike the preparation of food, wine doesn't require much labor to serve. Because it goes with the meal, it doesn't lengthen the time patrons sit, slowing table turnover. And since overhead is already figured into the price of the meals, the profits on wine are almost all net.

Restaurants, of course, often charge more than double or triple their wholesale price, which leads to a lot of grousing by consumers, who think restaurants are gouging customers. A business group on an expense account might think nothing of paying $60 for a bottle of Chalone Pinot Noir. But there are many who grow upset paying $30 for a Carneros Creek release that they can get for $12 at a Liquor Barn.

"People who should know better just don't seem to understand," says Verdon. "Restaurants are a low profit business, 5 to 10 percent. You have high overhead in rent and labor, and get very little from the food. The markup on liquor and wine is where many restaurants make whatever profits they get."

While Verdon agrees that some restaurateurs do mark up wines too much—his rule of thumb was twice and two and a half times wholesale—it's not exactly free money. "There are little costs associated with it, like washing glasses," he notes. "And then you have to hold it in inventory. Some wineries or wholesalers will offer you a 10 percent discount if you buy ten cases, or fifty cases. But you've got to consider that you might end up holding that wine too long. It's important for a restaurant owner to know whether his customers will buy those wines if you are to make a profit on them."

There is a certain art to selling wines in restaurants. Ideally, the entire serving staff will know how to cut tops off neck foils, handle the corkscrew and execute an elegant pour. In addition, tastings and discussions with the chef over what wine goes best with certain dishes can help them help the customers. It is in the interest of waiters and waitresses to move wine, if only because a 15 percent tip on a few extra $10 bottles per shift can add a couple grand extra to their annual income.

Wine stewards and servers alike can also help out the restaurant by steering customers toward certain brands, especially brands with which the restaurant is overstocked. But not too hard. Servers can stand on their heads trying to get patrons to try the Dover sole, and diners won't doubt the motives. But push a wine, especially an expensive wine, and customers are quick to grow suspicious.

Kevin Barron never recommends the most expensive

wine in the house. The British-born San Francisco resident, who has been a maitre d' at some of the city's best restaurants, likewise wouldn't recommend the cheapest wine. "I always start by recommending what's appropriate from the middle range," he explains. "If they then ask about the expensive wines, fine."

Barron thinks a big list is a dumb list. "Invariably, a restaurant with a large, pretentious wine list has a large and pretentious staff. But you don't want people staying at the table forever, and a big wine list almost guarantees someone will sit there studying it for ten or fifteen minutes."

Barron wants to help pick a wine that will make the customer happy. But he is also sensitive to the needs of the restaurant owner when an inventory of wine starts to approach an age where it will decline in quality, or becomes a financial drag. "In that case," he says, "I am perfectly willing to try and make that sale."

Customers can just say no to high wine prices. Rene Verdon has done it with suppliers. "When Opus One first came out," he explains, "they came around offering it for $480 a case. I said no. They came a week later, and offered it for $400 a case. If enough people say no, the price comes down."

These are street-fighting words vintners hate to hear. But in the merchandising battles, roughly one hundred California wineries are trying yet another tactic—private label bottling. While printing special labels and bottling wine for hotel chains and restaurants does nothing to build a winery's brand recognition—and can sometimes convey the impression that the winery is a flaky outfit—the technique has boosted sales volume for those that do it with skill and tact.

For example, Dennis Marion has put out Cincinnati wine, which is sold only in that Ohio city, and which commemorates Cincinnati's bicentennial. With sketches by a watercolor artist, the labels depict Cincinnati landmarks. Marion bottles three varietals for the special release: Cabernet Sauvignon, Chardonnay and White Zinfandel. In 1988 alone, Cincinnatians went through more than 4,000 cases.

The merchandising wine wars are still in the Neanderthal rock-throwing and club-thumping stage, primarily concentrated as they are on getting the right shelf space. Attractive labels and hand-printed shelf-talkers may represent a leap to bows and arrows and muskets. But as the street battles continue, more powerful, high-tech weapons will surely be brought to bear.

22
PROSE AND ETHICS IN DOUBT: THE SYMBIOSIS OF WRITERS AND WINE

"The bubbles from the pink blush of the champagne jettison to the top of the glass, picking up jewel-like intensity. As the bubbles hit the roof of the mouth, they explode, releasing the flavor of fruit and tickling like a feather. After the first swallow, the bubbles warm your insides, making you feel a little giddy. . . ."

Should a competent, professional journalist submit such purple prose to most magazines, it's liable to provoke an editor into filing a felony assault charge. Or at best, it would warrant an exceptionally cruel rejection note. But as the

311

above passage—lifted from a piece by a prominent Texas wine columnist—indicates, those who write about wine can get away with literary homicide.

Taken on the whole, wine writing in America does not begin to approach the art or craft applied to other topics, including sports, film or even business. A good many self-proclaimed wine writers simply cannot write, while a number of them know little or nothing about wine. Editors often put up with the ill-informed dreck because they want articles on vineyards, wineries and the beverage. Besides, pretty photographs can always carry the spread.

Writers who do have a working knowledge of the subject can be solipsistic to the extreme, and horribly arrogant in their assessment of a wine. They are, of course, entitled to an opinion. And those who review wines aren't really much different from film critics; the talent pool is similar, ranging from the superior Joe Bob Briggs to Pauline Kael and Gene Shalit.

Ask an educated, literate vintner about the quality of wine writing and he's likely to grimace, cringe and keep his mouth tightly shut. That's because winegrowers need the writers. Even a hack who spins a smarmy feature or profile generates publicity few wineries can afford to buy. More-over, critics have considerable influence in the marketplace, since many consumers rely on reviews to direct them in their purchase of wine.

This is, however, somewhat disconcerting in light of recent revelations concerning wine writer payola. Such improprieties were once common in many areas of journal-ism, although the freebie-taking has been purged from most. (Travel writing is a notable exception.) But selling words about wine is financially rewarding for relatively few scribes. Thus, there's the temptation for writers to look for free wine, lodging, junkets and more. Indeed, what the consumer reads about a wine is not necessarily what he'll get, since what the consumer reads may have been deter-mined by what the wine writer gets.

There are, to be sure, a handful of adept and knowledge-able writers covering wine, a fact that merely points up the deficiencies of their colleagues. The good ones are ethical and successful.

For example, bringing his background as a wine merchant to the topic, *Gourmet* magazine wine editor Gerald Asher is also an essayist of insight, wit and considerable style. His elegantly crafted columns would be just as enjoyable if the subject were adhesives instead of wine. Asher is able to write well on just about anything to which he turns his mind.

Anthony Dias Blue, while not the master prose stylist that Asher is—his work, in fact, borders at times on the smug or captious—nevertheless displays a solid and encyclopedic knowledge of his subject, which is combined with an excellent palate. Richard Nalley, the Copley News Service wine columnist, is a travel and feature writer based in New York, whose interest in wine is a relatively recent development. Still, he has displayed a remarkable aptitude as a quick study. His facile, unpretentious approach to wine makes it an accessible and enjoyable subject to the legions of Middle American readers whose newspapers subscribe to the Copley service.

Leon Adams, a contemporary of Louis Gomberg, calls himself "an old reporter who fell in love with the story of wine." He grew up in a California family that raised its own grapes and made its own wine. While covering the repeal of Prohibition for San Francisco newspapers in 1931, he was, at the age of twenty-six, one of the few writers in the nation who understood much about the stuff. Since then, Adams has become the leading wine historian in the United States, if not a piece of wine history himself. One of his books, *The Commonsense Book of Wine*, was first published in 1958 and is still in print in revised form. He's about to come out with the fourth edition of his landmark *Wines of America*, first published in 1973. In his straight-forward, reportorial style, Adams has written about nearly every winery in the country.

But for sheer influence, no one surpasses Baltimore's Robert Parker. If any wine writer has won the hearts and minds of the industry and consumer alike, it is Parker. More to the point, he has been practically beatified. To many wine lovers, Parker is St. Robert of the Vine. He has won the enthusiasm of the industry because he has so totally won the devotion of the consumer.

Parker isn't much of a writer, which he admits. His prose style is turgid and flat. Another wine writer says that Parker's writing "is terribly labored. I often imagine him sitting there, like a second grader with a crayon in his hand, tongue sticking out of the side of his mouth, trying hard to get the words down." Only a cement-head can't detect some jealousy of Parker's standing in the industry. And fine feature writing isn't what Parker is about. He is, for now, the most respected wine reviewer in America.

A former attorney, Parker developed an interest in wine during visits to Bordeaux and Burgundy. Soon after he was hired out of law school in 1974, he found his interests devolving increasingly on wine and away from corporate law. He left his practice after ten years, right after his retirement plan became fully vested. Even before he dropped out of law, he had begun a small newsletter called *The Wine Advocate*, which evaluated current releases. It was one of the first such publications truly oriented to the consumer, with no advertising. Parker's goal was to produce a guide that evaluated wine as mercilessly, dispassionately and objectively as the Consumer's Union rated cars, lawnmowers and electrical appliances.

Parker devised a rating system based on a 100-point scale. It was, he has averred, an inspired invention. Since it corresponded to the system used in education from grammar school to college, everyone in the country could understand it immediately. Wines that score 90 to 100 get A's. Wines that score between 80 and 89 receive B's and so on to 59 and below, which is an F Troop beverage. *The Wine Advocate* made lots of sense to lots of people, and a decade after its founding is the most influential wine guide in America.

Those who initially liked it a lot also helped make Parker a star. "Parker's early influence was created by New York retailers," says another prominent wine writer. "Like Malvolio, he had greatness thrust upon him. His big moment came when he was the first person to extravagantly praise the 1982 Bordeaux. He was busy yelling at the top of his tiny voice, and the marketplace generally ended up agreeing with him. But the retailers used Robert Parker to sell their wine. The majority of them have no professional savvy or pride in what they're doing; it was easier for them to put up signs saying Parker liked this or that, quoting *The Wine Advocate's* rating system. It was the retailers who made Parker a 'genius.' "

The same writer, however, agrees that Parker knows his stuff. "Give him his due. He tastes carefully, and I've never known him to give a really high mark to something inferior, or a really low mark to something superior."

Parker's palate is consistent, if idiosyncratic, and his research is formidable. He tastes and judges a tremendous number of wines, which probably means that more first-growth Bordeaux and Burgundy pass through his kitchen drain than slide down the gullets of customers at Lutèce. Most important, Parker claims he buys all the wines he tastes, and accepts no free bottles; ethically speaking, he is Caesar's wife. (Other wine writers have hinted that this may not be entirely true.)

Parker's own view of himself has grown to be somewhat Olympian. He is one of his best fans, despite the diffident politesse which he cultivates in public. Known to have disdain for fellow wine writers, Parker considers them fellow travelers in the industry—the California wine industry. His tastes in wine, on the other hand, seem decidedly Gallic, and he's especially fond of the wines from the Rhône and Bordeaux. While American wines can earn high numbers from Parker, his preference runs to the European vintages.

However, not everyone is charmed by Parker's scoring system. To them, it seems absurd to use such a precise measure when describing the taste, aroma and quality of wine. "It is disgusting to have consumers believe that there is a wine hierarchy that can be ranked from 0 to 100," says Agustin Huneeus. "Can you say that Mozart is better than Beethoven, and then give Beethoven a 73 and Mozart a 92? Now, I understand that Americans like things classified. I look for the little guy in *The San Francisco Chronicle*. [This cartoon figure signifies the reviewer's opinion of a movie, from wildly clapping to sound asleep.] But I know exactly what the review means, because I've learned the reviewer's taste. So do a lot of people, and purposely do exactly the opposite of what a critic recommends, because they are confident in their own likes and dislikes. But people are not as apprehensive about movies as they are about wine."

So, when Parker proclaims a wine Mozart, consumers flock to buy it. But John Foy, a writer and chef who has recently started a newsletter called *John Foy's Wine Odyssey*, believes that putting precise numbers on wine ignores a lot of considerations. "Ratings based on a system of 0 to 100 points . . . implies an exactness that does not exist and is misleading to the subscriber," Foy remarks starchily in a press release promoting his publication. He uses a ranking system based on letters, from AAA for the best to D, which connotes a grave lack of quality. In addition, Foy considers the price of the wine, and makes recommendations when he feels a release is a "must buy" for his readers. Parker also mentions prices and relative values in his tasting notes, but *John Foy's Wine Odyssey* is more like a well-researched stock market tout sheet.

Still, Parker can make or break a wine, and whether vintners like his numbering system or not, it's a powerful fact of life. "I'm the worst culprit," admits Huneeus with a laugh. "I get a 93 from Parker and the first thing I do is promote it like crazy." And that good review on a specific wine usually means that it will disappear from the shelves of wine shops in major East Coast cities a couple weeks after *The Wine Advocate* appears. Thus, there are plenty of winegrowers who like Parker, especially those who consistently win good reviews. But Parker has enemies. Naturally, some of his foes are merely the victims of their own sour grapes, but others raise legitimate questions about Parker's palate.

"The fact is that he is prejudiced against California wines for no legitimate reason," fumes one Napa Valley marketing director, whose wines have been tweaked by Parker. "He disparages the progress we've made here. He says we'll never compete with the French—and this after we've whipped their ass in blind tastings repeatedly. By turning people off to California wine, he's turning them off to great quality and great value. And what really takes the cake is that he's just one guy—one palate. And not a very good one at that. The guy has blind spots.'' Indeed he may, but Parker also has an enthusiastic readership, and even more who follow his recommendations. In fact, it's suggested that a goodly number of enologists make wine to suit Robert Parker's palate, instead of following their own instincts. And that is power.

After Parker, the nation's most influential wine writer is probably Frank Prial, a columnist for *The New York Times*. Unlike Parker, Prial can actually write. A veteran journalist, he served for many years as a *Times* foreign correspondent. If wading through Parker's descriptions of wine is purgatory, scanning Prial's clean, bright prose is an unmitigated pleasure. He writes with equal facility on wine, winemakers and the wine industry, and he even tackles his fellow wine scribes in print. In one column, Prial examined the state of wine books, focusing in particular on their evolution.

''The first reaction from the book trade to the American wine boom was an avalanche of coffee table books,'' he noted. ''We got bird's-eye views of every vineyard in Christendom and a few just over the line. And we got enormous enlargements of grape bunches to show us, presumably, how they look to the insects who try to get them before the pickers do. . . .''

Prial is nothing if not even-handed, and he chooses to praise those writers he feels deserve it. He has called Parker ''the hottest literary property to come out of Baltimore since H. L. Mencken and James M. Cain,'' in reference to Parker's studious tomes on the wines of Bordeaux and the Rhône. Prial's recommended wines also move product for retailers, although not with the same fury of Parker's Best Bets. And too, he writes for the New York market; Prial's sphere of influence is largely restricted to the circulation of the *Times*, although other papers around the nation do pick up his work.

However, since New York is the hottest wine market in the nation after California, Prial's columns are of significant and compelling interest to the industry. He is accorded tremendous respect, though for his retail influence and not for his considerable skills as a writer, which is a shame. Vintners may not quake and shake, genuflect and speak in tongues for Frank Prial—as they do in the presence of Parker—but they still roll out the red carpet and treat him like a visiting crown prince. That must amuse Prial; though he obviously loves wine and is intimately familiar with his subject, he is, at heart, a professional journalist, not a wine writer. As such, he is concerned with the meat of the subject, not the trimmings. Brush wars were once his beat; he now treats wine with the same incisive sense of inquiry and dispassion.

Wine writers can lead pleasant and privileged lives. Richard Nalley, for one, finds it quite agreeable. A soft-spoken thirty-year-old Georgian now living in New York, Nalley started out as a magazine free lance, specializing in travel pieces. Some of his early articles focused on the world's great viticultural regions, including Burgundy, Bordeaux and the Napa Valley.

"After I'd written a few pieces on wine regions, I found that I was developing a real interest in wines," he recalls. "I started studying the subject, and I began seeking assignments on wine and winemakers, instead of wine regions." When Dan Berger resigned his position as the Copley New Service wine columnist—Berger is now with *The Los Angeles Times*—Nalley was offered the slot.

"The money is hardly spectacular at Copley, but it does provide an excellent forum," says Nalley. "You're reaching readers in over 200 newspapers across the country. And these are generally people in small cities and towns—people who aren't exposed to wine that much, or information about wine. So it's a challenge to give them information they can use in clear, understandable terms. Too often, wine writers assume a mantle—they act as though they're part of a priesthood. They obscure wine, they don't clarify it. They're a barrier to the understanding and enjoyment of wine, not a means of access."

Nalley sees his job as one of "knocking down barriers, not putting them up. Wine writers are lucky people," he adds. "We get lots of free wine sent to our apartments for tasting and review, and we're sponsored on trips all over the world.

We do have an obligation—to the consumer first, and then to the industry. But we do need to provide information on wines and winemakers in an unpretentious fashion, so the consumer will know what in the hell we're talking about."

Nalley's misgivings about his peers, then, center primarily on their ability to communicate. "Really, a lot of them have very good palates," he avers. "Generally speaking, they know what they're talking about. Trouble is, nobody else does. They just aren't good writers. Their prose tends to be labored and inept, or, even worse, overblown and self-serving. It really turns people off."

Since wine writers can be critics more than journalists, many are inclined to frame mere opinion as objective fact. Those opinions at times border on the irrational, even the bizarre. In few other journalistic fields are bêtes noires pursued so ruthlessly, nor pet theories showcased so ostentatiously. The trouble, as far as the industry is concerned, is the fact that the peeves of certain writers can register in the marketplace.

As wine editor of *Bon Appétit*, columnist for *The Wine Spectator* and author of the most comprehensive analysis of individual releases of California wines yet published, Anthony Dias Blue is one of the most widely read wine writers in America. Blue usually favors a middle-of-the-road approach to wine critique; his columns are generally readable, informative and nonpartisan. At least they're nonpartisan until it comes to a Blue pet peeve, such as Sauvignon Blanc.

Considered one of the world's great white wine grape varieties by the general run of vintners, it can produce wines which are rich, full flavored and complex, or lean, herbaceous and crisp. First popularized in the U.S. when Robert Mondavi called his wine Fumé Blanc, Sauvignon Blanc is used to produce the great Sauternes and Barsacs of Bordeaux, the white wines of Graves, and the Sancerres and Pouilly-Fumés of the Loire. The great majority of winemakers—and wine lovers—around the world concur that Sauvignon Blanc is a grape most worthy of respect.

Andy Blue, however, seems to have a blind spot on Sauvignon Blanc. He periodically inveighs against the grape and the wine made from it. He labels the grape as a mediocre variety, and claims the wines made from it are simple, often vegetal in the extreme, and completely lacking in complexity and potential ageworthiness.

This may simply be that Blue's otherwise sound palate is unable to detect any of the desirable nuances that other competent tasters find in Sauvignon Blanc. There are, after all, folks who strongly prefer a regular Three Alarm chili to the Total Nuclear Conflagration variety, but at least they'll admit it. Blue, however, never prefaces any of the broadsides against Sauvignon Blanc with an advisory. Instead, his invective is presented as gospel, not personal sentiment. And this fact makes ulcer-ridden vintners who rely on Sauvignon Blanc start swilling Tagamet by the quart whenever Blue starts feeling contentious.

If wine writers are viewed with both hope and dread by winemakers, wine publications—the natural habitat of wine writers—provoke similar feelings. Newsletters such as Parker's *Wine Advocate* and *The Connoisseur's Guide* (published by Charles Olken and Earl Singer), restrict themselves solely to the review of current wine releases. Other publications, from *Vogue* to airline in-flight magazines, cover developments and personalities in the industry. *Wines & Vines* is largely a trade journal. It sees, hears and speaks no evil, except when it comes to neoprohibitionists and variegated leafhoppers. But *The Wine Spectator* is a unique beast, a splashy, oversized biweekly that is the most influential general wine publication in the industry.

The *Spectator* is published by Marvin Shanken. An overweight, effusive and temperamental New Yorker, he is a tireless self-promoter who displays a ready proclivity for flashy graphics and provocative headlines. The *Spectator* is no puff sheet. Its feature articles and news items examine all aspects of trade, from viticulture to distributors. And it seems to dote on exploiting troubles in the industry, whether it's the addition of ethylene glycol in certain Austrian wines or the acrimonious differences between California vintners and growers. The *Spectator*'s reportage irritates more than a few in the wine business.

"I think what Shanken really wants is to publish *The*

National Enquirer," complains one Sonoma winegrower. "It's the vinous equivalent of axe murders and aliens from outer space."

Yet others come to the *Spectator*'s defense. "They're objective, so that sometimes means they step on toes," says Bob Roux, a marketing analyst for Robert Mondavi. "And their format is pretty flashy. But they have to attract readers and advertisers, just like any other publication. Generally speaking, I'd say we're well served by the *Spectator*. They're a news publication, not a trade organ. They have their own agenda—they have to. But they do get the word out about wineries and wines, and that could only be good for the industry in the long run."

Regardless of their personal feelings about *The Wine Spectator*, winegrowers are unanimous in their desire to get into the magazine. It reviews a score or more new wines each issue. A wine picked for its Spectator Selection or Cellar Selection is virtually guaranteed to run up impressive sales in the nation's major wine markets, including New York, San Francisco, Los Angeles, Chicago, Houston and Miami. Any wine tapped for the tabloid's Best Buys or Highly Recommended categories can also expect enhanced sales.

The job of evaluating wine at the *Spectator* falls to three editors: Harvey Steiman, Jim Laube and Jim Gordon. They meet each week in San Francisco and taste and evaluate the new releases. All three possess sound palates; more important, their very number precludes the blind spots, off days and simple prejudices that can mar the evaluations by a Parker or Blue. *The Spectator* uses a 100-point system similar to Parker's, but the reviews are a consensus, not one man's opinion. As such, its reviews are perhaps the most reliable in the nation.

The Spectator also publishes some of the best, and most opinionated, wine columnists in the world, including Blue, Steiman, James Suckling and David Rosengarten. Often the columnists write about relatively innocuous subjects, such as the best wine to serve with hamburgers or crab cakes. Sometimes they pull out all stops and flay a wine, trend or a winery. At such times, the letters-to-the-editor department is invariably packed with outraged replies from aggrieved vintners and their fans. It is this willingness by Shanken and his staff to lance tender industry egos that makes The Spectator a singular publication in the wine business, and a valuable one.

The relationship, then, between wine writers and the wine industry is essentially a symbiotic one. With a few adversarial exceptions, it's like sportswriting and baseball many decades ago, where the scribes glorified the Babe's prodigious hitting, but ignored his less noble appetites. The fact that a highly regarded wine writer can sell wine is something with which the industry, however unhappily, must contend. Few other businesses support a coterie of journalists in such an intimate fashion, aside from the travel destination publicity game. Certainly, the observations of journalists covering the petrochemical beat seldom influence the sale of specific brands of chemicals and fuels.

At their best, wine writers are essayists and discerning critics. At worst, they are shills, know-nothings, or both. But the fact is that editors have indulged behavior by wine writers that would never be tolerated in a beat reporter; acceptance of free wine, lavish dinners and junkets abroad from the people they cover. In large part, this is due to the fact that wine writers are given paltry pay. Few papers or magazines pay more than a few dollars a column inch for wine prose, and most don't even provide expense accounts.

The writers are therefore at the mercy of the producers of the products they must evaluate. The best writers walk the fine line between reportage and promotion successfully. In the old days, the mores governing wine writers were loose. The industry was small, people didn't know much about wine, and cared even less. That's changed, and it is no longer desirable for writers to serve as de facto flacks for the industry. The marketplace is too sophisticated now, and too much money is involved. Just as there's a shakeout going on in the wine business itself, so there's a winnowing evidenced in the wine writing trade.

In the end, we can expect a fraternity of journalists who

know their craft and their subject, and who approach both objectively and professionally. That will be good for the consumer, and it will also be good, in the long run, for winegrowers; though many will no doubt long for the old days, when a good review could be had for a little schmoozing, a dinner and a few bottles of the good stuff from the back of the cellar.

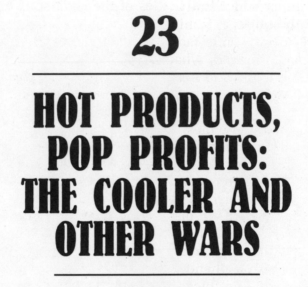

23

HOT PRODUCTS, POP PROFITS: THE COOLER AND OTHER WARS

In and out: it's a term that means profit in the wine business. Those wines that leave the winery quickly—as opposed to Cabernet Sauvignons and other varietals that must age in inventory—are called cash flow wines. From the premium perspective, cash flow wines may be unoaked Chardonnays and Sauvignon Blancs, which sell for a fairly good price, but stay in the winery for little more than a year before they're bottled and shipped. For vintners who have a market for such varietals, their return on investment may not be spectacular, but it rolls in much faster than with high-priced, well-aged releases.

However, there are other wines and wine-based products that fit the cash flow profile even more precisely, and they have become very big money-makers indeed. Most are sold at the lower end of the price structure, and are beverages that can quickly win legions of fans among consumers. They can also be exceptionally high-risk items for producers, for wine is as subject to fashion as any other business. But even as one novelty wine fades, another rises. And as Gerald Asher has observed, whatever arrives next is likely to be something "pink and fizzy." It's a pretty good bet, considering history.

In the 1960s and 1970s, the ultimate cash flow wines were the so-called pop wines. These were sweet decoctions that often had as much fruit concentrate—particularly pear syrup—in the fermenting base as grape juice. They were cloying, one-dimensionally fruity and, to the table wine drinker, simply terrible. But Americans, in large part young Americans, loved the quasi-wine. The first wave of such products included Bali Hai and Spanada, followed in short order by Annie Green Springs and Strawberry Hill. Cold Duck was also a phenomenon of this period, a red fruity sparkling wine produced by the bulk champagne process, but one that has stuck around.

These wines tapped a basic truism: the American consumer likes fruity, sweet, bubbly cold things to drink. They were not wines aimed at wine drinkers, but instead were targeted at consumers of soda pop and beer. Marketed to appeal to a product-driven consumer base, a segment of consumers whose tastes in everything—from togs to TV shows—changed often, such wines were very much products of their times. When the times change, many of the products die.

Yet the basic underlying tastes that fueled the products remain the same, which is why the cyclical appearance of topical wine products, if you will, is inevitable. At the upper end of this range of products, some beverages actually transcend the original trendiness which first blew a breath of life into them. They are distinctive, and secure a long-term niche. At the low end, packaging and marketing strategies mutate, but the basics remain the same—the liquid is sweet, fruity, colorful and best consumed cold. And for a time, such products can become incredibly hot.

No pop wine product has made such an impact on the marketplace as wine coolers, the hottest of the hot wine products. Their production has made a few people rich, depleted the pockets of a number of others, and caused the graph lines on the domestic wine industry to jump around like Little Richard in his salad years. Coolers caught on faster than VCRs, and in an exceptionally short time became a solid part of America's drinking culture.

Wine coolers got their commercial start in the early 1980s. Michael Crete, a Californian who liked to drink white wine mixed with fruit juices, had been complimented by friends on his impromptu wine creations. For years folks have mixed their own wine coolers, often using the likes of Spanada, Pink Chablis and Pink Ripple as a wine base. Crete, however, started wondering if there was a buck in it, and in 1981 went into partnership with R. Stuart Bewley.

The two men raised $150,000 from family and friends and plowed it into a derelict building in the Sacramento Delta town of Lodi. They whipped up a batch of Crete's Kickapoo joy juice, bottled it in recycled glass and sold it around Northern California. They called it California Cooler. The first year they sold 800 cases. The following year, they sold 85,000 cases. The year after that, 2.5 million. California Cooler was a phenomenon. In just three years it single-handedly defined an entirely new market segment.

By 1985, Crete and Bewley were moving more than ten million cases a year. They were offered $146 million for their company by Brown-Forman Corporation, the producers of Jack Daniel's whiskey. The two founders bailed out with their platinum parachutes, and California Cooler went corporate. But it was not alone. By then, Brown-Forman found itself going head-to-head with almost a hundred other cooler manufacturers, including two heavyweights who were to nearly blow California Cooler out of water: Seagram and the Gallos' Bartles & Jaymes brand.

Both the Gallos and Seagram decided to enter the wine cooler fray in 1984, when it became apparent that there were heaps of money to be made in it. Both companies realized that their products needed pitchmen, since they could hardly stand on their own merits as superior beverages, wine-based or otherwise. Seagram chose Bruce Willis. The Gallos created Frank and Ed; or rather, advertising wizard Hal Riney conjured up the avuncular duo. Other companies checked in with their own celebrity shills. Sun Country tried the aging and disinterested-looking Beatle Ringo Starr. Matilda Bay rolled out Grace Jones, sheep and koalas.

Willis, however, drove Seagram's Golden Wine Cooler to the top, as the company's sales surpassed those of California Cooler. But the smug and too-hip *Moonlighting* star played the role of the hare to Ed and Frank's downhome tortoises. Bartles and Jaymes crept up and eventually edged past Seagram. Meanwhile, California Cooler lagged a distant third.

At their peak, coolers were generating around $2 billion a year in sales, but winning in this market could prove a Pyrrhic victory. The sheer mass of product moved, the tremendous volume of dollars generated and the great expanse of shelf space devoted to coolers led a number of producers to assume that a new and permanent niche had been created. Such doesn't seem to be the case, for coolers could well have more in common with coonskin caps and hula hoops than a mature, self-sustaining product line.

As the big three began to dominate the scene, though, they began taking off the gloves and knuckling it out. This meant heavy discounting, with prices—and profits—going down about 10 percent. At the same time, cooler sales leveled off, and now appear to be dropping. The product could well be done in by the very demographics that made it.

Coolers appeal to the young, the very young, if not the prepubscent. Indeed, coolers are the favorite illicit drink among young teenagers, much to the outrage of anti-alcohol groups and the discomfiture of cooler manufacturers. Coolers are simply too fruity, sticky and sweet for mature palates, and are not a yuppie drink. But those qualities appeal to the fresh and plentiful taste buds in youthful palates. Unlike drinking beer and spirits, kids don't have to gag down a cooler to procure the desired buzz.

Nonetheless, people who grow up tend to outgrow coolers and similar products along the way. In ten years, suggest many industry analysts, coolers will be a kind of appendix; the beverage will still have a place, but it will be a very small, even vestigial one. It is easy to see the ghosts of Bali Hai and Strawberry Hill lurking behind the wild and crazy profile of the good-timing wine cooler. And that's just fine with lots of folks in the wine business.

Winemakers have generally avoided much of the trouble that periodically plagues beer and spirit producers. That's because wine is perceived as something which is upper crust, an emblem of culture that one sips and does not swill. Coolers, on the other hand, are seen as just another cheap high for thrill-seeking youngsters, and the entire industry is tarred with a very broad brush.

"The trouble with this," writer Elizabeth Erlich quotes a wine executive in a *Business Week* article on wine coolers and the abuse of alcohol by youths, "is it's putting wine beverages into the same level of concern as beer. We've always had a good relationship with regulators. Now they're going to be taking a harder look."

Coolers, of course, aren't at all the same as table wine. Wine is but one ingredient in them, along with a lot of fruit juice, citric acid, sugar, artificial flavors and stabilizers. Not only that, but some coolers have no wine in them at all; these are grain-based, which further muddies consumer perception about the whole product line. Wine statistician Lou Gomberg cautions industry members who are hopeful that today's cooler-swilling youngster will be tomorrow's serious collector of reserve Cabernets.

"It ain't necessarily so," he explains. "It could go either way, and in all probability it will go toward sodas and beer and away from wine. Sweet drinks just do it for young people. When I was a kid, it was sarsaparilla. The products change with the times, but the underlying basic appeal remains the same—sweet, cold, carbonated beverages are and always will be the drinks of choice for the young."

Gomberg sees only one possible "bridge," as he calls it, that could carry cooler consumers to real wine. "This is simply the fact that the word 'wine' is featured on most cooler packages. The drink itself isn't much of a bridge. But the word, in a small way, could lead to a limited crossover into the true wine market. But even that chance is dwindling as more and more coolers become spirit or grain-based.''

If coolers seem to be cooling, that isn't the case for another pop wine phenomenon, White Zinfandel. This wine is a case of the little engine that could—and did.

It is a summer morning in the offices of Offenbacher Inc., a small advertising firm in Sonoma County that handles the merchandising for Sutter Home Winery. Doug Offenbacher is grimly listening to a tape at the behest of a Bay Area musician, a song extolling the virtues of White Zinfandel to a raucous, heavy-metal score. The chorus is insistent, vaguely sinister and more than a little irritating, since the singer's voice is distinctly adenoidal and the guitar riffs are nothing short of deafening:

"If I live to tell, my White Zinfandel, my White Zinfandel, my White Zinfandellll . . ."

Offenbacher looks at one of his employees and manages a wan, sickly grin, and turns to the musician. "Well," he says, summoning up as much vivacity as he can, "I'll run it by my client and see what he says. We'll get back to you."

"You'd better make it quick, man," responds the musician, "or somebody else may have it by the time you make up your mind. I'm taking it around to other people. Beringer. Fetzer . . ."

"Gee, if you get an offer from them first, then I guess you'll have to take it," Offenbacher says, politely but firmly escorting the musician to the door. "But we do appreciate the opportunity you gave us to hear it first."

Artists, writers, musicians and similar ilk are always hitting up advertising agencies. But what was unusual about this exchange was the subject of the colloquy. A decade ago the Zinfandel variety itself was moribund. Five years ago, White Zin was a very minor category. Today it's the hottest premium wine in America. True, it's one of the cheapest, but it's still a cork-finished varietal wine. Around eight million cases of it are sold annually, at a winery profit in excess of $200 million. White Zinfandel has arrived, a fact signified by the rock paean written to it, however atrocious.

According to wine writer Bob Thompson, White Zinfandel was made in the Napa Valley more than a century ago. Robert Louis Stevenson mused over the wine during his peregrinations through the North Coast wine country. More recently, Thompson claims, Ridge Vineyards made this century's first commercial release of White Zin in 1970. That may well be, but the real story of the blush varietal started with Bob Trinchero of Sutter Home.

Trinchero, of course, started out making White Zinfandel in the style of a good Chardonnay—dry, oak-aged and somewhat austere. But it was when he turned it into a fruity and sweet wine, a pseudo-pop wine, that White Zin took off. Sutter Home did it largely without advertising or an extensive merchandising budget; White Zinfandel made it because of consumer demand, not industry promotion.

Wine critics, for the most part, were not as charmed with White Zinfandel as consumers. Most dismissed it as "candy" and "soda pop." One writer, however, differed from the majority. Oz Clarke, one of England's most widely published wine writers and a respected Shakespearean actor, praised White Zinfandel as "a delightful quaff" and predicted that it would continue to swallow shares of the lower end of the American premium wine market.

He was right, much to the chagrin of his peers, who had predicted an early and ignominious decline of the category. Like Topsy, White Zinfandel just grew and grew, until it was so big that nobody could afford to ignore it—least of all wineries that had previously disparaged it. Many forgot their old prejudices as they embraced the variety, in particular the fact that it is a true, in and out, cash flow, profitable wine. Even that industry paragon of quality, Robert Mondavi, acceded to the craze.

"I remember Fred Franzia talking to Bob Mondavi at a dinner," reminisces one Napa Valley wine executive who required anonymity. "Fred is one of the big names in bulk wine production and distribution. He obviously doesn't have any qualms about making White Zinfandel, or anything else that can be sold for a profit. So Bob was saying how he got into White Zinfandel because his son, Michael, had been urging him to do it, and how he had finally decided he could make a White Zinfandel that reflected his concern about making only the finest wines, and the sanctity of the family tradition for quality and all. And Fred was just laughing at him. He says: 'Bullshit, Bob, tell them the real reason—you're making White Zinfandel because you can make money at it, right? M-O-N-E-Y, right? Go ahead, tell them.'

"And Bob denies the hell out of it," continues the executive, "and manages to stay calm while he's doing it. But you can tell he's pretty p.o.'ed at Fred, though. And the thing is, Fred was right. Bob makes a damn good White Zinfandel, but hey, it's still White Zin. It ain't reserve Cabernet. He got into it for the same reason other people are getting into it—there are just ungodly profits in the variety. You bring the grapes in, sell the wine in less than a year—no oak, no holding the wine in inventory—it's a winemaker's dream. And you sell it as a premium varietal, at a premium price."

More than 120 wineries now make White Zinfandel. Sutter Home is still king of the mountain, accounting for almost half the White Zin made, but others are coming on fast. Mondavi now makes close to 500,000 cases annually of the limpid pink libation, and Beringer is producing more than 600,000 cases. "White Zin has been a tremendous profit center," says Beringer executive Tor Kenward. "It's certainly bought us a lot of French oak barrels, we've even used the earnings from it to put in a $1 million research facility for Cabernet Sauvignon and Chardonnay, and it continues to fund research."

Even small, boutique wineries have determined that White Zinfandel represents cash flow, and they've also championed the varietal. Consequently, where Caterpillar tractors were tearing out old stands of Zinfandel vines just a decade ago, the variety is now being planted or budded over at a rapid rate. That includes large tracts in the Sacramento and San Joaquin valleys, where Sutter Home has proven that acceptable Zinfandel fruit may be produced in very warm climate zones.

Along with the plonk grapes that go into wine coolers, the Zinfandel plantings are a boon to the long-squeezed Central

Valley growers. Normally, wines made from their grapes retail for between $3 and $6 a gallon. Sutter Home will be able to sell Central Valley White Zin in cork-finished, premium varietal bottlings for $3 to $4 a fifth, or between $15 and $20 a gallon retail. Zinfandel grapes, even if used in a blush wine, are certainly worth more than Thompson Seedless and Tokay.

Some producers are now touting White Cabernet Sauvignon, most notably Sterling and Vichon. Using Cabs to make a blush wine seems a horrible waste of good grapes. The relatively stiff price and oxymoronic associations with red, rich Cabernet have made this product a less than stellar success. But in any event, the blush wines fit the pink and fruity profile of a hot-selling pop wine.

There are fads in the high end of the wine market as well as the low. For example, the big, powerful, alcoholic Cabernets of a decade ago have yielded to more restrained, medium-bodied and complex wines. The Petite Sirah, an excellent red varietal, has faded in popularity as winegrowers push Cabernet. There's a chance that it could almost totally disappear from store shelves; or, with some publicity and promotion, make a comeback. But one of the more significant examples of shifting fortunes for a product is the rise, fall and resurrection of American sparkling wine.

There's been a sparkling wine industry in this country almost as long as wines have been made. Napa Valley sparklers were enjoyed in San Francisco, Chicago and New York in the late nineteenth century. They crashed along with still wines during Prohibition. More recently, New York champagnes from the Finger Lakes region have enjoyed a solid share of the market, especially on the East Coast. Throughout the 1940s, 1950s and 1960s, New York sparkling wines made from *Vitis labrusca* hybrid grapes were the only real alternative Americans had to the true champagnes from France.

That essentially changed with the 1973 arrival of Domaine Chandon, the Moët-Hennessy subsidiary. Just as Americans were beginning to drink more pricey vintages, Moët noted that the U.S. had few premium sparkling wine producers. Except for the New York sparklers and a few hard-to-find labels, Korbel was the only substantial line in the nation. There was also Cold Duck, which sparkled, but does not come close to being a real champagne.

Prior to the mid-1970s, most American sparkling wine was produced through the Charmat process, a procedure that involves putting the wine through its secondary fermentation in large vats. This yields a serviceable, but not a superior, wine. For that, the *méthode champenoise* must be used, a process that entails inducing secondary fermentation in the bottle; a costly method that demands a great deal of labor.

Domaine Chandon, of course, brought French skill in *méthode champenoise* to the U.S. The company aimed to produce wines that were between the top French champagnes and the zany Cold Duck, in both price and quality. These days, Domaine Chandon executives will tell visitors and inquisitive journalists that their goal is to produce the finest sparkling wines in the world. Yet their marketing strategies—and their product—belie those words. Domaine Chandon produces very good wines, but they are not equivalent to the vintage champagnes of the mother house. But then, they're not as expensive, either. Chandon's sparklers sell for between $9 and $13 a bottle, depending on the retail outlet, which is considerably less than the top end posted for the Moët-Hennessy line, which can carry mid-to-high double-digit price tags.

The company's sales soared. That was too much of a temptation for other sparkling wine houses; other foreign ventures in Sonoma, Napa and Mendocino counties sprouted like mildew in a Seattle closet. Mumm opened Domaine Mumm; Piper Heidsieck started a joint venture with Sonoma Vineyards; Freixenet checked in with Gloria Ferrer Vineyards, a sprawling Spanish-style champagne facility in the Carneros District.

Jack Davies had made excellent champagne at Schramsberg Vineyards since the early 1970s. Korbel had long dominated the mid-range of the category for *méthode champenoise* style sparklers, and even now accounts for about 70 percent of all domestic *méthode champenoise* sales. But with Domaine Chandon contributing some much-needed panache to this business, still more players began jumping in. In fact, more than fifty premium producers now offer sparkling wines in California alone, and several Oregon and Washington wineries have also entered production.

Consumers responded favorably, even as prices increased in the early 1980s. Finally, though, the boom crashed, or at least stalled dramatically. Much of it had to do with price resistance.

"Here you had a time of a strong dollar, and domestic producers were charging up to $25 a bottle," recalls one wine retailer. "You could get some excellent champagnes for that; I mean real champagnes, from the Champagne region of France. You also had a lot of product, both in terms of quantity and new labels, coming out at the same time. As usual, the industry overestimated the potential market. Sure, Americans were drinking more sparkling wine, they just weren't drinking enough to cope with this upsurge in supply, especially at those inflated prices."

There was also some consumer confusion about the products. By French law and professional courtesy in other countries, only those sparkling wines which come from Champagne can be called champagne. That didn't stop numerous American producers from labeling their products as champagne, including the Gallo brothers, whose André Champagne has more in common with Koala Springs soda than it does with champagne. This struggle over nomenclature is actually codified in a treaty, first drawn up by France in 1891, that gives the French the sole right to use the name "champagne" on a wine. The U.S. refused to sign when asked to do so in 1911, and refused again when the issue was formally broached in 1927 in The Hague, in 1934 in London and 1958 in Lisbon.

Given this history, it's unlikely the U.S. will ever sign, since "champagne" has become a generic term in this country. But it's still a generic term that implies quality, something "sparkling wine" does not. So the less-than-sophisticated consumer may well buy a lousy bottle of "champagne" to celebrate his girlfriend's birthday and pass up a superior bottle of sparkling wine, all the while thinking that he was springing for the good stuff.

Domestic producers of premium sparkling wine have been feeling the pinch from several directions. Not only do they compete with the expensive, true champagnes of France, but increasingly they are being hammered by moderately priced sparklers. Spanish producers began pouring great amounts of *méthode champenoise* sparkling wine into the country in the late 1970s, and still have a firm hold on their market share. When one can buy an excellent Spanish *méthode champenoise* sparkling wine for $5, it doesn't make sense to purchase a California sparkler of similar quality for twice the amount.

Then there are the lower quality products that ride the term "champagne" and get served at all those birthday parties. One such successful brand is called Cook's, a cheap, mediocre sparkler produced by the Guild Cooperative of Lodi, which had been remarkable only for being so unremarkable for so many years. Backed by a strong television advertising campaign, however, Cook's has recently taken off; it sold slightly more than 500,000 cases in 1986, and one million in 1987.

However, when sparkling wine sales hit the wall several years ago, many domestic producers were forced to slash prices. While Domaine Chandon and a handful of quality producers kept prices stable, others without the reputation for quality and value took a beating. But on the whole the recovery of the sparkling wine segment has been surprisingly swift. In 1987, the sales of Hanns Kornell grew 63 percent over the previous year's, Korbel and Domaine Chandon each had 19 percent boosts, and Piper Sonoma grew 17 percent. By holding the line in price and maintaining value, the nation's sparkling wine producers should be able to continue growing at a satisfactory rate, while consolidating market shares at the expense of imports.

It seems safe to say that domestic premium sparkling wines have transcended the pop phenom category, although with their rapid growth in the 1970s they certainly behaved like one. Sparklers are now a strong and legitimate market genre.

Fad wine products will, however, continue to come and go in the U.S. This reflects both the youth of the American wine industry and the outlook of its customers. European winemaking styles, for the most part, are not susceptible to dramatic flux, since Europeans have been making and drinking wine for centuries. They have defined the types and styles of wine that are best suited for each area, and consumer taste has reinforced those definitions. Too, Europeans are wedded to tradition. That, obviously, is not the case with Americans, since we have relatively little in the way of tradition—save for an appreciation of a good hamburger and a Fourth of July fireworks display—to root us.

So, for the foreseeable future, wine fads will continue to be a wild card in the marketplace. For vintners, the category is analogous to junk bonds. They can make a killing; they can also lose their shirts.

Section Seven

EPILOGUE: A TROUBLED HORIZON

24

A TROUBLED HORIZON

More than most movers and shakers in other industries, wine business bigwigs have consistently demonstrated short-sightedness in addressing potential problems. This has locked them into boom-and-bust cycles of grape and wine supplies, the eschewing of long-term marketing programs in favor of raking off short-term profits, and, in many cases, a simple refusal to grasp objective economic reality. The portrait of the empyrean winemaker still holds plenty of allure for newcomers and some old hands alike. The hubris that such an image engenders can—and does—lead to disastrous consequences, from palatial, overly leveraged wineries to downright reprobate and foolish pricing policies.

Still, in some ways, things are looking up for the industry, particularly in the premium segment. The weak dollar has temporarily scotched much of the demand for pricey European vintages. Even wine lovers on the Eastern Seaboard—who have long been the most ardent buyers of imported wines—have turned to California Cabernets and Chardonnays as their international buying power has shrunk. However, there are plenty of problems facing the entire industry, and the future bodes much wailing and gnashing of teeth if looming bugaboos are not addressed.

One which is very basic and very visible is the neoprohibition movement. Made up of a loose confederation of Christian temperance advocates, Mothers Against Drunk Driving and similar groups, and self-styled pro-health agitators, the movement is basically anti-alcohol. As with the original Prohibition cause, some see demon rum in all such beverages, a sinful and ungodly drink that dissipates the body and soul. A newer wrinkle is the war against drunk drivers, a class of folk no one seems to like. But perhaps the strongest component in this coalition is the health cabal, a growing force that seems determined to reclassify alcoholic products as environmental toxins rather than beverages.

Robert Mondavi, always willing to play St. George to any number of real or perceived dragons, has launched himself and his winery into the fray against the latter element. The point Mondavi tries to make is that wine is not an alcoholic beverage per se, even though it contains alcohol. It is, instead—or so the claim goes—a food. At the very least, it's a moderate beverage ideally suited to the consumption of food. This is a distinction the anti-alcohol and anti-drunk-driving lobbyists have not been able to make. But unless that distinction is made, wine will continue to be hammered as ruthlessly as distilled spirits and beer.

Medical studies conducted on the deleterious effects of alcohol are mixed. Heavy drinking, of course, wrecks one's liver and vaporizes brain cells. But the medical debate isn't about alcoholism and binges, but moderate use. Some studies hint that the equivalent of one or two glasses of wine each day may contribute to oral and esophageal cancer. Others indicate that such quantities can aid in lowering hypertension and the risk of a heart attack.

It was only a decade ago that many gynecologists and obstetricians recommended that expectant mothers drink a glass of wine each evening for its mildly relaxing qualities. But according to recent claims by researchers studying Fetal Alcohol Syndrome, almost any alcohol, taken at any point in the pregnancy, can harm a fetus. While the research is clearly frightening, it appears somewhat alarmist; scientists admit that they've yet to detect adverse consequences from light drinking. Still, alcohol during pregnancy is obviously on the way out.

But there are just enough questions about alcohol and health to keep the debate burning. It is a squabble that will not disappear anytime soon, and the wine industry must be prepared for a prolonged lobbying effort.

Too, there are other concerns about the constituents of wine that have nothing to do with alcohol. The use of sulfur in wine as an antioxidant has caused considerable furor among public health advocates. Free sulfur can and does cause severe allergenic reactions among a limited number of people. By federal law, wine bottles must now post the advisory that the product enclosed "contains sulfites."

Another concern is urethane, a reasonably potent carcinogen that is produced naturally in wine in minute quantities during the fermentation process. Canada currently limits urethane content in wine to 30 parts-per-million (ppm) for table wine, 100 ppm for fortified wines and 400 ppm for fruit brandies. Many U.S. health groups are pressing the federal government to adopt the Canadian standard for American wines. In a recent test of about 300 California wines, about 10 percent exceeded the Canadian thresholds. That may not seem like much, unless you are one of the winery owners whose product doesn't make the cut. A 10 percent displacement in the wine industry would be chaotic, and this could occur if the urethane issue ever gains a full head of steam.

Of special concern to vintners is the approval by Congress of the Alcohol Labeling Amendment to the Omnibus Anti-Drug Bill in late 1988. By 1990, federal law will require health warning labels on all beer, wine and spirits containers sold in the U.S. Many people in the industry agree with Buena Vista's Marcus Moller-Racke, who called the legislation "The greatest threat . . . facing the wine industry."

This isn't entirely correct; the most significant problem facing the industry isn't labeling, but a failure to expand the consumer base. Still, Moller-Racke points out that no other country requires such warnings, and the labels could give foreigners the impression that American wines can cause birth defects while foreign wines are safe.

Obviously, this new legislation has rendered the debate that characterized Vintage 2000 academic. Also worrisome to vintners is the probability that excise taxes will soon be levied against their problems to help alleviate the national debt.

The wine industry can weather the storm brewing over the health issue with a long-term program of well-funded lobbying and advertising. It can marshal its own cadre of pundits who believe in the healthful benefits of the beverage. Their case is by no means a loser. Indeed, a 1981 Kaiser Permanente study examined the drinking habits of 8,000 people over ten years. It determined that moderate drinkers—those who consumed two glasses of wine or its alcohol equivalent a day—were 27 percent less likely to expire from all causes than either teetotalers or heavy drinkers. A 1985 Stanford University study found that moderate drinking increases the high density lipoprotein (HDL) content in the bloodstream. The "good" kind of cholesterol, HDL may reduce the risk of cardiovascular disease.

The numbers, then, are there for the wine industry to exploit. Whether it does in an efficacious manner is another matter entirely. Certainly, the opposition is well organized and fanatically dedicated. And it wouldn't even take another bout of full-fledged Prohibition to hamstring the business; in these health-conscious days, the mere perception that wine is somehow harmful might be almost as catastrophic.

Paradoxically, even as some may shun wine because it contains alcohol, others may turn away because it contains too little kick. Distilled spirits—particularly white spirits such as gin and vodka—may well be experiencing a popular resurgence. After years of schmoozing over glasses of white wine, upscale drinkers, young or otherwise, are rediscovering the joys of a good, stiff drink. So says Faith Popcorn, the New

York-based trend expert whose cultural forecasting batting average has CEOs clamoring for her next prognostication. Popcorn predicts that within the next few years, the vodka martini will be the drink of choice. Granted, it's less wimpy than the house white.

The wine industry is faced with a tough and thorny dilemma: how to stay trendy without seeming too wicked. Obviously, new strategies are called for; wine will have to be portrayed as a healthful, accessible, everyday beverage that is suitable for a wide variety of situations. The closest anyone has come to this strategy is Almadén, whose TV ads show attractive, unpretentious, everyday folks enjoying wine with everything from a hot bath to hamburgers.

In the words of Lou Gomberg, this is just the kind of thing that creates a "picture" of wine in American consciousness, a vision that has been sorely lacking. It is just the kind of image that Gomberg has been urging the industry to project for some fifty years, to link wine with meat loaf, an evening of lively conversation, a family picnic and so on. But the whole industry has to do this, not just Almadén, which, after all, makes jug wines.

The industry also must contend with market problems from other, less obvious quarters. While the future belongs to premium producers, they must somehow find ways to stand out from the crowd, an especially difficult task in light of consolidation and concentration of distributors. Many individual wineries are destined to be lost in the shuffle.

Another matter related to sulfites in wine is California's Proposition 65, the Safe Drinking Water and Toxic Enforcement Act, which the state's voters passed in 1986. It requires all businesses to warn consumers about "products containing chemicals known to the state to cause cancer or other reproductive harm or birth defects." Eventually, the state will publish a list of more than 200 chemicals, some of which are used in agriculture. The rub is that minute quantities of such chemicals could conceivably end up in wine. The amount could well be as little as a few parts-per-billion. If the public isn't warned of the harmful chemicals, on a label or by a sign in a store, the Act contains "bounty hunter" provisions that will enable members of the public to sue a producer or retailer.

Some in the state view Prop 65 as a full-employment bill for attorneys. But the real problem here is that scientists don't have the slightest idea of what exposure levels trigger cancer in humans, and even how. Is the cancer the result of repeated exposures, or does the "one-hit" theory— where it takes only a single chemical molecule striking the wrong cell at the wrong time—apply? Killing mice with massive doses of cancer chemicals is easy, but figuring out whether a part-per-million or -billion is "known" to cause problems in humans is another question.

The questions create uncertainties, and the upshot is that the Act, which also prevents the release of chemicals into ground or surface water, could limit the amount and variety of pesticides grape growers may use on their crops. That may be good news to environmentalists and people who live next door to vineyards, but it poses problems for growers who are rarely more than a step ahead of the next destructive pest.

In addition, a newly amended program to enforce the federal Endangered Species Act also has provisions that could restrict pesticide use. "It should be recognized that due to the Endangered Species Act, pesticide use may be jeopardized in 910 of the 3,050 counties in the United States," says Dr. Irwin Sherman, the Dean of the College of Agricultural and Natural Sciences at the University of California at Riverside. Although grapes usually require far fewer applications of pesticides than most other food crops, such legislation could have a dramatic impact on grape-growing regions, particularly the San Joaquin Valley.

Lawyers are partially responsible for another form of wine industry trouble. The high cost of liability insurance has curtailed wine tastings in many states. In Texas, for example, large tastings, some involving up to a thousand people, were once the rule in this most expansive of states. No longer. Big tastings are bye-bye, and the much smaller tastings that are held feature more food than wine, something of a problem when the objective evaluation of wine is the primary goal of the event. The problem is that tasting sponsors are now slapped with the same insurance rates as bar and restaurant owners, rates that have skyrocketed since victims of intoxicated drivers have won huge judgments against those who served the booze to the drunks.

As wine becomes harder for consumers to taste, it will be harder for vintners to sell. Score a point for the neoprohibitionists.

Another travail is far more insidious. It's also difficult to address. The industry calls it "bottle variation." It means bad wine, a wine that has spoiled because it wasn't bottled properly. The problem can be fairly common among vintners who don't maintain rigorous quality control standards. Anthony Dias Blue has estimated that undesirable bottle variation can run as high as 8 percent. He points out that for a business that is "currently in a fight for its life," each spoiled bottle is a "black mark for the industry." While consumers take this more seriously than vintners, it would behoove the latter to pay more attention to quality control, for they are losing potential repeat customers.

One of the biggest perennial threats to the American wine industry comes from abroad. Despite the weak dollar, Europeans have not given up on the American marketplace. They can't afford to, given the massive overproduction of wine in recent years. Europe is a wine lake, and it has to drain somewhere.

Unlike the American industry, wine in the European Economic Community receives a good deal of government subsidy. Although Common Market nations have made a much ballyhooed 1.1 billion-gallon product cutback, Europe still produces far too much wine. Most of this is mid-to-low-quality stuff. But the EEC plans to push its members to replant areas stripped of vines with better varieties. The current threat on the low end will creep upward toward the already stressed fighting varietal segment. This is the category where the domestic industry can least withstand more competition.

And Europe isn't the only player in this game. Excellent wines are being made in Australia, Chile and Argentina, and are being imported to and sold in the U.S. in increasing quantities. With liberal trade laws, America is more awash in wine than ever, and demand is by no means keeping up with supply.

Not quite so dire is the continuing imbroglio over appellations. The system works well in Europe, but the modern American wine industry is really only five decades old, and consumers here aren't as savvy about wine as Europeans. That hasn't stopped growers and vintners from championing viticultural regions such as Stag's Leap, Sonoma Mountain, the Alexander Valley and the Carneros with the same enthusiasm French vintners evince while touting Margaux, Vosne-Romanée, Chablis or Graves. The trouble is, Americans don't know what the American winegrowers are talking about. Even reasonably knowledgeable wine consumers have no firm concept about any appellation that gets more specific than the Sonoma or Napa valleys.

Growers and vintners may make more money by pushing Carneros or Stag's Leap to the limited pool of consumers who do understand. But it's doubtful that a complex appellation system contributes anything to the long-term stability of the industry. At this point, it probably confuses more than it helps, and what the industry needs most is clarity, not further obfuscation.

The Gordian knot of state liquor regulations could also use some simplification. Some current laws covering the movement of wine across state lines seem better suited for toxic waste than a beverage. To date, this issue has been a major target for cooperative industry lobbying and spending, and the business has had some success. It is now easier to sell wine in food stores in more states, and California now allows wineries from other states to sell directly to California residents in two-case lots, provided the favor is reciprocated. But much of the regulatory tangle remains, and it strangles the effective marketing of wine to a significant portion of the American public.

On a more basic level, there are some questions about the perception of the beverage itself. After two decades of hype, glitter, huzzahs and honking, some analysts think that Americans may be simply bored with wine. Certainly that emblem of yuppiedom, the glass of generic white wine, has faded as a cultural icon. True, high quality whites and reds alike are up in sales, but this reflects the maturation of an established market more than a new influx of customers.

The biggest problem facing the wine industry, then, is the long-term appeal of the beverage itself. Colonial governments struggled with this before the American Revolution, and so did Thomas Jefferson, who never did convince his fellow Americans to abandon spirits and beer for the temperate quaff. Winegrowers in the 1800s pondered whether America would ever become a nation of wine drinkers. Winegrowers in the 1980s are just as puzzled about why their product never really takes off.

Many think the industry had its chance to change this in the late 1960s and early 1970s, when consumer interest began to run hot and high. That moment was not seized. The wine business failed to close ranks and work in concert, to fund the kind of promotion and advertising campaign that would make a real and permanent difference. Instead of using that momentum to build the image of wine as an everyday beverage, as natural to drink with burgers, hot dogs and pizza as is beer and soda, the industry blew it by doing the opposite. It made wine seem like the drink of a specialized and recondite fraternity that only the extremely astute, talented and wealthy could penetrate.

Americans may always feel this way about wine. But if nothing else, the wine industry may take comfort in that fact that for most things, what goes around comes around. The cycle for the wine business could well be headed down, but the chance to make America a nation of wine drinkers will come again. Whether or not the people who produce and sell wine make better use of it than they have in the past remains to be seen.

Index